The Hangman's Record

Volume One 1868 - 1899

STEVE FIELDING

Chancery House Press
15 Wickham Road, Beckenham,
Kent, BR3 2JS, England

Copyright ©	1994 Steve Fielding
First Published	1994
All rights reserved	No part of this book may be reproduced, stored in a retrieval system, or transmitted, in any form or by any means, electronic, mechanical, photocopying, recording or otherwise, without the prior written permission of the publisher.
ISBN	0 900246 65 0
Published by	Chancery House Press 15 Wickham Road Beckenham Kent BR3 2JS UK tel 081 650 7745 fax 081 650 0768
Cover design	Simone Riley
Pictures	HM Prison Service Museum Hulton Deutsch Collection Ltd

WEST SUSSEX LIBRARIES	
7568167	364.66
MACAULAY	06 Mar 1998
1st CW	Init M.	2nd	Init
3rd	Init	4th	Init

Database typeset by BPC Whitefriars Ltd.
Printed and bound by BPC Wheatons Ltd.,
both members of The British Printing Company Ltd.

Chancery House Press

Chancery House Press is an imprint of the well established and respected publishing house, CBD Research Ltd.

Its aim is to provide an outlet for non-fiction publications of an esoteric or specialist nature, to assist serious researchers and the dedicated hobbyist.

We welcome any proposal - in the form of a preliminary letter - for reference works of a singular nature that will extend what is intended to be a diverse and eclectic range of publications.

Contents

Author's Preface	vii
Acknowledgements	ix
Introduction	xi
The Executioners	xv
The Development of the Scaffold	xxxi
Analysis: 1868-1899	xxxiii
The Cases: 1868-1899	1
Victim Index	263
Method Index	277
Executioner Index	285
Hanged Index	293

Author's Preface: Why The Hangman's Record?

I set about writing this book when I found a conspicuous gap in the subject of British executions. Although several similar books have been written over the years with varying degrees of inaccuracy, no one had attempted to put together a definitive list of the criminals who paid for their crimes on the scaffolds in British prisons.

What I have put together is a complete list of every person hanged in Great Britain since 1868, the year when executions ceased to be public occasions and retreated behind prison walls. This first book covers the period up to the turn of the century; some of the cases have become classics, while other lesser known ones, just as notorious, were sometimes overshadowed by events of the day.

In preparing a work of this size I have been forced to discipline the length of the entries to accommodate every case. As a lot of the work was done in my home town of Bolton, using local papers, there will therefore naturally be a slight northern bias, but I do hope readers from the south will find enough information on their local cases to sustain interest.

I will add at this point that while all information has been double checked wherever possible, I have struggled to find anything other than the bare facts on one or two cases, usually the "domestic murder in Dorset" type of thing, when there is nothing else to record other than the most basic facts. In particular, a number of the less sensational cases from Ireland were barely recorded in English newspapers.

Should readers notice any glaring omissions or oversight then I would be pleased if they would contact me, through my publishers, so that any error can be corrected.

Steve Fielding
Bolton
Lancashire
England
1994

Acknowledgments

Numerous people have helped to make this book possible and I am indebted to the following: First and foremost, Lisa Moore for her unfailing support and encouragement, and help with the proof reading and illustrations. Mark and Anne-Marie Harris for their valued advice and help with the computer. Syd Dernley, former public executioner, for his knowledge and technical detail; while Tony Homewood and Tim Leech both generously supplied valuable information from their own research.

I would like to thank Jeremy Beadle who kindly loaned me a number of out of print books from his personal library. Thanks also to Marie at Clifford Elmer books, and Margot Armitage at Crookes Books, for helping to supply research books at reasonable prices!

The vast majority of the work for this book was done at Bolton library's Archives and Local Studies room, and at Farnworth library, and I would like to thank the staff at both libraries for all their patience and help.

Finally I would like to thank my parents, William and Lilian Fielding, for their continued love and support.

Introduction: From Courtroom to Scaffold

"The sentence of the Court upon you is, that you be taken from this place to a lawful prison and thence to a place of execution and that you be hanged by the neck until you are dead; and that your body be afterwards buried within the precincts of the prison in which you shall been confined before your execution. And may the Lord have mercy on your soul. Amen."

Since the middle ages the above death sentence was passed in British Courts on people convicted of murder. The words changed little from when it was first used until the death penalty was abolished in the late 1960s.

During the period of reformation in the 1860s, which culminated in the passing of the Capital Punishment Amendment Act 1868 (31 VIC c 24), capital punishment was abolished for all offences except treason, piracy, arson in the Royal dockyards, and murder. It was the last offence which brought the vast majority of people to the scaffold.

The crime of murder carried a mandatory death sentence until as late as 1956, and as a result many juries were reluctant to find a person guilty of murder if there was any doubt. They would usually add a recommendation for mercy although any action as a result was totally at the discretion of the Home Secretary and his advisors.

There were no executions carried out after 1868 for any offences other than murder and treason, the latter occurring mostly during and after the Second World War.

Once charged with murder, the prisoner was tried at the County Assize Court, which sat at regular quarterly sessions, like a college term. Therefore, a person could be tried within days of an offence being committed if it was prior to the court sitting, and likewise he could face a lengthy remand if the next session was not due to sit for many months.

The courts were visited by a selection of Judges – usually two for each Assize – who would stay in the town for the duration of the session. There were usually a couple of towns in each county that served this purpose, and most had their own gaol for carrying out executions, hence towns like Carlisle, Hereford, and Bodmin etc featuring in the text.

Moves were afoot as early as the turn of the century to streamline the number of prisons which could be upgraded into efficient centres of execution with a purpose built scaffold kept ready for use when needed. This would do away with the need of local carpenters having to construct a gallows at short notice. (The prison authorities were known to sometimes recruit workers from the ranks of convicts to assist, and this has often been cited as the reason for the "non-execution" of John Lee at Exeter in 1885 – see "The Executioners" chapter).

Once the judge had passed the death sentence, and the chaplain had concluded it with an "Amen", the prisoner would be ushered from the dock to the cells.

In the mid 1800s, the death cell was often nothing more than a dungeon; dank and dark, usually cut off from natural light. The condemned man would be watched closely to lessen the chances of him pre-empting the sentence. His diet would be the usual prison food of gruel, water, and occasionally meat and potatoes.

The time-span between sentence and execution in 1870 was, on average, a fortnight, although this was gradually lengthened until by the turn of the century the term "three clear Sundays" was well in use. The decision to allow three Sundays between sentence and execution was thought to be long enough for any new evidence that might alter the verdict to appear, while not stretching out the painful wait for certain death any longer than necessary.

On the morning of the execution, the prisoner would be visited by the chaplain and after breakfast, they would move to a holding cell near or adjacent to the scaffold, where the condemned would receive any sacraments or religious blessings that he may require.

At five minutes before the hour, the hangman would enter the cell, and after shaking hands, would pinion the prisoner. Executioners William Marwood and James Berry both used a cumbersome body belt which was fastened around the condemned man's waist. The arms would then be secured to straps fixed to the belt, leaving the prisoner's arms crossed over his stomach.

Once secured, the procession would be formed. The chief warder would take the lead, followed by the chaplain, the prisoner and hangman (with assistant, if one was being used). They would be flanked by eight warders, four on either side, while bringing up the rear would be the Governor, the Sheriff, two wand bearers, and the prison surgeon.

On reaching the drop, the final scene would see the chaplain standing to one side reciting the Litany for the Dying, while the hangman adjusted the noose and secured the prisoner's legs. Two warders took up positions on planks placed across the drop and they would offer support if the condemned man showed signs of collapse. Watching from one side would be the official witnesses, which included several members of the press.

The lever would then be pushed and the floor would collapse. The body would hang for one hour before being taken down. This was a legacy from the old days when it was rumoured that some prisoners were buried alive, the actual hanging having failed to kill them. Therefore, to remove any doubt, it was decided to let the man hang for this length of time.

Burial would take place within the confines of the prison, as the body was then the property of the state. There was usually some mark in the prison wall beside the body to identify who was buried where.

The Executioners

William Calcraft gained a place in the history books as one of the longest serving executioners on record. Between April 1829 when he was granted his first appointment, and May 1874 when he was finally pensioned off, Calcraft carried out the vast majority of first public, then latterly private, executions in Great Britain. Officially he was the "Executioner for the City of London and Middlesex", but as it was usual among many local authorities to appoint the London hangman, Calcraft's services were often requested at various prisons throughout the land.

Calcraft was born around 1800. Horace Bleakley's book *Hangmen of England* states the hangman's birthplace as being Baddow, Essex, but in an interview given shortly after his retirement Calcraft said he was born in Barnet.

After serving an apprenticeship as a cobbler he succumbed to the lure of city life and moved to London where he married. He tried his hand at many varied occupations, one of which was as a hawker of meat pies and this often took him to the public executions carried out at the London gaols of Newgate and Horsemonger Lane.

Discovering a new interest and fascination in hanging, he made the acquaintance of the two hangmen of the day: James Foxen and his sometime assistant Thomas "Old Cheese" Cheshire. Calcraft claimed that while he was running a coffee stall at Finsbury Park, Foxen had stopped by, and while chatting had told him he was giving up his calling as he was "queer in health." Later, when he heard that an assistant hangman was required for a triple execution at Lincoln, Calcraft applied for and was offered the job.

When Foxen died in 1829, it would have been usual to promote his assistant to number one, but Cheshire had gained a reputation as a drunkard who frequented seedy drinking dens and mixed with the low life, so the authorities let it be known that they were looking for a new man to take over. Calcraft offered his services and from a short list of two was accepted. For the next thirty or so years, he perfected the art of strangulation by allowing the condemned drops of between one and two feet.

Despite the nature of his business and the class of people who flocked around him at executions, Calcraft was a strict churchgoer and devoted to his wife and three children. He was described as an animal lover who gave generously to charity. In 1855, he bought a house at Shoreditch and spent many hours tending his garden, of which he was immensely proud.

It was partly as a result of the sickening spectacle of a Calcraft execution, and the increase in unruly crowd behaviour, that eventually persuaded Parliament to sanction private executions in 1867, although it was probably as much of a relief to the executioner as this article from a newspaper in 1868 describes:

> "The execution on Thursday, (August 13th 1868) marks the disappearance of Calcraft from public life, he will henceforth be surrounded in the mystery of his terrible office, and the rising generation of criminals who take an interest in the matter will have to ask their seniors what type of man he was, and to trust in their imagination for a picture of him.
> To no man will this mystery be more welcome than Calcraft himself. He has shown on more than one occasion, that his dread of facing a crowd is only inferior to the victim's dread of facing the gallows. At Manchester where he had something more than the prospect of a public execution before him he is said to have shown more signs of weakness than any man put to death. He shuffled about the prison yard and seemed loath to mount the gallows' steps and the sweat fell from his face.
> It is a great gain in every sense to have lost sight of him for after all he constituted perhaps the most unwholesome part of the spectacle of public executions. The more than prejudice – the hatred of the crowd against him – was no doubt a most unjustifiable feeling, seeing that as the mere instrument of justice and of judgment he was neither to be hated or to be loved; but it existed in such intensity that there was no prospect of it ever being lessened. The effect was extremely injurious, even to the poor kind of morality that public executions were supposed to prompt.
> The passive feeling of awe with which men might be disposed to look upon a criminal going to a righteous doom was changed to an active feeling of disgust and horror when they beheld the man by whom he was to be put to death, and there was too much reason to believe that they left the precincts of the prison with this feeling uppermost in their minds."

Unfortunately, the Capital Punishment Amendment Act of 1868 did not legislate for a change in technique which was still not much more than a crude improvement of the lynching on a tree branch. The collapsing platform, which had replaced a stool kicked from under a condemned man, was shrouded with a black curtain intended to shield the swinging man from view, but the drop was never long enough for it to be of any use, as Calcraft was still content with his usual short drops.

Despite the public being denied the chance to witness whether the execution was carried out without a hitch, the presence of members of the press ensured that when anything untoward occurred, as it frequently did when Calcraft was in charge, they wasted no time in informing their eager readers of the full gory details.

Although the hangman was still entitled to the victim's clothing and possessions, in January 1873 Calcraft was the subject of a confidential government circular sent to Governors of English prisons asking them to prepare accurate accounts of all pre-requisites enjoyed by the hangman whenever he visited for an execution. The return was required, it was stated, with a view to checking the veteran official's duty return, and if necessary surcharging him on any items that he may have "under-estimated or overlooked."

Eventually time caught up with Calcraft, and though he protested he was still able to perform his duties, the authorities now had a good enough excuse to put an end to the legal strangulation he had administered, and to adopt the methods now being practised by a new hangman in Lincolnshire.

Calcraft claimed he never kept a diary and once a criminal was dispatched he thought no more about him, quoting that: "As soon as I have done it, it goes from me like a puff of tobacco smoke." He died at his home in Hoxton, in December 1879.

Although most local authorities used the London hangman when an execution was to be carried out, several chose to retain their own man. Staffordshire always had their own executioner and the most noticeable was **George Smith** of Dudley.

Smith was born to respectable parents in 1805 but was disowned by his family when he fell into bad company as a youth. It was while serving a term of imprisonment at Stafford Gaol, for failing to maintain his wife and child, that he was offered the chance to become an executioner. In April 1849 three men were to be hanged and Calcraft was hired to carry out the sentence. On arriving at the gaol the Governor inquired whom he planned to use as an assistant. Calcraft asked if a warder could be found who could stomach the job, and when no-one volunteered, the Governor lined up a selection of the less dangerous convicts and explained that if one would assist the hangman, he would offer a pardon. While others pondered the question, Smith stepped forward and when Calcraft surveyed the man's build, he nodded his approval and Smith began a new career.

Calcraft was impressed with his new assistant, and with a number of executions coming up, he offered Smith the position of his regular assistant. He was built of much sterner stuff than his new "guv'nor," particularly when it came to hanging women, and on one occasion he had to support Calcraft when he almost fainted after hanging a young girl at Bristol.

Smith applied for the position of "Executioner of Staffordshire" and received the appointment. Calcraft, by virtue of his national fame, was being offered almost every execution and as such was regularly "double-booked". In these instances, he would often recommend that Smith be appointed. Smith's chief moment of glory came in 1856 when he hanged Dr Palmer, the infamous Rugely poisoner. Local resentment towards the poisoner, who had decimated his family to finance a gambling habit, was such that he was tried in London, but on conviction was returned to Stafford for execution. Calcraft offered his services but was warned off by Smith for "trespassing", and pointed out that he was the Executioner for Staffordshire.

Smith continued assisting Calcraft whenever needed and hoped to succeed him on retirement. Unfortunately for Smith, Calcraft showed no sign of hanging up his ropes and the appearance of other men on the scaffold pushed him further down the list. Resigned never to take over as number one, Smith carried out his last execution in 1873 and died on April 4, 1874.

The death of Smith and the superannuation of Calcraft led to a flood of applicants whenever a particularly gruesome murder occurred, and one such letter was published in December 1874 after a murder at Burton:

" "For the Town Clarke Solicitor Stafford."
December 13th. Sir, I write to you to no whether anyone is enagaged for the place of Smith to hang at Stafford, as I ham at your service anytime. I shall be obliged if you will try to place in office of Smith, I will com down to see you any day for imfamason.
Derect to Mr ——, Boot and Shoemaker, —— Lane, Derby."

Thomas Askern, from Maltby, was the choice of the Yorkshire authorities, who like Staffordshire, preferred their own executioners than using the London hangman. The main reason for this trend, which lasted until abolition, was simply a matter of economics. The council wouldn't justify paying out travelling expenses to a southerner when a local man could do the job just as well, and wouldn't require a lengthy expense account. Askern carried out executions in the north of England and Scotland from 1853, but rarely ventured south of Leeds, the execution at Lincoln in 1868 seeming to be the exception. He averaged only one or two jobs a year, and after botching an execution at Leeds in 1877, his services were no longer required and he died in the following year.

The most mysterious character in the annals of the executioner must surely be **Robert Evans.** Even his name is subject to question. Several conflicting accounts of his life have been written but it seems safe to say he was of Welsh origin. One source quotes him as being the son of a lawyer, and that he trained but never practised as a doctor; another reports that he was a farmer from Deeside, North Wales.

Some claim that he paid Calcraft for the privilege of assisting. He did assist Calcraft in his last job and there is a letter in the National Library of Wales from the Governor of Newgate offering him the position, adding that Calcraft had chosen him for the job.

What is known is that when he received the offer to carry out an execution on his own, he went under the name of **Anderson.** The first appointment for Mr Anderson was at Kirkdale in January 1874. He favoured a short drop and seemed to many to be no more competent than the old bungler Calcraft, who had badly botched the last job at the prison. He was in action a week or so later at Gloucester but any hopes he had of attaining the mantle that the recently pensioned off Calcraft had relinquished, were shattered by the promotion of William Marwood, who charged up the list by virtue of his new technique of dispatching instant death.

Anderson possibly carried out the double at Liverpool in 1874. He did perform a triple at Liverpool in January 1875 and this is his last recorded execution. He was described as being of average build, aged around forty, closely shaven and with deep set eyes. He dressed in a black frock coat and wore a black skull cap.

Although Anderson only performed a handful of executions, he was well known in the Merseyside area where his name was feared by young children who were often threatened that: "Mr Anderson will have you." His reluctance to socialise with anyone connected with either the job or at the prison ostracised him from his contemporaries, and like the others on the list he lost out to the emergence of Marwood. He was reported to have met up with both Calcraft and Marwood – the only time the three got together – while Marwood was in Liverpool to hang Heap in 1875, but he then seemed to drift into obscurity as easily as he had appeared on the scene.

William Marwood was born at Horncastle, Lincolnshire, in 1820. Like Calcraft, he was a cobbler by trade, but unlike his predecessor he wasn't drawn by city life and was content to ply his trade until well into middle age. He was reported to have had a keen interest in hanging but claimed never to have witnessed a public execution. He began experimenting with a series of drops designed to impart instant death and as reports of sickening scenes at executions began appearing in the press with sad regularity, he wrote to the Governor of Lincoln Prison explaining his methods. Eventually he was granted an interview and after a demonstration that met with their approval, Marwood was engaged in the execution of William Horry in 1872.

It has often been reported that it was Marwood alone who had instigated the long drop, but some credit must go to the executioners in Ireland who had devised and put into practice a similar theory a few years earlier. The idea was to use a drop, based on the weight of the prisoner, designed to break the man's neck. The calculation had to be exact or there could be the horrific sight of a decapitation. The first recorded case of this happening using the long drop was at Dublin in 1870, when an unnamed executioner using a drop of fourteen feet, succeeded in ripping the prisoner's head clean from his shoulders.

As Marwood's new methods proved to be a success his fame spread among the hanging circles and he was offered more jobs. He was still down the pecking order behind Smith, Askern, and Anderson but as these three advocated the short drop and its sickening consequences, once Marwood had a chance to display his methods, the authorities decided to do away the primitive style and adopt the new.

By 1875, Marwood was the undisputed number one executioner in Great Britain. Marwood preferred the term "executioner", and would never allow anyone to address him as a hangman. He scornfully termed Calcraft as a hangman and added that: "Calcraft 'hanged' people, I 'execute' them." He kept a small number of ropes in his cobbler shop that boasted his grand title of Crown Office, and would delight in explaining to the ever growing list of customers the difference in his method over Calcraft and the other "Jack Ketchs." (Jack Ketch: a notorious hangman and executioner, appointed around 1663 and dying in 1686). Marwood's fame soon became nationwide and he was the subject of the children's riddle:

"If Pa killed Ma, who'd kill Pa?"
"Marwood."

Marwood was the first southern executioner to gain appointments in Yorkshire, but when he was called to hang Walker in April 1878, he made one of his rare blunders which could have done a lot to destroy the credibility he had built up over the years.

He had no real rival across the country, and the only other man getting regular work was **George Incher,** of Dudley. Incher had received his first engagement in March 1875 when the authorities at Stafford needed an executioner to replace Smith. Marwood was otherwise engaged and hearing of their plight, Incher arrived at the gaol to take up the position. His clothing was so tattered that he had to be given a suit from the prison stores before he was deemed suitable to work on behalf of the state. Incher had apparently carried out the job to everyone's satisfaction and was on call at the prison for several years.

The only other time Incher ventured out of the Black Country on government business was to assist Marwood at the quadruple execution of the "Lennie" Mutineers in 1876. At the end of that year, he was sent to gaol for a month after committing a felony. He carried out an execution in the spring of 1881, and what became of him from then on is a mystery.

Another hangman who makes a brief appearance was a man called **Stanhouse,** from Gainsborough. He carried out an execution at Cork in August 1879, again possibly because Marwood couldn't attend due to a prior arrangement. There is no record of Stanhouse performing any executions in England.

Once Marwood was appointed, it is worth noting that the annual number of executions went up considerably. This may be due to a reluctance of officials to sanction a death sentence which in all probability would be horrifyingly carried out, but with new efficient methods of execution, the burden of sending a man to his death may have rested easier on the conscience. Whatever the reasons, there was a noticeable increase in sentences carried out from 1875.

Marwood's last year as an executioner coincided with the Phoenix Park murders in Dublin, and as a result he made a number of trips to Kilmainham to hang the five condemned, as well as making visits to Cork,

Galway and Tralee. Marwood took these trips in his stride unlike Calcraft, who showed great reluctance at having to face up to the hostilities of an Irish crowd. He was content that the protection of two detectives afforded him by the Irish authorities was sufficient.

At the end of August, Marwood fell ill with inflammation of the lungs, caught whilst on government business and rumour quickly spread that he had been "got at" by the Irish Invincibles. The illness was further complicated when jaundice set in, and after lingering for a few days, Marwood died on 4 September 1883. His passing was mourned in the national press but when speculation grew that he had been murdered, the local coroner took the step of ordering an inquest which showed that the executioner had died from pneumonia, complicated by liver disease. He was buried at the Trinity Church beside his home on Church Street, Horncastle.

On 3 December 1883, The Times carried an article relating to the execution of Henry Dutton, the Liverpool ironworker hanged for the murder of his wife's grandmother. The hangman who carried out the sentence was **Bartholomew Binns,** a former Gateshead coal miner, then running a small shop in Dewsbury, who had recently taken over from Marwood as the official Hangman of England. Many people had applied for the post, but he was one of only three selected for an interview, and the one eventually offered the post.

Binns carried out his first execution at Wandsworth in November 1883 – although he was reported to have assisted Marwood on a number of jobs – and another three in the same month before he received the offer of executing Dutton.

He arrived at Kirkdale Prison, Liverpool, three days before he was needed to carry out the task, and set up court in a cheap hotel. For the next two nights he held impromptu lectures on all matters relating to his craft, often inviting questions from the hordes of customers who had flocked into the bar-room, and the more the drink flowed the more open he became in his replies.

On the morning of the execution, Binns horrified warders at the gaol by turning up just an hour before he was required, with a friend in tow. Both men were still hung over from a weekend of drinking and the warders refused entry to the other man even though he claimed to be the assistant. Binns shook hands with the prisoner before he placed the noose around his neck and pulled the lever. The man fell into he pit and thrashed around. The drop had obviously failed to break his neck and the doctor had to wait several minutes before he could pronounce the prisoner dead.

At the inquest carried out later that morning, the doctor told the Governor that the execution had been badly carried out. He claimed that the hangman, who had since left the prison, had turned up drunk and used the wrong type of rope needed for a correct execution. The Governor forwarded a report to the Home Office stating that the execution had not been a success, and complaining about the hangman's conduct but, remarkably, Binns was still allowed to officiate for another three months.

On 10 December, Binns was involved in an incident at his shop in Dewsbury. A hawker called selling songs lamenting the demise of Patrick O'Donnell, whom Binns was due to hang the following week. Binns refused to buy one from him and the man left, only to return later in a drunken state, claiming to be the son of O'Donnell and threatening to shoot the hangman. Binns summoned assistance and ordered the man be locked up. When the case came to court, the magistrate said that Binns was a Government official and must not be annoyed. The man was ordered to pay a fine and when he refused he was sent to prison.

On 3 January 1884, Binns was in trouble himself when he was in court for travelling by train on 21 December, between Huddersfield and Dewsbury, without paying his fare. He was accompanied by his assistant, Alfred Archer, and both were returning from London where they had dispatched O'Donnell. The men were alleged to have alighted from the express and retired to the refreshment room for twenty minutes. When asked for their tickets, both claimed that they hadn't travelled on the train. In his defence, Binns said that he had been unable to purchase a ticket because there was a crowd at the station and someone had recognised him as the hangman. Both were fined twenty shillings, or a month in prison.

After the execution, at Liverpool, of McLean in March 1884, the Governor again reported that Binns had made a mess of the execution and this time he was sacked. Binns had supposedly arrived at the gaol drunk, and fearful that the hangman would botch the job, the officials had sent for Samuel Heath, who had assisted Binns in a double execution at Liverpool five days earlier. At the inquest after the execution, Binns denied he had turned up drunk and blamed a long train journey combined with hunger as the cause of his falling asleep after the one drink he had partaken before reaching the prison.

Binns left the gaol and visited a friend at Runcorn to whom he claimed that the Governor and doctor seemed to have a vendetta against him and that he couldn't do any right in their eyes.

Six months after his dismissal, Binns appeared at Wakefield Police Court where he accused his mother-in-law of stealing a watch from him.

There seems to have been some bitterness after Binns' wife had left him because of his continuing hanging experiments on cats and dogs. The mother-in-law told a reporter that she was going to inform the RSPCA of his torturing of defenceless animals.

Binns took to travelling in side-shows, explaining his method of execution to curious locals for a few pence until the police put a stop to his gruesome trade. He also continued to assist at one or two executions in Ireland until the turn of the century when he completely disappeared from the public eye.

Former Bradford policeman **James Berry** was one of those short listed for the post on the death of Marwood; but the intervention of a member of his family, who wrote to the prison commissioners requesting that Berry be passed over as he would bring shame on his family, persuaded them to favour Binns with the appointment.

At the time of his application in 1883, Berry, a native of Heckmondwike, had a wife and three children. He had served with both the Yorkshire and Nottinghamshire police forces, before resigning earlier that year to become a salesman. Berry claimed that he knew Marwood well and had assisted him on several jobs, including Charles Peace, but there is no record of his name appearing at executions before 1884, and it is more than likely just a boast to establish his credibility. Berry received his first appointment in March 1884 at Edinburgh, and in his book *My Experiences As An Executioner,* he admitted to suffering greatly from nerves before this first job. Berry was assisted by a man who assumed the name Richard Chester, a 36 year old wagoner, who regularly accompanied Berry during the next year or so.

Berry worked along the same lines as Marwood but went one step further in devising a calibrated table of drops so that it could be seen at a glance what drop the condemned should be given. Like all new systems however, there were flaws and in 1885 Berry had two dreadful experiences which could have shaken a less determined man out of the trade. These two mishaps took place in the same year that Berry had his most dramatic scene on the scaffold when an event occurred that passed down into English folklore:

John Lee was a nineteen year old footman from Babbacombe, Devon, who was convicted on circumstantial evidence of the murder of a Mrs Keyse, his elderly, wealthy, employer. The prosecution had alleged he had battered her to death after she cut his wages. Lee was taken to Exeter prison to await execution which was to be carried out in a coach house on a hand-built scaffold. Berry tested the equipment and although he remarked that it seemed poorly constructed, he decided to carry out the execution as planned.

On the morning of 23 February, Lee stood pinioned and noosed, a matter of seconds from death. Berry pulled the lever and when the trap failed to open, first Berry, then a number of warders stamped on the doors in a vain attempt to force them open. Lee stood motionless while all around was panic. Eventually he was led from the drop and taken to a room aside from the scaffold while an examination of the drop was carried out. A few alterations to the boards and the drop fell as previously tested. Lee was returned to the scaffold and the congregation was horrified to find a repeat of the earlier incident. When the drop refused to fall for a third time, the Governor postponed the execution and later Lee's sentence was commuted to life imprisonment. He was released from gaol in 1905 and emigrated to America, where he outlived his executioner.

Berry was a deeply religious man and would often send the condemned prisoner a lengthy poem he had copied from a Dorset paper which began:

"My brother – sit and think,
While yet on earth some hours are left to thee,
Kneel to thy God who does not from thee shrink,
And lay thy sins on Christ, who died for thee."

There are six more stanzas of this painful verse which Berry subjected his customers to until one Governor deemed it the responsibility of the chaplain and not the hangman to pray for the soul of the condemned and it was stopped.

Once he had settled into the routine of carrying out executions, Berry began to use an assistant less and less, and except for when he was to perform a double execution he usually worked alone, knowing that he had the aid of a burly warder if he needed help. Berry was only once called to hang three men together, when he executed the Netherby Hall murderers at Carlisle in 1886. For this job, he was assisted by a Charles Maldon, who was later identified as Sir Claude de Crespigny, a magistrate from Maldon, Essex. He had persuaded Berry to allow him to assist by paying him ten pounds, as it was likely in the near future that he would be required to witness executions by virtue of being appointed a sheriff for his native county. Questions were later asked in Parliament about the ethics of appointing a man who had abused his royal standing to secure a position that many from a working class background would never have been granted. The Home Secretary replied that provided the job was carried out satisfactorily then Sir Claude was as entitled as the next man to perform the task.

The last minutes of some of Berry's victims were recorded in his autobiography which was published shortly after his retirement. Berry also kept extensive scrap books into which he would paste cuttings relating to his commissions, and like Marwood he also modelled for Madame Tussauds.

It was another horrific episode on the scaffold that finally convinced Berry to hang up his ropes. When he went to hang Conway at Liverpool in 1891, he had a disagreement with the prison surgeon, Dr Barr, the same man who had given Binns so much grief. When the drop caused the neck to lacerate, spraying the pit with blood, Berry decided to call it a day. He had already agreed to carry out an execution at Winchester the following week and this was to be his last execution.

On his retirement, Berry embarked on a tour of music halls giving lectures of his methods but this was not a success and by the turn of the century he was pleading to be reinstated on the list. After one lecture at Edinburgh he was attacked in a public house, and when he left to seek help he was set upon again in the street. A man was remanded for the attack but it had shaken Berry up and as a result he cancelled many of his appearances. Berry died at his home in Bradford in October 1913.

The man who replaced Berry as the number one hangman was **James Billington,** a barber from Market Street, Farnworth, a small town on the outskirts of Bolton. Billington had applied for the job around the same time as Berry and had been appointed as the executioner for the county of Yorkshire. It was unusual for the normally thrifty Yorkshiremen to employ a Lancashire man, who would have to travel and therefore run up an expenses account, when they had the option of using Berry who lived in the county and had already carried out executions. Whatever the reason, Billington received the commission for Yorkshire, and for the next eight years he averaged one job a year, almost exclusively at Armley Gaol.

Billington was a twice married father of six born in Bolton in 1847. His early occupations included working as a piecer in a mill where he earned the nickname "Jimmy Armhole", and as a pub singer before he took over the barber shop at Farnworth.

Billington was credited with reducing the pinioning time at executions from five minutes to a matter of seconds. When the use of a scaffold built on ground level became commonplace in 1890, the whole process of pinion, procession and drop now took less time than it took Marwood to secure the prisoner in a body pinioning belt.

Billington's one dread was speaking to the reporters who flocked to his shop whenever he was engaged on a famous case. Many is the time he would leave someone half shaved if he thought the curious customer was a journalist. He assumed the name "Higgins" when on official business and would report to the prison dressed in a smart top hat and coat, carrying his equipment in a little black bag. He was also fond of wearing a little black velvet peaked cap, or a similar skull cap.

In his early years as a hangman Billington primarily worked alone, but from January 1892 he was usually accompanied by an assistant, the first of whom was **Thomas Henry Scott.**

Scott was a native of Huddersfield and is credited as being a former assistant of Berry's. There is no record of any such instances and the first mention of Scott is at Ireland in April 1892. Scott assisted Billington on a number of occasions around Britain and was in action as a number one in January 1893 when he hanged a man at Londonderry. It was reported that a large crowd pelted Scott with rotting vegetables as he made his way to the prison in a cab. Following a precedent set earlier in the century, the authorities at Stafford declined to use the recognised hangman and appointed Scott for themselves. He averaged a couple of jobs a year, usually one at Stafford and one in Ireland. Scott received some publicity of an unwelcome kind when he was the victim of a robbery while travelling to an execution at Liverpool in 1895.

On arriving at Lime Street Station, he shared a taxi with a young woman of questionable virtue, Winifred Webb, and instead of heading directly for the gaol they chose to cruise around the city for a while. On reaching his destination and after bidding farewell to his companion, Scott discovered that he had been robbed of two pounds nine and sixpence, and a pair of spectacles. Amazingly, when he called at the police station to report the theft, he found Miss Webb at the front desk reporting that she herself was the victim of a robbery by two strangers. Police promptly arrested the woman and she was remanded in custody.

Scott continued to carry out executions into the next century and on one or two occasions in Ireland he used Binns as an assistant.

For the next few years, Billington continued to be assisted by fellow Lancastrians. The first to join the list was William Wilkinson, who changed his surname to Warbrick when he learned his parents weren't married. Like Billington, he was a native of Bolton and there appears to have been some rivalry between them.

Another assistant was Robert Wade, a native of Accrington who appeared on the list in 1895. He vied with Wilkinson as Billington's main assistant, although both men were used when Billington hanged three men at Newgate in 1896. Wade was the assistant at Reading in 1899 and the Governor noted that he appeared rather nervous and dazed. He also added that Wade did very little but appeared on good terms with Billington. By this time Wade was also living in Bolton.

Around 1897, Billington left the barber shop and took over as the landlord of the Derby Arms at Churchgate, Bolton. It was also in this year that the first of Billington's sons was added to the list. Thomas was his eldest boy and he first assisted his father at Lincoln in July. In the following year, **William Billington** was added to the list and although junior to Thomas both in age and experience, it was William who was engaged to carry out an execution at Lincoln in 1899 when James Billington was unavailable. At the close of the century, there were six men on the official Government list of executioners, and with the exception of Scott they all lived in Bolton.

Official List of Executioners: 1899

Executioners:

    James Billington   Thomas Scott   William Billington
    Churchgate   Mold Green   Churchgate
    Bolton   Huddersfield   Bolton
    Lancashire   Yorkshire   Lancashire

Have all satisfactorily conducted executions, have assisted at executions, and have received official training at Newgate Prison.

Assistants:

    Thomas Billington   Robert Wade   William Warbrick
    Churchgate   Chorley New Road   Pole Street
    Bolton   Bolton   Bolton
    Lancashire   Lancashire   Lancashire

Have all assisted at executions, and have received official training at Newgate Prison.

The Development of the Scaffold

A scaffold specially constructed to hang a condemned man was first used around the turn of the 19th century. Before this time, a prisoner was taken to a gallows – which could be nothing more than a tree – on the back of a conveyance such as a horse, cart, or similar; noosed and pinioned and on removal of the conveyance, dropped into space. This had replaced the more conventional method of kicking a stool from beneath the person's feet, as is often seen in films portraying witchcraft executions in the middle ages. Another popular method was to use a ladder from which the condemned was "turned off".

In 1818, a collapsing scaffold was first used in Northampton and proved so popular that by the following year, almost every prison used a similar idea. Initially, the gallows was a platform around six to eight feet high, reached by a staircase of usually thirteen steps. The platforms varied, but were on average ten feet square and comprised of two upright beams, a cross beam, trapdoor and lever.

The beam was around eight feet high and had a chain hanging down, onto which the rope was attached. The trap doors also varied, some counties preferring a single trap door, others a pair of double doors. The latter proved to be the more popular and later became standard. (All further descriptions apply to the double door drop).

The gallows was operated by the pushing of a lever which released a large hinge on one of the doors, causing it to fall. This system was used until well into the 20th century when a more modern system superseded it.

The rope was around five eighths of an inch thick. Various hangmen, notably Bartholomew Binns, used thicker ropes, but when the Home Office drew up guidelines in 1885, they stipulated what thickness the ropes should be.

Up until James Berry's time, the hangman could supply his own ropes and would often dispose of them at a healthy profit. This practice was later stopped and all future ropes were produced by a London ropemaker, who supplied the state until the 1970s. The rope was usually Italian hemp, and thirteen feet long. Woven into one end was the noose which, in the 20th century, was covered in a soft leather to prevent burn marks on the skin. Woven into the opposite end was a brass eye-let through which a shackle passed and attached the rope to the end of the chain.

By the 1880s, an execution chamber was becoming more and more popular, although many still erected a scaffold in the prison yard. The scaffold was reached by a flight of steps which was not always easy for a prisoner to manage, especially one stricken with terror. It also proved difficult for the warders to get the man onto the drop if he tried to struggle.

The simple answer was to have the condemned cell and drop on the same level. The first attempts at this saw the digging of a deep pit in the yard over which the scaffold was placed. Other ready made pits were used, especially in Scotland, where the gallows was erected over various openings such as ventilation shafts and stairwells.

In 1890, the three storey scaffold housed inside a wing of the prison was first used. The lower level acted as a pit and received the falling body. The ceiling contained the bolt and doors of the drop. The first floor was the execution chamber, and the upper floor housed the beams and chains.

The condemned man still had to make his way from the cell to the drop and this was often fraught, with the prisoner sometimes having to be dragged whimpering with fear. The natural progression was to have the cell situated in close proximity to the chamber, thus cutting down the time between hangman entering the cell to the body being suspended on the rope.

Although this became standard by the middle 1900s, many prisons carried on with their outdated equipment until new Home Office regulations decreed modernisation.

Analysis: 1868-1899

The first thirty one years of private capital punishment in Great Britain saw 525 people hanged in 499 executions. A difference exists between these figures as one 'execution' sometimes featured two or more executees, and in the case of the "Lennie" mutineers in 1876, the only quadruple execution of the period.

All were hanged for murder, and there were 337 instances of homicide. Uxoricide (the murder of one's wife) was the second most popular 'victim group' with 122 such crimes. There were forty cases of infanticide (for the purposes of this book, infanticide has been defined as the murder of any child of five years or under). The remaining groups are small: patricide: 7; sororicide (the murder of one's sister): 4; matricide: 3; and fratricide: 1.

26.5% of all murders the condemned carried out were perpetrated under the influence of alcohol, or related in some way, such as the squabble over a drink in the case of Edward Gough who was hanged in January 1874.

Of the 122 uxoricides, 41% of the husbands were inebriated when they committed the crime. Conversely, of the fifteen murderesses hanged, none were recorded as being alcohol related. Some of these women murdered out of jealousy, notably Mary Ann Britland (hanged August 9th, 1886) who went to quite severe lengths to get her man. Others killed for that always popular motive of claiming the insurance money.

Firearms were responsible for more deaths than any other weapon. The second most common tool was the knife, which was used more to slit than to stab, the latter method being edged into fourth place behind batterings with a blunt instrument. Axe attacks, physical beatings, strangulation, and poisoning were all mildly popular, but the most bizarre method is probably murder by abortion as perpetrated by Alfred Thomas Heap, who was hanged in April 1875 at Liverpool.

Jack the Ripper's busy three months in London in 1888 prompted various associations among executed men. William Waddell, who was hanged in December 1888, committed a murder in the Ripper's style. Hanged in April 1889, William Henry Bury claimed he was Jack, with some justification; while Dr Thomas Cream (hanged November 1892) maintained he was the killer when he couldn't have been. Lastly, Frederick Butt, who wore the rope in December 1889, appeared to think Jack the Ripper was a game anyone could join in!

November 1887 saw the youngest person hanged when seventeen

year old Joseph Morley stood on the gallows. The following year in December, Samuel Crowther became the oldest at seventy one.

Many of the condemned showed extreme fortitude prior to and at the moment of execution, such as Robert Taylor in December 1874. Equally, and hardly surprisingly, to some the prospect of the gallows instilled sheer terror, none more so than Alfred Sowery who, among other things, had to be dragged to the rope when he was executed at Lancaster in August 1887.

Disability was no guarantee of escaping the gallows. August 1873 saw Laurence Smith executed at Cavan, Ireland, although he didn't see a thing as he was blind; and Henry William Young was hanged in May 1887 despite having only one leg.

Certain occupations, it appears, increased one's chances of meeting the hangman. Of the cases where a prisoner's trade was known, labourers, colliers, soldiers, and sailors respectively were easily the most popular; while shoemakers and tailors, both professions which utilised sharp instruments, also had numerous killers among their ranks.

More executions were carried out in the month of August than any other in the 1868–1899 period. William Marwood pushed the lever on more occasions than any other hangman, notching up 164 executions, comfortably ahead of James Billington who had 124 to his credit, who himself was two ahead of James Berry. William Calcraft officiated at 40 private executions as well as many public hangings prior to 1868.

Newgate Prison in London was the scene of the most executions, followed by Liverpool, Manchester, Leeds, Durham, as detailed on the following two tables:

Executions per Prison 1868-1899

Armagh	3	Edinburgh	4	Mullingar	2
Aylesbury	4	Exeter	5	Newcastle	4
Bedford	2	Galway	9	Newgate	50
Belfast	2	Glasgow	6	Northampton	6
Birmingham	6	Gloucester	9	Norwich	7
Bodmin	2	Greenock	1	Nottingham	13
Bristol	4	Hereford	3	Omagh	2
Cambridge	2	Horsemonger Lane	5	Oxford	6
Cardiff	2	Huntingdon	1	Perth	1
Carlisle	4	Ipswich	4	Reading	4
Carmarthen	3	Isle of Man	1	Shepton Mallet	3
Carnavon	1	Jersey	1	Shrewsbury	2
Cavan	1	Kilkenny	1	Sligo	1
Chelmsford	11	Knutsford	4	St Albans	3
Chester	4	Lancaster	5	Stafford	9
Clonmell	3	Leeds	23	Swansea	3
Cork	9	Leicester	6	Taunton	5
Cupar	1	Lewes	4	Tralee	4
Derby	8	Limerick	2	Tullamore	2
Devizes	4	Lincoln	12	Usk	3
Dolgelly	1	Liverpool	39	Wandsworth	18
Dorchester	3	Londonderry	1	Warwick	8
Dublin	14	Maidstone	17	Wexford	2
Dumbarton	1	Manchester	28	Winchester	14
Dundee	1	Mayo	1	Worcester	7
Durham	21	Morpeth	2	York	9

Executions per Prison 1868-1899

Newgate	50	Exeter	5	Belfast	2
Liverpool	39	Horsemonger Lane	5	Bodmin	2
Manchester	28	Lancaster	5	Cambridge	2
Leeds	23	Taunton	5	Cardiff	2
Durham	21	Aylesbury	4	Limerick	2
Wandsworth	18	Bristol	4	Morpeth	2
Maidstone	17	Carlisle	4	Mullingar	2
Dublin	14	Chester	4	Omagh	2
Winchester	14	Devizes	4	Shrewsbury	2
Nottingham	13	Edinburgh	4	Tullamore	2
Lincoln	12	Ipswich	4	Wexford	2
Chelmsford	11	Knutsford	4	Carnavon	1
Cork	9	Lewes	4	Cavan	1
Galway	9	Reading	4	Cupar	1
Gloucester	9	Tralee	4	Dolgelly	1
Stafford	9	Newcastle	4	Dumbarton	1
York	9	Armagh	3	Dundee	1
Derby	8	Carmarthen	3	Greenock	1
Warwick	8	Clonmel	3	Huntingdon	1
Norwich	7	Dorchester	3	Isle of Man	1
Worcester	7	Hereford	3	Jersey	1
Birmingham	6	Swansea	3	Kilkenny	1
Glasgow	6	Shepton Mallet	3	Londonderry	1
Leicester	6	St Albans	3	Mayo	1
Northampton	6	Usk	3	Perth	1
Oxford	6	Bedford	2	Sligo	1

1868

Cases where no executioner is recorded are multiple executions, and readers are asked to refer to the entries before or after for details of the hangman.

1868

August 13th: Thomas WELLS (18)　　　　　　　　　　　　　　　　Maidstone

On 1 May 1868, Edward Walshe, the station master employed by London South Eastern Railways at Dover Priory Station, summoned Wells into his office, and before the Area Superintendent, Henry Cox, reprimanded him for disobedience and his continuing poor standard of work.

Wells, whose duties included cleaning and working as a porter, received a lecture and a warning that if he was called into the office again he would be dismissed. It was the latest in a long list of cautions the young lad had received and he became convinced that the station master was victimising him.

Wells left the office but returned a few minutes later brandishing a gun that he used for shooting birds, and which he kept concealed at the station. He entered the office as Walshe and Cox were discussing him, and pointing the gun at Walshe, shot him through the head. He fled from the scene and was arrested in an empty railway carriage where he had made a half-hearted attempt to hide from the police.

He stood trial at Kent Summer Assizes held at Maidstone. The defence counsel tried to show that the prisoner was suffering from insanity, the result of an accident he sustained while working at the station when he was almost crushed by a train. This was rejected and he was sentenced to death by Mr Justice Wills.

Wells had been due to get married in August but instead was hanged by William Calcraft and George Smith. The execution was the first to be carried out in private but was in fact witnessed by sixteen journalists who were able to relate to their readers later that day that Wells died hard, struggling on the end of the rope for several minutes.

September 8th: Alexander Arthur MACKAY (19)　　　　　　　　Newgate

Early on the morning of 8 May, cafe proprietor George Grossmith left his shop at Norton Folgate to go out on business. Still on the premises were his wife, his son Walter (11), and Alexander Mackay, who was engaged in some menial work.

Shortly before 9am Walter left for school and minutes later neighbours heard screams coming from the cafe, which they believed to be Mrs Emma Grossmith. The voice cried out 'Oh, don't!', three times, followed by, 'Oh, John, you'll kill me!' (although christened Alexander, Mackay was known as John). A neighbour, admitted by Mackay, found Mrs Grossmith lying in a pool of blood in the kitchen. She had been battered to death with a rolling pin and a poker. The neighbour asked Mackay if he had done it and he said that he hadn't. Mackay then said he would go and find Mr Grossmith and rushed from the house.

Emma Grossmith died in hospital a week later but the police were unable to locate Mackay for several weeks because he had been arrested on a minor offence and was locked up in the cells at Maidstone prison. He was eventually recognised from a photograph circulated by the police and charged with murder.

Sentenced to death at the Central Criminal Court on 21 August, he was hanged by Calcraft and Smith. He was so overcome with fear at the end that he had to be dragged to the drop whimpering in sheer terror.

December 28th: Priscilla BIGGADYKE (29)   Lincoln

Although Richard Biggadyke, a Lincolnshire well-sinker, earned a reasonable standard of living from his work, he and his wife supplemented their income by taking in two lodgers.

Richard would go to work early in the mornings leaving his wife in bed, and he gradually began to suspect that she was having an affair with one of the lodgers, a man called John Proctor. On 30 September, Richard came home from work at the normal time, ate his tea and settled down by the fire. Within minutes he collapsed in agony and died the following morning.

His doctor was mystified at the sudden death of a hitherto healthy patient, and had the stomach contents analysed. Large traces of arsenic were found. Mrs Biggadyke, who was known to keep arsenic in the house, claimed she had seen Proctor put some powder in her husband's drink. He was arrested but later released through lack of evidence. Police continued with their enquiries and eventually the grieving widow was charged with the murder of her husband. She was later convicted and sentenced to death.

Her execution was carried out by Yorkshire hangman Thomas Askern. Mrs Biggadyke, in a faint, had to be assisted to the scaffold and when the drop fell she struggled violently for several minutes before eventually succumbing.

1869

Cases where no executioner is recorded are multiple executions, and readers are asked to refer to the entries before or after for details of the hangman.

1869

January 19th: Martin Henry VINALL (22)　　　　　　　　　　　Lewes

Aka Martin Brown, convicted at Lewes Assizes of the murder of an elderly labourer.

On 9 October 1868, David Baldey travelled into Kingston to collect wages owed to himself and his two sons. A search was carried out when he failed to return home that night, and the next morning his body was discovered in Lewes. He had been beaten about the head, shot, and robbed of the wages.

Vinall, who had lodged with the old man up until August, was an immediate suspect. He tried to evade arrest by joining the Royal Artillery, but was soon apprehended. He confessed that he had committed the crime, but that Baldey was not the intended victim, claiming that his target had been a wealthy shepherd called Tupper, whom he had hoped to ambush and rob, and he had killed Baldey by mistake. Hanged by Calcraft.

March 23rd: John DOLAN (37)　　　　　　　　　　　Durham

Sentenced to death at Durham Assizes on 27 February, for the murder of Hugh John Ward at Sunderland on 9 December 1868.

Dolan and Ward lodged with Dolan's girlfriend, Catherine Keehan, at a house on Union Street, Sunderland. On 8 December, Ward and a friend went out drinking. Dolan had also gone out drinking and returning to the house at 1.40 am he sent Mrs Keehan out for some more beer.

Ward later returned home, made some comment to Keehan, and went to his room. While Dolan sat drinking his beer, he suddenly jumped up and attacked the startled woman. She screamed out for Ward to help her as Dolan attempted to drag her into his bedroom. Ward came down and the two men began to fight on the stairs. Mrs Keehan rushed out to fetch the police, who came to the house but left after finding the disturbance had died down.

No sooner had they gone than the two men began to fight again and, in fear, Mrs Keehan jumped from a window to seek out the recently departed officers. When they returned they found that Dolan had fatally stabbed Ward with a shoe–maker's knife and he was taken into custody and charged with murder.

Hanged by Calcraft.

1869

March 23rd: John McCONVILLE (23)   **Durham**

On 30 January, Philip Trainer, an Irish labourer, was shot dead outside a Darlington public house. He had, until a few days earlier, been a member of a secret Fenian society but left the group after disassociating himself from their subversive activities.

Shortly before midnight John McConville, another Irish labourer, got into an argument with Trainer and challenged him to a fight outside the pub. As a crowd streamed out, McConville fired into it, fatally wounding Trainer.

A similar incident had occurred the previous week when another former group member was seriously wounded, with a man named Finnigan arrested for that attack. McConville was convicted on circumstantial evidence, and hanged alongside **DOLAN** [above] by Calcraft.

March 29th: Michael James JOHNSON (20)   **Manchester**

On Boxing Day, 1868, the landlord at the Cambridge Arms, Salford, evicted Johnson from the pub because he was drunk and being abusive to other customers.

A police officer arrived but after promising him that he would go home to bed, Johnson returned to the pub and asked the landlord to come outside and fight. An itinerant musician and casual barman in the pub, Patrick Nurney, told Johnson that he would be wise to go home and went to close the door, but as he did so Johnson drew out a knife and stabbed him fatally in the shoulder. He was arrested the next day hiding under a bed in his cousin's house.

Convicted at South Lancashire Assizes and hanged by Calcraft.

April 20th: William SHEWARD (57)   **Norwich**

A tailor who murdered his wife Martha (56) on 15 June 1851 by stabbing her to death with a pair of scissors. They had had a quarrel over money and he committed the crime in a rage, then set about dismembering the body which he successfully disposed of.

He remarried in 1862 and by 1868 he was running a public house in Norwich. During a trip to London he got drunk and in a fit of remorse walked into a police station and confessed to the murder. He was able to say where his wife's remains were and a search produced body parts belonging to an elderly woman. When he sobered up he tried to retract his statement, but was convicted and hanged by Calcraft.

August 12th: Jonah DETHERIDGE (20)   **Dorchester**

Sentenced to death at Dorset Assizes on 22 July for the murder of a prison warder.

On 23 March, Jonah Detheridge a native of Wednesbury, Staffordshire, was part of a work party at Portland Prison, Dorset. He was breaking stones in the quarry when he was berated by assistant warder James Trevett who complained about the standard of his work. Trevett, who was popular with both staff and inmates, told him to do the work as he had been shown and gave him some extra duties, which he refused to do.

An hour later Detheridge crept up behind the warder and beat him to death with his pick–axe.

Hanged by Calcraft.

October 11th: William TAYLOR (24)   **Exeter**

On 31 July, Taylor, a Birmingham born private in the 57th Rifles Regiment stationed at Raglan Barracks, Devonport, was among several soldiers told to report for extra drill by Corporal Arthur Skullen (35).

Taylor came onto the drill square without his knapsack and the Corporal told him to go and fetch it. Taylor put down his rifle and walked off, but Skullen bawled at him to pick up the weapon, which he then did. When he reached his room he loaded the rifle, walked out onto the parade and shot Skullen in the head.

He was disowned by his relatives, including his wife and young son, and received no visitors in his cell before being led to the scaffold in faltering steps and sobbing loudly. He was hanged by Calcraft.

1869

November 15th: Joseph WELSH (42)　　　　　　　　　　　Maidstone

Joseph Welsh and John Abrahams had been having a long standing dispute over money. Welsh, a married man with six children who earned his living as a painter, was accusing Abrahams of owing him money for some work he had carried out. When he refused to pay, Welsh took him to court at Greenwich, where the ruling was in favour of Abrahams.

Later that day the two men were drinking in a pub and exchanged words, whereupon Welsh pulled out a clasp knife and stabbed Abrahams in the chest. He was immediately arrested and when Abrahams died in hospital on the following day, was charged with the murder.

Sentenced to death at the Old Bailey and hanged by Calcraft.

December 13th: Frederick HINSON (32)　　　　　　　　　　Newgate

Hinson, a carpenter, shared a house with a Maria Death at Wood Green. They lived together as man and wife despite the fact that he already had a wife in his native Scotland. During the autumn of 1869, he began to suspect that Maria was having an affair with a man called William Boyd.

On 4 October he waited for them outside Wood Green station and as they walked out he savagely attacked Boyd, whose life was saved when a passer-by dragged off the crazed man.

Boyd fled from the scene as Hinson dragged Maria home, where he pulled out a gun and shot her in the chest before beating her about the head with the butt. Satisfied that she was dead, he reloaded and went off in search for Boyd. Hinson found him in a stable where he coldly shot him dead, before making a weak attempt to cut his own throat.

Hinson was immediately arrested by a passing policeman and charged with the double murder. He was sentenced to death at the Central Criminal Court on 26 November and later hanged by Calcraft.

1870

Cases where no executioner is recorded are multiple executions, and readers are asked to refer to the entries before or after for details of the hangman.

1870

January 10th: John GREGSON   **Liverpool**

On 13 October, 1869, Gregson, a Wigan collier, took his wife and two children for a day out and when they returned home later that afternoon, he was drunk. After tea, he told his wife he wanted her to pawn some of her clothes so he could buy more drink. His wife replied saying she wouldn't pawn clothes for drink, especially when the children needed feeding, and in a drunken rage Gregson savagely kicked her about the head and chest with his heavy, iron soled clogs. A neighbour who tried to drag him off also received a kicking.

    Mrs Gregson, who was covered in blood, was later put to bed but never recovered from the beating, and died three days later in hospital. He pleaded manslaughter through provocation at the trial, at Liverpool Assizes on 20 December, but after a lengthy retirement the jury found him guilty. He was hanged by Calcraft.

March 28th: William MOBBS (19)   **Aylesbury**

Soon after Christmas 1869, Mobbs was sitting next to a nine year old boy on a park bench at Linford when he asked him what he thought would happen if he was to kill. The young boy replied that he was sure to be hanged, whereupon Mobbs pulled out a knife and stabbed him several times in the neck.

    Mobbs later confessed to a policeman. He had become obsessed with murder after seeing a picture depicting the scene of the killing of Fanny Adams in 1867 by Frederick Baker. (Baker was hanged on Christmas Eve the same year).

    Mobbs was hanged by Calcraft.

May 27th: Lawrence SHEILD   **Tullamore**
           Margaret SHEILD

A brother and sister convicted and hanged together for the murder of a farmer, Patrick Dunne, on 26 February.

    As Dunne was walking home from a pub, he came across the couple standing in the road watching him approach. Reaching them, they bid him goodnight but when he returned the greeting, Margaret pulled out a gun and shot him in the chest. As he fell to the ground, she shot him again, before cutting his throat with a knife. Dunne was able to make a full statement before he died, in which he identified his attackers.

Lawrence Sheild was arrested as he tried to board a ship at Queenstown, and when his sister was in custody, they both stood trial. It was alleged that the motive for the crime stemmed from an incident several years old, when a group had attacked Dunne's house in search of weapons, and as a result he had shot and wounded one of their number.

Executioner unknown.

July 28th: Andrew CARR   Dublin

A discharged army pensioner convicted on his own confession of the murder of his paramour at Bulls Lane, Dublin on 16 June.

The couple shared a hovel in one of the city's slum areas, and after a drunken quarrel Carr cut her throat then told a policeman what he had done. He claimed it was a revenge attack after she had caused him some personal injury earlier in the year.

His plea of insanity failed and he hanged at Richmond (later Mountjoy) Prison. The executioner, who retained his anonymity by concealing his features with a black mask, gave the man a drop of fourteen feet, despite advice from a doctor that eight feet feet would be sufficient to kill the prisoner. When the drop fell, the doctor was proved right as Carr's head was ripped off.

A report later that day in the local press stated that if the public had seen this first private execution in Dublin, it would surely have been the last.

August 1st: Walter MILLAR (31)   Newgate

On 9 May, a man called at the house of Reverend Elias Huelin (35), claiming to be his nephew. He ordered the removal of some furniture which included a trunk. Neighbours later reported that Huelin and his aged housekeepr, Mrs Ann Boss, had disappeared and enquiries led the police to a furniture warehouse where the bodies of the missing couple were discovered; they had ropes around their necks and had been battered to death with a blunt instrument.

Walter Millar, a plasterer from Chelsea, was identified as the man who had organised the removal of the goods, and in spite of his claim that he was merely acting as an agent and was innocent of any crime, he was charged with the double murder.

He was tried at the Old Bailey in July, convicted on circumstantial evidence and sentenced to death.

He tried to cheat the hangman by hurling himself head first at a stone wall in an attempt to bash his brains out but succeeded in only causing cuts and bruises, and had to be carried to the gallows tied to a chair. This caused Calcraft to give him a drop that was shorter than intended and as a result Millar struggled for several minutes on the rope.

August 8th: John OWEN (38)   **Aylesbury**

Aka John Jones, a Wolverhampton born drifter convicted of mass murder, claiming Emmanuel Marshall and six members of his family at Denham village, Middlesex, as his victims. Marshall was the village blacksmith and had previously employed Owen as a casual worker. On 22 May he gained entry into the house and systematically beat to death each member of the family before stealing Marshall's best suit, then after smashing up a portrait of the man he crept out into the night. Owen was seen leaving the house and soon arrested.

The motive for the murders was a grudge he bore against the blacksmith believing that he was being paid an unfair wage.

After being sentenced to death he asked to spend the last two nights of his life in the coffin which he was to be buried in, and on the morning of his execution he threatened to punch Calcraft in the mouth for not having the courtesy of visiting him in the cell on the previous day.

August 15th: Thomas RADCLIFFE (26)   **Dorchester**

Edward Bly was a warder at Portland prison in Dorset. On 20 April he was in charge of seventeen convicts in a work party when he was threatened by Radcliffe, a petty criminal from Wigan serving a seven year sentence, and another convict, after he ordered them to do some task.

Later, while Bly wasn't looking, Radcliffe crept up behind him and struck him with a shovel. Radcliffe was then overpowered by other convicts and detained before the guards reached the scene and restored order.

Bly died on 15 June from blood poisoning caused by the wound and Radcliffe was charged with murder.

Hanged by Calcraft; Radcliffe was the second man hanged in a year for the murder of a guard at Portland Prison (see **1869, August 12th: Jonah DETHERIDGE**)

1870

October 4th: George CHALMERS (45)   **Perth**

A vagrant convicted on 8 September, at Perth Circuit Court, for the murder of John Miller, a toll keeper who lived alone at Blackhill Toll Barr, near Braco.

Miller was last seen alive by a local shepherd on the evening of 21 December; the following morning his body was discovered with horrific head wounds and a blood-stained crow-bar beside it. Miller's house had been ransacked, and his watch, some money, and some of his clothes had been stolen. The murderer had left behind some of his own clothing and a local policeman recognised them as being worn by a tramp who had recently been released from Alloa gaol after serving ten days for theft.

A description was circulated for Chalmers but it was six months before he was arrested in Dundee after a suspicious policeman had questioned him. When detained, Chalmers denied the crime but was found to be wearing some of the dead man's clothing.

Hanged by Calcraft.

October 11th: Margaret WATERS (35)   **Horsemonger Lane**

A Brixton 'baby-farmer' convicted of the murder of several young children, whom she killed variously by starvation, strangulation, and suffocation.

In March 1870, she was remanded at Lambeth County Court on a charge of neglecting and failing to provide food for her adopted child. Subsequent investigations revealed the bodies of other children she had taken for adoption and who had since died.

The frail widow of seven years pleaded guilty to the murder of five children and was hanged by Calcraft.

1871

Cases where no executioner is recorded are multiple executions, and readers are asked to refer to the entries before or after for details of the hangman.

1871

April 3rd: William BULL (21) — Bedford

Sally Marshall was a weak old woman, of low intelligence, who lived alone in a cottage at Little Slaughton. The local boys would often tease her by throwing stones at her window and knocking on her door, which would bring her running into the street screaming and swearing as they ran off laughing.

On the night of 29 November, William Bull had been out drinking and on leaving the pub he walked home with a friend. As they parted company, Bull told him that he was going to call on Sally and cause a 'to-do'.

Next morning a neighbour found the door open, and when he looked inside he found her beaten to death on the floor. Neighbours told police that they had heard screams but as they were used to hearing them, paid no heed.

Bull was arrested two days later and traces of blood were found on his clothes. He was convicted at Bedford Assizes, sentenced to death by Mr Justice Campbell, and confessed his guilt before he was hanged by Calcraft.

April 24th: Michael CAMPBELL (28) — Chelmsford

A Berwick born tailor and former soldier, convicted of the murder of Samuel Galloway (49), a retired dock worker.

Campbell and three accomplices were disturbed by Galloway as they tried to break into his home on Cannon Street, Stratford, on 8 February. Galloway spotted one of the men climb over a fence and gave chase, but the three men and one woman waited for him to approach, caught him, and while two held his arms, a third struck him on the head with a blunt instrument.

Mrs Galloway witnessed the assault and was able to identify Campbell as the assailant; when Galloway died ten days later Campbell was charged with murder. He admitted his guilt but denied any intent.

Hanged by Calcraft.

1871

July 31st: Richard ADDINGTON (38)   **Northampton**

On 29 May, Addington, a Northampton shoemaker, and his wife attended a village festival where he indulged in an all day drinking session and had to be helped home in a drunken state. The next morning they quarrelled about his conduct and to escape his temper, Margaret Addington went out into the garden. A neighbour heard Addington shout at his wife to come inside and when she refused, he stormed into the garden and dragged her back into the house where he cut her throat with a shoe knife. The neighbour, who had witnessed the incident from his own garden, summoned the police and Addington was arrested.

His defence maintained he was insane, as a result of being kicked in the head by a horse twenty years earlier, but he was found guilty and hanged by Calcraft.

August 17th: William COLLINS   **Clonmel**

Convicted of the murder of John Ryan at Glassdrum, County Tipperary, on 31 March. The crime was committed in full view of a house owned by Patrick Hayes, in which were Ryan's wife, mother-in-law, and some friends.

Collins attacked Ryan as a result of a long standing feud, and as Ryan called for help, Patrick Hayes rose but was halted by his wife, who thought it was a ploy to lure her husband outside as he too had had a fierce row with Collins. Eventually, when someone else went to Ryan's aid, it was discovered that Collins had almost severed the man's head with a knife.

Collins fled but was soon tracked down, and police found a piece of skin stuck in Ryan's mouth fitted a wound on Collins's hand. He pleaded not guilty to the crime but confessed after sentencing.

The executioner was probably Calcraft.

1872

Cases where no executioner is recorded are multiple executions, and readers are asked to refer to the entries before or after for details of the hangman.

1872

January 8th: Frederick JONES (20) Gloucester

On 10 December 1871, Emily Gardner was walking home with her elder sister Alice from a large house in Cheltenham where Alice was employed. They were accompanied by a young baker, Fred Jones, who had been courting Emily for several months. As they reached the street where Alice lived, the sisters parted and Jones promised to see Emily safely home.

Less than an hour later, Jones walked into a police station and admitted that he had killed his sweetheart by cutting her throat. Her body was found at the house. Jones claimed he was drunk and had committed the crime through his jealousy of a man who lodged with Emily and her father.

Tried at Gloucester Assizes and sentenced to death by Mr Justice Keating on 22 December 1871.

Hanged by Calcraft.

March 18th: Edward ROBERTS (35) Oxford

Roberts, an Oxfordshire gardener, lodged with a Mrs Meyrick at Whitney and had become enamoured with her daughter Ann, even proposing marriage to her but she turned him down. Later, when he discovered she was in love with another man, he swore that he would kill her.

On 30 July, Mrs Meyrick was at church leaving her daughter and lodger alone in the house. While Ann was mopping up some water from the kitchen floor, Roberts went into the garden shed, returned with an axe, and struck her on the head.

Despite her horrific injuries - he had sliced off the top of her head - she survived for several days. Roberts, who had gone at once to the police and confessed, was charged with murder, convicted and hanged by Calcraft.

April 1st: William Frederick HORRY (28) Lincoln

A Staffordshire publican found guilty of the murder of his wife Jane on 18 January.

They had been married for five years and lived happily until September 1871 when he became a heavy drinker, caused by jealousy of his wife talking to customers in the bar. She left their home in Burslem and went to stay with relatives in Boston. He followed her and pleaded for her to come home; she refused and he shot her dead.

He pleaded insanity at the trial but the prosecution proved that he had purchased the gun at Nottingham on his way to Boston, thus showing that the crime was pre-meditated.

Hanged at Lincoln Castle by William Marwood who was officiating at his first execution.

August 1st: John KEWISH   **Isle of Man**

A middle-aged self confessed sheep rustler convicted of the murder of his father at Sulby.

On 28 March, John Kewish senior was found dead in a field with four chest wounds which the police thought had been caused with a pitchfork. Evidence led the police to his son who was charged with, and later convicted of, his murder. In the condemned cell, Kewish confessed that he had shot his father four times and that he had died instantly.

It was the first execution on the island for thirty years and there was much trouble building a scaffold for Calcraft to hang the man on. Firstly, there was a great deal of reluctance by the island's carpenters to build the scaffold; and secondly, when a Castletown contractor finally agreed to undertake the task, it was discovered there were no plans or drawings to aid construction as no one had ever witnessed an execution.

Eventually the Governor of Kirkdale forwarded a blueprint and the execution went ahead as scheduled in the grounds of Castle Rushen at Castletown.

August 12th: Christopher EDWARDS (34)   **Stafford**

A locksmith who brutally murdered his wife, Rosanna, at Willenhall on 20 April.

In a fit of drunken jealousy, he beat her brains out with a poker. Her screams alerted neighbours who rushed in to find her dead on the floor, while the Edwards' two children lay asleep in an adjacent room. He had frequently beaten her and she had taken to carrying a knife to stave off any threat of assault.

The jury at Staffordshire Assizes on 28 July took less than ten minutes to return a guilty verdict. The judge said he had never come across a case of less provocation. Hanged by George Smith.

1872

August 12th: Charles HOLMES   **Worcester**

A labourer sentenced to death at Worcester Assizes on 22 June for the murder of his wife at Bromsgrove.

Holmes earned a respectable living at a Bromsgrove quarry, and his wife also received a good wage working in the forge at the village nail works. They had lived quite happily with their young crippled son, until relations between them floundered when he took to drink.

On 7 March, Holmes was drinking in the Rose and Crown pub, when his wife came in and summoned him home. At the house, neighbours heard him shout that if she didn't fetch his supper he would 'make her fit for a coffin.'

She took the next day off work, and together with her son, went to stay with friends. When Holmes came home and found her gone, he went to the friends' house and tried to persuade her to return. Four times that night he called at the house and each time she refused his request to come home.

Finally, he went to the house just as she was taking the child upstairs to bed. Holmes called out to his son and asked him if he would like some pocket money. Mrs Holmes carried the child towards her husband who stood at the door and as they approached, the boy held out his hand. Holmes reached into his pocket but instead of pulling out money, he withdrew a razor and slashed his wife across the throat, killing her instantly and covering the boy in blood.

He made no effort to escape and admitted his guilt. Hanged by Calcraft, he was the first person to be hanged at Worcester for almost forty years, and died after a brief struggle.

August 13th: Thomas MOORE (52)   **Maidstone**

A former soldier who had served with distinction in the Crimean and Indian wars, where he had earned medals for bravery, strangled his wife after a quarrel at Ashford on 1 June.

The Wednesday before the murder he met his wife, from whom he was separated, by appointment and on the next two days he went to work and behaved as normal. On the Saturday he met her by chance and offered to walk her to her father's home; along the way they sat down for a rest, during which time he claimed he had an overwhelming desire to kill her.

He accused a member of her family for inciting trouble between him and his wife. His unsuccessful defence was insanity.

August 13th: James TOOTH (42)   **Maidstone**

A Royal Marine sentenced to death for the murder of drummer boy George Stock (17), at Marine Barracks, Chatham.

Tooth had been in the army for twenty years and had risen to become an NCO, but had been downgraded after a drunken incident at the barracks. He had made an attempt to reclaim his former rank but his fondness for drink let him down.

One day during the spring, Stock was asked to search for a ring that had been lost by one of his corporals. He was unable to find the ring but was seen with a half-crown, which, when questioned, he said he had been given by Tooth. Tooth was then suspected of stealing the ring and carpeted by his superiors. Realising that he had lost any hope of regaining his promotion, he went out and got drunk.

On the following morning, he spotted Stock emerging from church and crept up behind him. Before the boy could do anything to defend himself, Tooth took out a knife and cut his throat. He was immediately detained and when he stood trial later that month, he pleaded guilty through insanity.

After conviction, he wrote a letter to Stock's older brother, who was a corporal in the same regiment, and asked for forgiveness, which was granted.

August 13th: Francis BRADFORD (19)   **Maidstone**

On 31 May, Daniel Donahoe reported Bradford to his superiors for causing a disturbance, and as a result Bradford was reprimanded. Later that night as Donahoe slept in the barrack room, Bradford crept in and butchered his colleague with a bayonet. He was detained at once and claimed he was glad Donahoe was dead as he wouldn't be able to cause grief for anybody else.

Hanged beside **MOORE** and **TOOTH** [above], in a triple execution carried out by Calcraft and Smith. Bradford died hard and struggled for over ten minutes at the end of the rope, while the other two died instantly.

1872

August 26th: William LACE   Taunton

Sentenced to death by Mr Justice Mellor at Wells Assizes on 5 August, for the murder of his wife on 23 April.

Fuelled by drink and an accusation against his wife, he kicked her repeatedly and savagely for over an hour before she fled to a neighbour's house and died later from her wounds. He acknowledged his guilt when arrested.

Hanged by Calcraft.

December 9th: Augustus ELLIOT (31)   Newgate

On 14 September, Ellen Moore a 22 year old prostitute, was visited at her room in Hoxton by Augustus Elliot, an old boyfriend whom she had known for four years. They enjoyed each others company and were seen together in various pubs and cafes.

On the afternoon of 16 September, the landlady at Ellen's lodgings heard a series of shots and rushed upstairs to find the couple lying wounded on the bed. Ellen whispered 'Gus done it' before dying.

Elliot was nursed back to health and charged with murder. He was tried at the Old Bailey and claimed that he had shot her because she refused to emigrate with him to America. On 20 November he was found guilty; hanged by Calcraft.

December 30th: Michael KENNEDY (58)   Manchester

Early in October, Kennedy purchased a pistol and ammunition. On October 8, having spent the afternoon in a pub, he returned home to find his meal not ready. Later he asked his wife of 36 years, Ann, for a kiss, but she told him she didn't kiss drunken men. In a rage he shot her dead.

He pleaded insanity at the trial but evidence was shown that he had bought the gun earlier in the week and the prosecution claimed that this was enough proof that the crime was premeditated.

Kennedy's defence claimed that he had become upset at the death of one of his children and when he later lost his job he began to drink heavily. The combination of alcohol and an old head injury had the effect that, after a drinking session, he became madly dangerous.

He was found guilty of murder and hanged by Calcraft.

1873

Cases where no executioner is recorded are multiple executions, and readers are asked to refer to the entries before or after for details of the hangman.

1873

January 7th: Edward HANCOCK (50)   **Warwick**

On 13 November 1872, Hancock, a butcher, returned home from a neighbouring village the worse for drink and quarrelled with his wife, of whom he was very jealous.

Tired of their constant rows, she told him she was leaving and walked out. Hancock followed but failed to persuade her to return, whereupon he stabbed her with a knife.

Sentenced to death at Warwick Assizes on 18 December, he was hanged by George Smith.

January 8th: Richard SPENCER (60)   **Liverpool**

Spencer was a fishmonger who kept a shop in Liverpool. Elizabeth Wharton, many years his junior, lived with him as his wife. In August 1872 the business collapsed and they moved to a house in Everton.

On 8 August they went to bed sober after a night out. In the morning she was woken with a sharp blow to the head and cried out: 'Richard, what are you doing?' He told her that he wanted them to die together; she replied saying she wanted no part of his suicide pact, and fled to a neighbour's house. She returned home later to find him nursing a head wound, and without warning he pulled out a gun and shot her. Following her death three days later, Spencer was charged with the murder.

He claimed that the shooting was accidental but was found guilty and sentenced to death by Mr Justice Mellor, who added that Spencer had no chance of a reprieve. Hanged by Calcraft.

January 13th: Hugh SLANE (22)   **Durham**
                John HAYES (29)

On the evening of 26 November, Slane went into a Spennymoor tobacconist shop run by Joseph Waine (33) and began to quarrel with a customer called Wilson. Slane accused Wilson of causing a disturbance in a public house. Wilson replied that he was mistaken because he hadn't been in the pub and was certainly no troublemaker. Slane insisted that he was the man, and eventually Waine had to intervene saying there must have been a mistake and asked him to leave.

Slane asked the tobacconist for a box of matches which, after purchasing, he threw into Waine's face before dragging him into the street. He whistled for his friends who were waiting around the corner and together they kicked him to death on the pavement as Waine's wife watched helplessly.

Four men stood trial for the murder and all were sentenced to death. Terence Rice (19) and George Beesly (27) were granted a reprieve on 5 January. Slane and Hayes were hanged by Calcraft.

March 24th: Mary Ann COTTON (40)   **Durham**

A thrice married former nurse convicted of the murder of several members of her family.

In 1853, she met and married her first husband William Mowbray, who worked as a coal miner. In the next five years, they had four children: all died at a very early age from gastric fever. Her husband, who had left the mines to go to sea, also died from the same complaint. Using the insurance money, she moved to Seaham Harbour, where she met and had an affair with a married man, Joseph Nattress, before moving to Sunderland and becoming a nurse.

There she began another affair with one of her patients, George Wade, whom she married following his discharge from the ward. Soon, he also died from gastric fever, after making out a will to his new bride. Next, she married James Robinson, and they had four children, all of whom also succumbed to gastric fever.

She went on marrying and murdering until July 1872, when a doctor discovered traces of arsenic after the death of one of her many children. A total of twenty bodies were exhumed and examined; arsenic was found in each of them.

Mary Cotton was convicted at Durham Assizes at the beginning of March 1873. She gave birth to her last child five days before she was hanged by Calcraft.

August 4th: Henry EVANS (45)   **Aylesbury**

Sentenced to death at Aylesbury Assizes in July for the murder of his wife, Annie Seabrook-Evans.

Evans lived with his wife at Oving, where she supported him with her earnings as a dressmaker. He was a drunkard and as a result they frequently quarrelled.

On Saturday 22 March, Evans went to his father's house which was directly opposite his own, and said his wife had locked up and left, taking the key with her. He repeated this tale to many people, and spent the weekend in his parents' spare room. On Monday morning, he left town in a pony and trap.

Neighbours became suspicious at reports of Mrs Evans' sudden and unexepected disappearance, and decided to investigate. The door to the house was forced and Annie Seabrook-Evans was discovered battered to death.

Evans was located, found to be in possession of her key, and was seen to be wearing trousers with faint blood stains. He was convicted after a short trial and hanged by George Smith.

August 4th: Benjamin HUDSON (24)   **Derby**

A collier sentenced to death at Derby Assizes on 15 July, for the murder of his wife, Elizabeth. She was found battered to death with a hedge stake at West Handley, near Stavely.

Mrs Hudson had left her husband on Easter Sunday, ten days before the murder. On 24 April, Hudson was seen in the area, and later that night her body was found battered to death in a field. He was soon arrested and charged with murder.

At his trial, Hudson pleaded guilty to causing her death but was instructed by his counsel to change the plea to not guilty. It did him no good and he was hanged by Calcraft.

August 19th: Edward WALSH   **Mayo**

A publican from Castlebar convicted of the murder of his heavily pregnant wife on 27 April.

While drunk, Walsh asked his wife and mother of five children, for the keys to the tap room at their public house and as she went across the yard to get them, he followed her and beat her to death with a large stick.

He pleaded insanity at his trial but was convicted and hanged by George Smith.

August 20th: Laurence SMITH (45) Cavan

A blind farmer convicted of the murder of Patrick Lynch, at Lackermore, Co Cavan, on 3 July 1872.

The two men had a quarrel over a piece of bog-land as they walked back from a Ballyduff public house. Smith was alleged to have pulled out a knife and stabbed Lynch eighteen times. He pleaded self-defence but was found guilty of murder and sentenced to death.

When the hangman, George Smith, drew the bolts to collapse the platform, the witnesses were horrified to find the prisoner's feet touched the floor, and the executioner had to pull the rope up about two feet to cause death by strangulation. Smith died in great agony. Witnesses claimed the hangman had used a rope that was far too long.

August 26th: Thomas Hartley MONTGOMERY (32) Omagh

A police inspector convicted of the brutal murder of William Glass, a bank cashier at the Northern Bank, Newton Stewart.

Shortly after 4pm on 15 July 1871, a cleaner found the man's body in a pool of blood behind the counter. He had been battered to death with a hammer. Missing from the safe was over a thousand pounds in notes, although the thief had left behind a large amount of gold. Montgomery, the sub inspector at the local police station in Newton Stewart was identified by two witnesses who saw him enter the bank at the approximate time of the murder; he was also seen later to wash his soiled coat in a stream, and his suspicious behaviour after the crime was reported attracted the attention of his fellow officers.

Despite a strong case put forward by the prosecution, his first trial held before Mr Justice Lawson at Omagh Assizes was concluded on 22 July 1872, with the jury twice failing to bring in a unanimous verdict.

A retrial was ordered at the next sitting of the Assizes and this time Montgomery was convicted and hanged by Smith & Marwood.

September 8th: James CONNOR Liverpool

A powerfully built London boilerman sentenced to death by Mr Justice Brett on 16 August for the murder of Sheffield born James Gaffrey and the attempted murder of William Metcalfe on Monday 11 August.

Connor had been drinking and visited a music hall in Liverpool. On leaving the theatre, he made conversation with Mrs Mary Shears, the wife of a ship's steward, and asked her to join him for a drink. When she refused he began to get violent and accused her of stealing money from him.

Gaffrey and Metcalfe were walking down Mill Street, Liverpool, when they saw Connor strike the woman. They rushed over and asked him what was going on and during the ensuing row, Connor struck Gaffrey in the face. When Gaffrey responded by punching him back, Connor drew a knife and stabbed him behind the ear, then turned on Metcalfe, wounding him.

Connor pleaded manslaughter through provocation but was convicted of murder.

Hanged by Calcraft who was assisted by Marwood. It was another in the long line of botched executions by the aged hangman. Connor was pinioned in the usual fashion and took his position under the beam. As Calcraft pulled the lever, the rope snapped under the strain and Connor fell into the drop, landing in a heap on the floor where he squirmed about in a great deal of pain and unable to move due to his bindings. A new rope was fetched, Connor was brought up and then dropped a second time.

1874

Cases where no executioner is recorded are multiple executions, and readers are asked to refer to the entries before or after for details of the hangman.

1874

January 5th: Thomas CORRIGAN (23)   Liverpool

On 3 November 1873 Corrigan, an Irish born loafer and occasional dock worker, returned home after drinking all afternoon and went to bed. On waking, he heard his mother moaning about his girlfriend sleeping in the house, an arrangement his parents disapproved of. He went downstairs and demanded his supper but when told it wasn't ready he knocked his mother onto the floor and began kicking, stamping and jumping on her, all while his father and a couple of neighbours stood by!

When his mother crawled upstairs to bed, he followed, and threw her back downstairs, this final act too much for her to take and she died. No one had dared interfere with Corrigan but when he walked out into the street, a policeman was called and he was arrested.

He was convicted at Liverpool Assizes and after sentence of death was passed, Mr Justice Quain told him to expect no mercy. Hanged by Calcraft. A witness at Kirkdale prison said; 'He died hard.'

January 5th: Charles DAWSON   Durham

On 13 September 1873, Dawson, an ironworker, and Mrs Martha Jane Addison, whom he lived with at Darlington as man and wife, went out drinking with three people they shared a house with. Dawson became angry because he found his shirt collar too tight and punched Mrs Addison. She left him to go drinking with some of her own friends, and later in the evening when Dawson saw her, he knocked her to the ground with a bottle and stamped on her, causing fatal injuries.

He pleaded manslaughter at his trial but was convicted of murder.

January 5th: Edward GOUGH   Durham

On 7 July 1873, Gough, a pitman, called into a pub at Sunnyside, County Durham, and ordered a small porter. James Partridge, also a pitman, was drinking with a group of friends, and told him not to order a small drink, rather he should buy a drink big enough for them both to share.

Gough drank up and left the pub but later returned with a friend and challenged Partridge to a fight. They went outside and as Partridge took off his jacket, Gough rushed over and stabbed him in the groin.

He pleaded guilty of manslaughter under provocation, but was convicted of murder.

1874

January 5th: William THOMPSON (26)   **Durham**

A pitman convicted of the murder of Mrs Jane Thompson (20), with whom he lived at Anfield Plain. They had travelled into Newcastle during the afternoon of 4 October and began to argue after he saw her talking to another man.

They returned home and got ready to go out that night. When her father, who lived with them, went on ahead to the pub, he again started an argument over the man he had seen her talking to earlier. They made up and went out drinking, but later whilst drunk he accused her of being unfaithful and cut her throat.

Thompson was hanged along with **DAWSON** and **GOUGH** [above] in a triple execution carried out by William Marwood.

January 12th: Charles Edward BUTT (22)   **Gloucester**

Butt managed a small farm for his widowed mother at Arlington, and for many months he had been paying attention to Amelia Phillips, the sister of a neighbouring farmer. On 18 August 1873, he invited her to accompany him to a cheese fair, but she refused, saying that she had already accepted an invitation from another young farmer. Next day he shot her dead as she walked out with the other man. Butt fled from the area but was arrested three days later in Abergavenny, and brought back to face trial.

January 12th: Edwin BAILEY (32)   **Gloucester**
              Ann BERRY (31)

Bailey was the manager of a shoe shop in the Clifton area of Bristol, whose wife had left him due to his adultery.

In the summer of 1872, he seduced one of his customers, a servant girl named May Jenkins, and when in January 1873 she gave birth to a child, she took a summons out against Bailey after he refused to admit to being the father and to pay any maintenance. The court ordered him to pay five shillings per week for the child, which he sent to a police officer at Horsfield.

Ann Berry worked for Bailey and was much enamoured by him; they began an affair while her husband was serving a prison sentence. She paid May Jenkins a visit and persuaded her to accept a health tonic for the baby. When the child began teething, the young mother administered the medicine. It contained a lethal dose of arsenic.

35

Bailey and Berry were caught, convicted and hanged, together with **BUTT** [above], by Anderson. At the time of their executions, Ann Berry's husband was still in Gloucester Prison for petty theft.

March 31st: Thomas CHAMBERLAIN   Northampton

John Cox Newitt was a wealthy farmer who occupied a lodge at Wood Burcote, Towcester. On the night of Sunday 30 November 1873, he and a servant girl stayed home while the rest of the family went to church.

At around 8pm, Thomas Chamberlain, a local shoemaker, entered the kitchen of the house armed with a cutlass and attacked the young girl. Newitt was alerted by the sound of the struggle and rushed into the kitchen whereupon Chamberlain let go of the servant and started to attack him instead. The girl was able to flee and raise the alarm.

The police found Newitt's body hacked to pieces on the kitchen floor and Chamberlain, who was known to the servant girl, was quickly taken into custody and charged.

Hanged by Calcraft.

May 25th: John GODWIN (27)   Newgate

A hearth-rug maker convicted of the murder of his wife Louisa (27), at Islington.

Godwin, his wife, and their two children occupied a room in a house on Kinglands Road, Islington. On 22 April, a neighbour heard noises coming from their room. She knew that Godwin was in the habit of ill-treating his wife, and thinking that he was beating her up, she knocked on the door. Godwin refused to open up, saying that there was no trouble and that everything was fine.

The neighbour, Sarah Wilkins, then went back upstairs but watched over the landing for someone to leave. Moments later, Godwin left the room whereupon Mrs Wilkins entered and found Godwin's wife dead in a pool of blood. She had been battered to death with a piece of wood later found under the bed.

Godwin was soon arrested, and after conviction he was hanged by Calcraft and Anderson. It was Calcraft's last execution.

1874

June 29th: Frances STEWART (48) — Newgate

A widow sentenced to death by Mr Justice Blackburn for the murder of her one year old grandson Henry Ernest Scrivener at Chelsea.

Mrs Stewart threw the child into a river at Poplar in a jealous rage after being asked to leave her lodgings at her daughter and son-in-law's house. Stewart had warned her daughter that she would 'make your heart ache, like you have made mine.'

At her trial she claimed that the child had fallen into the water by accident but could offer no reason why she had failed to go to its assistance.

Mrs Stewart became the first grandmother to be hanged for the murder of her grandchild, the sentence being carried out by William Marwood who gave her a drop of under three feet.

August 10th: John MacDONALD — Exeter

A discharged marine convicted of the murder of his paramour, Bridget Walsh, at Stonehouse, Plymouth.

On Sunday 28 June, MacDonald quarrelled with Mrs Walsh - whom he had lived with while her husband was at sea - over some furniture they had bought and disputed the ownership of. A fierce row ensued during which he pinned her to the ground with one hand around her neck, while brandishing a poker in the other. Fortunately her life was spared - temporarily - when her son came home and dragged him off.

Next day, MacDonald bought some lead acetate poison, and after paying off some debts, he burst into her house and battered her to death with a bed post. He then made two attempts to end his own life. First he drank the poison, then while waiting for it to take effect he cut his own throat. He was arrested before he could finish the job and removed to prison where he recovered, despite a third attempt at suicide when he tried to starve himself to death.

He pleaded insanity at his trial held before Mr Justice Brett at Devon Lammas Assizes in July. After being convicted, he admitted that he killed her because she had provoked him with her unfaithfulness.

He made a will shortly before his execution leaving eleven pounds which he asked to be used to pay for her funeral.

Hanged by Marwood.

1874

August 18th: William JACKSON (29)   York

William Jackson was a soldier discharged from the 77th Regiment after serving in India. Soon after moving back in with his parents, he began to have frequent arguments with the family. These altercations were mainly caused by Jackson's heavy drinking.

After one particularly fierce series of rows, he packed his bags and told his parents that he was leaving home, and on 5 May he set out for Ripon. On the journey he came across his sister Elizabeth (16); the next morning her body was found dead in a field with a cut throat. From letters on her person the police suspected that Elizabeth's boyfriend was the murderer and he was detained but later released when other evidence led them to her brother.

Jackson was later detained and charged. No motive was clearly established but he was convicted, and hanged by Askern inside York Castle.

August 24th: James Henry GIBBS   Usk

Sentenced to death by Mr Justice Lush at Monmouth Assizes for the murder of his wife at St Mellons.

On 3 June, Mrs Gibbs's fearfully decomposed body, partially eaten by insects, was discovered in a ditch in the grounds of a farm in Llanrumney Hall, near Cardiff. Investigations led the police to her husband, a butler at the hall, and he was later charged with her murder. The state of the body made it difficult for doctors to be certain of the cause of death but Gibbs probably killed her by cutting her throat, as there was evidence of neck injuries on the rotting corpse.

He protested his innocence and maintained fortitude in the death cell until the hangman, Marwood, called for him to leave. Gibbs then broke down and began to wail pitifully as he was assisted to the scaffold by two warders where he had to be held erect until the drop fell.

August 31st: Henry FLANAGAN (22)   Liverpool

Convicted after a two day trial of the murder of his aunt, Mary Flanagan (53), at Liverpool.

It was alleged that, while drunk, Flanagan broke into her house and attempted to rape her, before strangling her and fleeing with her purse containing three sovereigns. He boasted to a friend that he had stolen some money, and was later arrested for murder.

Hanged on the same morning by Marwood as **WILLIAMS** [below], but not together. Flanagan was hanged first, while Mrs Williams was held in a cell adjacent to the drop. She was brought to the scaffold once Flanagan's body was taken down and the trap reset.

August 31st: Mary WILLIAMS (40)   **Liverpool**

Sentenced to death at Liverpool Assizes on 12 August for the murder of Nicholas Manning (26), a labourer from Bootle, who died from gunshot wounds received on the night of 20 April.

Mary Williams was a married woman who lived with her husband at 60 Raleigh Street, Bootle. Manning lived with his parents at number 50.

On the night of the shooting a disturbance took place between Manning's sister and Mrs Williams, which resulted in some windows of the Manning house being smashed. Later, Nicholas Manning was confornted by Mary Williams who threw a mug at him, shouting that he had hit her earlier. As they stood face to face arguing, she produced a gun and shot him in the chest before fleeing. Manning died three days later. A search of the Williams house revealed a large quantity of firearms and ammunition.

At her trial she protested her innocence by claiming her husband shot Manning, but to no avail.

October 13th: John Walter COPPEN (37)   **Horsemonger Lane**

Coppen, a coffee house keeper, was addicted to drinking in excess and on the night of 27 August he again returned home drunk. Seeing the condition that her husband was in, his wife Emma Skevington-Coppen (35), refused to share his bed and slept in another room.

The next morning Mrs Coppen was getting ready to leave after breakfast when her husband rushed at her with a butcher's knife he had borrowed earlier from a neighbour, and stabbed her.

At his trial at the Old Bailey, Coppen claimed that he had been aggravated into carrying out the crime, which was not premeditated. The evidence of the knife being procured on the morning of the attack suggested to the jury that the crime was planned and they returned a guilty verdict.

Hanged by Marwood, who gave him a drop of five feet.

1874

November 16th: Thomas SMITH — Winchester

A private in the 20th Hussars, sentenced to death at the Old Bailey by Mr Justice Lush on 28 October, for the murder of a Captain Bird at Aldershot.

On 13 September, the officer had inflicted a punishment drill on the young soldier which he resented, and in a rage he shot Bird dead. His defence claimed it was an accident and that there was no malice between the two men, while the prosecution proved the opposite.

Hanged by Marwood.

December 28th: Hugh DALEY — Durham

On 7 November, Daley, a married man from Dinton, a small mining village near Durham, returned home drunk and was assisted to bed by his wife and a neighbour.

Later that evening Phillip Burdey, a single man, called at the house to see Mrs Daley. A few minutes later Daley woke, rushed downstairs, and chased Burdey out into the street brandishing a poker. Cornering his victim, he rained blows on him with the poker for over two hours until he died.

Sentenced to death on 14 December; he was hanged by Marwood.

December 29th: Robert TAYLOR (21) — Stafford

On 23 November, Mrs Mary Kidd (57) and young Sarah Hollis (8), were returning from the market at Yoxall, near Burton. On approaching Coppice Wood, near Hoar Cross, they spotted Taylor, a Wigan born miner, sitting on a gate.

Mrs Kidd asked Taylor if he was going to sleep, to which he answered 'No.' 'Why don't you go home then,' she replied, with Taylor answering that he had no home to go to. Mrs Kidd and the girl walked on and soon they were followed by Taylor who asked for half-a-crown. She told him she didn't have that much money and gave him tuppence.

Angered at the small amount, he told her he would cut her throat, then took out his knife and chose to stab her in the neck instead. A passing cart caused him to flee but he was later picked out by Sarah Hollis in an identity parade.

Taylor was tried at Staffordshire Assizes and admitted his guilt under questioning. He showed no fear in the condemned cell and ate a massive last breakfast which included over a pound of meat. He ate his meal with a wooden spoon and scratched upon it a drawing of a man hanging on a gallows. After finishing his feast, he called for Marwood to 'Snap me off quick.'

1875

Cases where no executioner is recorded are multiple executions, and readers are asked to refer to the entries before or after for details of the hangman.

1875

January 4th: James CRANWELL (59)   Newgate

Cranwell was a shoemaker who rented a room in a house on Great James Street, Lisson Grove. On Saturday 17 October 1874, he invited his girlfriend, Emma Bellamy (30), to his room for tea. Shortly after her arrival she said she felt tired and Cranwell told her to lie down in the bedroom while he prepared the tea. As she dozed, Cranwell crept into the bedroom, locked the door behind him, and struck her several times with a hammer. She pleaded for mercy, but Cranwell said: 'No, you have deceived me,' and proceeded to cut her throat with a large knife.

Neighbours had become alarmed at the noise from his room and saw blood stains on him when he walked out of the room, prompting someone to find a policeman. When the officer returned he found Emma at the foot of the stairs; she had staggered from the room and collapsed.

Cranwell immediately confessed that he had tried to kill her because he thought she had been unfaithful. Emma was taken to hospital where she died the following week.

Tried and convicted at the Old Bailey in December, Cranwell was hanged by Marwood.

January 4th: John McGRAVE (20)   Liverpool
Michael MULLEN (17)

Condemned to death, together with a man called Campbell, for the murder of Richard Morgan whom they kicked to death as he walked from the ferry down Tithebarn Street in Liverpool, with his wife and brother on 3 August 1874.

As the family walked past a gang of men, Michael Mullen asked Morgan for sixpence to buy some beer. Morgan brushed him off and told him to get a job, to which Mullen replied: 'My job is taking money off passers by,' and then he and the rest of the gang attacked.

Mullen, McGrave and Campbell were sentenced to death by Justice Mellor on 14 December at Liverpool Assizes. Campbell, whom the jury had recommended to mercy, was reprieved two days before execution.

(In September 1877, Thomas Mullen and Mary McGrave, brother and sister of the two hanged men, were involved in a similar incident, when a friend kicked a man to death on a Liverpool street corner after he had gone to assist his wife who had been caught up in a quarrel. The gangs responsible were called Corner Men, and it was a very common crime in the nineteenth century).

1875

January 4th: William WORTHINGTON (33) Liverpool

Worthington was a Wigan boatman who lived with his wife and daughter on a barge moored in Liverpool.

On the night of 29 August, screams were heard coming from the yard adjacent to the mooring point. A passer-by saw Worthington's wife stagger from the yard covered in blood. The police were called but they decided they couldn't interfere between man and wife and simply ordered the couple to go home. Mrs Worthington's body was later found on the boat where they lived - she had been beaten to death with a poker.

Convicted at the same Winter Assizes as the two Corner Men, **McGRAVE** and **MULLEN** [above], and hanged in a triple execution by Anderson.

March 24th: John McDAID Sligo

Convicted of the murder of Edward Ferguson, a retired butter merchant who was found beaten to death at his home in Sligo on 31 October 1874.

The old man had not been seen for several days and when his niece called on him she found the house locked. She ordered the door to be forced and the body was discovered. Missing from the house were numerous valuables.

Hanged by William Marwood.

March 29th: Richard COATES Chelmsford

A soldier sentenced to death at Essex Assizes on 8 March for the murder at Purfleet of a young girl, Alice Boughen, whom he beat to death after attempting to violate her.

He killed the child in a school closet then carried her body down to a riverbank, intending to throw it into the water. He was unable to lift it over a railing near the river and returned to the school. He was seen carrying the body back and was arrested.

He confessed his guilt in the condemned cell and blamed it on drink.

Hanged by Marwood.

1875

March 30th: John MORGAN (19)   Maidstone

A bandsman in the 82nd Regiment convicted at Maidstone Assizes, of the murder of John Foulson on 6 March.

The two soldiers were in the same regiment stationed at Shornecliffe camp, and on the night of the crime they were sitting in a hut with two young drummerboys. Morgan gave one of the boys a sum of money to go and fetch some sweets and both the drummers left. Within seconds of them leaving the hut, Foulson rushed out clutching his neck and dashed into another hut where he picked up a pen and wrote 'Morgan done it.' He died within minutes from the hideous gash, his last action being to point accusingly at his killer who had now entered the hut.

Morgan denied the crime, claiming that Foulson had committed suicide, but this was easily disproved by cuts to the victim's hands, caused while trying to fend off the blows.

Morgan wrote a last letter from his cell asking his former comrades to forgive him for the shame he had brought on the regiment. He was hanged by Marwood.

March 30th: John STANTON (22)   Stafford

Stanton had been married just six months when he got into a quarrel with his uncle, Thomas Nield, in a Stafford public house. After finishing his drink he went home, returned with a shoemaker's knife, and fatally stabbed his uncle.

He was sentenced to death on 10 March. Marwood was unable to carry out the execution as he had accepted another engagement so the County Officials tried to locate another hangman.

Unable to find an experienced executioner, they turned to George Incher, a local man, who travelled from the Black Country to officiate. He turned up at the gaol in a tattered and torn suit and had to be fitted with a set of clothes from the prison before he carried out the execution.

Stanton, who was lame, managed to climb the steps to the scaffold unassisted, but being only a small man the short drop failed to break his neck. It was reported that he took a long time to die.

April 9th: John RUSSELL — Clonmel

On 22 August 1874, William Sandford was seen leaving a public house in the company of several men. They headed out towards a field where his body was discovered the next morning. His skull had been smashed to pieces with a large stone. The men had attempted to drag the body across a railway line, presumably to throw it into the adjacent river but had left it when several people appeared.

Sandford had been murdered for the five pounds he was known to have been carrying; Russell was identified as one of the men with him when he left the pub and arrested.

Hanged by Marwood.

April 19th: Alfred Thomas HEAP — Liverpool

An unqualified chemist and druggist convicted at Manchester Assizes of the murder of Margaret McKivett (26), who died after he tried to procure her an abortion.

On 13 March, Miss McKivett and her mother visited Heap at his shop in West Gorton, Manchester. Heap's housekeeper, Mrs Julia Carroll, watched them go upstairs and claimed she heard them struggle. Later they came down and the women left. Mrs McKivett and Heap met up in a pub later that day and she paid him one pound.

During the next few days the woman's condition deteriorated so much that Heap was summoned. He jeeringly told her she musn't die on him, but on 18 March she passed away.

Heap was arrested along with his housekeeper, who was later released. Evidence was brought into court that Heap had been involved in a similar case in 1867, and although the victim had recovered, he had still served five years on an attempted murder charge.

Hanged by Marwood.

April 19th: William TOBIN — Cork

Convicted of the murder of Mrs Joanna Cotton, a farmer's wife, in August 1874.

Tobin was a released convict who had been roaming the country. During the summer of 1874, three people were murdered in the north eastern part of County Cork, and two days after the third murder, Tobin enquired in a town as to the whereabouts of a farmer called Cotton. He called at the farm and, finding the farmer away, struck Mrs Cotton with a pitchfork, killing her instantly. He was spotted by her young daughter, who fled for her life as he gave pursuit.

Tobin was arrested soon after, still holding ten shillings he had stolen from Mrs Cotton. Marwood was unable to attend as he had accepted an engagement in Liverpool, so Tobin was hanged by an American sailor serving a short sentence at the gaol for desertion. The execution was carried out efficiently and Tobin died almost at once.

April 26th: William HALE   **Bristol**

A barge-owner, with a successful business, sentenced to death by Mr Justice Lush on 5 April, for the murder of his wife at their Bristol home in August 1874.

In 1872, Mrs Hale's alcoholism soured their previously happy marriage and soon they were constantly quarrelling. On 28 August 1874, Hale returned home from the pub at midnight and found his wife sitting on the doorstep. They were both drunk, and she told him she wouldn't come into the house with him. Despite his persistent requests she refused to go to bed; finally, Hale went inside, returned with a table knife and stabbed her twice in the neck.

He pleaded provocation through drink but was convicted, and hanged by Marwood.

July 27th: Jeremiah CORKERY (20)   **Warwick**

On 7 March, PC Lines and PC Fletcher called into a Birmingham public house and arrested a man for burglary. As they took the man away, a group of his friends, led by Corkery, began taunting the officers and as they headed from the pub, one shouted: 'Let's give it to the pigs.'

One of the men was seen by a witness to draw a knife during the disturbance, and both officers were subsequently stabbed. Although the witness couldn't positively identify the man, he claimed that the attacker had been struck over the head with PC Lines' truncheon. Corkery received treatment for a head wound later that night.

A group of men, including Corkery, was paraded before the wounded officers as they lay in hospital, but he wasn't picked out as the assailant and was released.

1875

On 20 March, PC Lines died and soon after Corkery was arrested and charged with the murder. He protested his innocence but was convicted despite the victim being unable to identify the attacker and a lack of any other evidence linking him with the crime.

He was convicted at Warwick Assizes by Mr Justice Field, and declined the court's offer of mercy as he maintained his innocence. Four other men indicted for the riot were sentenced to life imprisonment.

Corkery was hanged by Marwood.

August 2nd: Michael GILLINGHAM (22)   **Durham**

A respectable young man sentenced to death at Durham Assizes by Baron Huddlestone, for the murder of John Kiegoam, a young Irishman.

Without any provocation, Kiegoam was set upon by a gang of six youths at Darlington on 10 April, and witnesses testified they saw Gillingham strike the man about the head with a sharp instrument, which punctured his brain over the eyebrow.

August 2nd: Elizabeth PEARSON (32)   **Durham**

Convicted of the murder of her elderly uncle, James Watson (74), by mixing rat poison in his medicine, at Gainford, County Durham.

Mrs Pearson was alleged to have persuaded her mother-in-law to purchase some 'Battles Vermin Powder' which she said she needed to kill mice. Soon after this, her uncle became poorly but after three days, he appeared to be getting better. On 15 March, the doctor visited the sick man and proposed administering a tonic which he left for Watson to take later.

When the old man died that afternoon, the doctor ordered that the contents of his stomach be analysed, and traces of strychnine were found. Mrs Pearson was the only person who had attended the sick man that day, apart from the doctor, and she was arrested for the murder.

She was tried before Mr Justice Archibald at Durham Assizes on 8 July. The prosecution's claim that she had murdered her uncle in order to gain possession of his furniture was accepted by the jury, and she was convicted and sentenced to death.

1875

August 2nd: William McHUGH   Durham

Sentenced to death at Durham Assizes on 13 July for the murder of Thomas Mooney at Barnard Castle.

Early on the morning of 11 April, a witness saw McHugh and another man, William Gallagher, dragging Mooney down to a yard, where he was then thrown over a wall into the River Tees. As the victim was either drunk, or insensible through a blow to the head, he was unable to swim and drowned in the murky water.

Gallagher had refused at the last minute to help McHugh throw the man into the river, and as a result he was acquitted, although the judge censured him for not stopping McHugh committing murder.

Hanged alongside **PEARSON** and **GILLINGHAM** [above] by Marwood.

August 9th: Peter BLANCHARD (26)   Lincoln

Blanchard, a Lincolnshire tanner, had been trying in vain to court Louisa Hodgson (22) but she wouldn't go out with him, partly because he wasn't liked by her parents, and also because she had recently began seeing another man in the town.

On 7 March, Louisa and her new boyfriend were walking home from church when they came across Blanchard. He walked down the street with them until he reached his front door, where he pulled out a knife and stabbed Hodgson through her heart. He was immediately detained and admitted he had committed the crime through jealousy.

Hanged by Marwood.

August 11th: Joseph Phillip LE BRUN   Jersey

A unique execution because it was carried out in public as the island of Jersey was not covered by current legislation.

Le Brun was convicted on 8 July for the murder of his married sister, Nancy Laurence, and of the attempted murder of her husband. It was alleged they were shot because of a family quarrel.

Le Brun protested his innocence rigorously, and was accompanied through his last hours by a priest who was a member of the Plymouth Brethren who seemed to share his view.

The condemned man was led through the streets to Gallows Hill with the rope in place around his neck. The hangman was reported to have been Marwood. When the drop fell, the priest stood on the trap with his arms spread wide crying: 'He's innocent! He's innocent!'

August 16th: Mark FIDDLER (24)   Lancaster

Fiddler, an unemployed spinner, and his wife Dorothy (22), quarrelled often and as a result she left him. He sold their house and its contents and proceeded to fritter away the money on drink before calling at his wife's lodging and begging her to forgive him. When she refused, her cut her throat and then his own. Sentenced to death on 27 June.

When the drop fell, the white hood that was placed over Fiddler's head turned bright red as blood began to ooze from the neck wound he had self-inflicted. If the drop had been a few inches longer it would have torn his head from his shoulders.

August 16th: William McCULLOUGH (36)   Lancaster

McCullough was an engine fitter, and he and his wife shared a house with William Watson (62) and a woman who acted as his wife.

On 29 March, McCullough had come home drunk and asked his wife for some money so that he could purchase more drink; when she refused he began to beat her. She fled into Watson's room and cried for help. As Watson tried to calm the drunken McCullough down, he was fatally stabbed.

Hanged alongside **FIDDLER** [above], by William Marwood who gave them both a long drop.

September 6th: William BAKER   Liverpool

On 10 July, Baker, the landlord of a Liverpool public house called The Railway Vaults, was drinking in another local pub with a group of friends. At closing time, they headed for one of the illegal drinking dens that littered the city's docklands. On reaching their destination, they were angry to find the owner of the 'club' refusing them admission.

The time of their arrival had coincided with the departure of another group of men, one of whom, Charles Langan, had recently fallen out with Baker. Langan's party followed the others away from the club and as they reached the main road, Baker called Langan over and after an exchange of words, he pulled out a revolver and shot him dead.

Baker was immediately detained, and when he stood trial a few weeks later his defence pleaded that he was guilty of manslaughter, caused by drink, but he was convicted and sentenced to death.

September 6th: Edward COOPER (33)   Liverpool

Sailors Edward Cooper and Edward Jones were both serving aboard the British ship 'Coalbeck' which had left Liverpool on 23 January bound for the Chilean port of Valparaiso.

All was well until some ill feeling developed between the two men. On 24 April, Jones, acting for the second mate, gave Cooper, a native of New Orleans, an order which he scornfully refused to obey. Angry words ensued which concluded with Cooper offering Jones to go on deck and 'Fight it out like a man.' As they squared up Cooper drew a pistol and shot Jones dead.

Cooper was detained and brought back to port to stand trial. His defence that he was attacked and cut by the victim was contradicted by various witnesses, and he was convicted and sentenced to death by Mr Justice Archibald.

Hanged alongside **BAKER** [above] by Marwood.

October 5th: Patrick DOCHERTY (21)   Glasgow

Convicted of the murder of John Miller, a miner, by striking him over the head with a hoe, near Rutherglen Bridge.

On 1 May, three men and a woman were dancing on the bridge. They had been drinking. They were later joined by Docherty and his sweetheart, and soon afterwards Miller climbed onto a wall and watched them. Miller and Docherty then exchanged words, after which the fatal blow was struck.

Docherty was tried before Lord Neaves at the Glasgow Circuit New Court on 14 September. He pleaded not guilty. The prosecution claimed it was a deliberate act of murder while the defence argued the blow was struck merely on impulse.

He was hanged by Marwood after a petition for a reprieve was refused.

October 19th: David WARDLAW   Dumbarton

An aged shoemaker convicted at Stirling Court on 28 September of the murder of his wife at Bonhill, Dumbarton. He pleaded not guilty and told the court he had argued with his wife, mainly through drink, for over twenty years and had no recollection of the crime. She had been battered to death with a hammer.

The jury found him guilty by a majority of 11-4 and he was sentenced to death. Three petitions failed to save him and he became the last man hanged at the prison.

His execution was carried out by Marwood who caused a great deal of controversy among council officials when he submitted his bill for expenses, which included over a dozen bottles of bitter beer, two bottles of whiskey, two bottles of brandy, one bottle of sherry and a bottle of port, half of which he consumed on the morning of the execution.

December 21st: William SMEDLEY (50)   Leeds

Smedley, a Sheffield knife-maker, had been widowed several years earlier but had started living with an Elizabeth Firth as man and wife. At the end of August she told him she no longer wished to share his house on account of his poverty. He had been unable to work due to his failing eyesight.

On 31 August they were drinking in a pub together and at the end of the evening he walked her to her new home. When they reached the front door she refused to let him in, sending Smedley into a jealous rage. He drew out his razor, grabbed her by the hair and cut her throat, so severely that he almost severed her head. He then turned away and walked to the local police station where he gave himself up.

Hanged by Thomas Askern.

1875

December 21st: Henry WAINWRIGHT (37) — Newgate

A well respected London shopkeeper charged in September with the murder of his former mistress.

Outwardly, Wainwright was a church going family man who ran a successful hardware shop in Whitechapel, but unknown to his wife and family he was leading a double life. He had courted Harriet Lane (22), and after she fell pregnant with his child, he set her up in a flat. Later that year she gave birth to a second child.

Wainwright carried on his double life, maintaining his two illegitimate children with an allowance of five pounds a week, while bringing home money for his wife. Eventually this arrangement tired him; first the expense of having two dependants began to tell on his account, and then Miss Lane took to drink. An awkward liability, he decided to be rid of her. He shot her in the head, cut her throat, dismembered her and buried the parts under the floor of his workshop.

He was declared a bankrupt soon afterwards and had to give up tenancy of his shop. He decided to remove the remains of his former mistress and rebury them in a safer place. The task of conveying the parcelled up remains was entrusted to an unsuspecting friend who became curious to their contents; when he opened them he informed the police of his grisly discovery.

Wainwright was arrested, and following conviction, hanged by Marwood.

December 22nd: John William ANDERSON — Newcastle

In August, John Anderson, a young clerk, gave up work and took to drink, and as a result relations with his wife became strained. They argued constantly and she threatened to leave him unless he got a job.

On 27 August they visited a neighbour and appeared on good terms, but later, when they returned home, another neighbour heard screams from their house. When the disturbance was investigated, Mrs Anderson was found lying in a pool of blood: she had been stabbed seven times. Anderson gave himself up immediately.

Hanged by Marwood.

December 23rd: Richard CHARLTON   Morpeth

A farm labourer sentenced to death by Mr Justice Denman at Durham Assizes for the murder of his wife.

After the birth of their first child in the spring of 1875, Sarah Charlton left her husband because she became tired of him coming home drunk, and went to live with her sister at nearby Dinnington.

On 5 June, Charlton went to his sister-in-law's house armed with his gun. After failing to persuade his wife to return home, he shot her dead and seriously injured his sister-in-law before turning the gun on himself.

He was incapacitated for a time, due to his self-inflicted wounds, but after conviction was able to walk firmly onto the scaffold where he was hanged by Marwood.

1876

Cases where no executioner is recorded are multiple executions, and readers are asked to refer to the entries before or after for details of the hangman.

March 28th: George HUNTER (23) — Morpeth

On 9 December two young pitmen, George Hunter and Williams Woods, were out shooting birds in a snow-covered forest. Later they called into a public house for a couple of drinks.

As they left the pub to walk home, Woods walked slowly behind and threw a snowball at his friend. Hunter warned him that if he did it again he would shoot him. Woods then threw another at him, to which Hunter responded by raising his gun and shooting him dead.

Hunter lived with his aged parents, and had signed a petition earlier that day asking for a reprieve for **CHARLTON** [above]. He was taken into custody and charged with murder.

He maintained that it was an accident and that he thought the gun was empty; despite the lack of evidence that the crime was premeditated he was convicted and hanged by Marwood.

April 4th: Thomas FORDRED (48) — Maidstone

Sentenced to death at Kent Assizes for the murder of his paramour, Mary Ann Bridge (27), at Margate.

Fordred was alleged to have kicked her to death as they returned home drunk from a pub. He maintained that although he was responsible for her death, he was innocent of murder as she had merely fallen while they were fooling around. A doctor maintained that death had been caused by kicks to the head and chest. It was alleged that earlier in the evening, witnesses overheard him threaten to beat her brains out if he caught her going with another man.

Hanged by Marwood.

April 10th: George HILL — St Albans

Convicted of the murder of William Thrussel, his illegitimate son.

Having been served a maintenance order by a court, while drunk he lured mother and child through a deserted field on the pretext of showing them a house he had rented on their behalf, and then attacked them both with a hammer, leaving them for dead. The mother recovered and her evidence convicted him. He expressed remorse after sentencing.

Hanged by Marwood.

1876

April 24th: Edward DEACON — Bristol

Deacon, a shoemaker, had been married for nine years but had been separated from his wife at various times in the last five years, due mainly to his drunkenness.

Shortly before Christmas 1875 they made another attempt at a reconciliation, but no sooner had they got back together than she threatened to leave if he didn't curb his drinking.

On 23 February, he borrowed an axe from a neighbour, at his wife's request, and began to chop some logs for the fire. Whilst engaged in the chore, his wife began to curse him, and in a rage he struck her with the axe.

He pleaded that he had acted in self-defence after she had attacked him with a kettle, but the testimony of his step-daughter was enough to convince the court of his guilt and he was hanged by Marwood.

April 25th: Joseph WEBBER (63) — Cardiff

Sentenced to death at Cardiff Assizes for the murder of Edward Stelfox.

Early on the morning of 13 March, Stelfox was fishing on private land at East Moor, Cardiff. He had paid for permission to use the water but also fishing on the same stretch was Joseph Webber, who was in possession of no such authority.

When a bailiff came round later that morning, Stelfox complained about Webber encroaching on his territory. On hearing this, Webber picked up his double-barrelled shot gun and some duck shot, then went over to Stelfox. After a short exchange of words Webber emptied both barrels at the man, who died minutes later.

Hanged by Marwood.

April 26th: John DALY (47) — Belfast

A coal carrier sentenced to death by Baron Fitzgerald for the murder of Margaret Whiteley, whom he kicked to death at his home in Belfast on 15 September 1875.

The deceased was a relative of Daly's and the crime was committed while they were both drunk.

Hanged by Marwood.

1876

May 23rd: George KADI   **Newgate**
              Pascaler CALADIS
              Matteo CORGALIS
              Giovanni CACCARIS

Spanish born Pascaler Caladis, and three Greeks - Matteo Corgalis, George Kadi and Giovanni Caccaris, were sentenced to death at the Old Bailey by Mr Justice Brett, for their part in the murder and mutiny aboard the British ship 'Lennie'.

    The men were part of a scratch multi-national crew, recruited in London in October 1875. They were taken across to Antwerp and set sail later that month, but within five days some of the crew had begun to show signs of unrest and insubordination which came to a horrific climax on 31 October. During the night they systematically massacred almost everyone aboard by shooting, stabbing and beating them to death, sparing the life of a steward whom they ordered to set sail for Greece.

    They were eventually captured by a British vessel and taken into custody. Eleven men stood trial, but eventually proceedings against the majority were dropped and only four were convicted.

    They were hanged side by side by Marwood and Incher in the largest mass private execution.

May 31st: Thomas BARR (45)   **Glasgow**

A twice married travelling bookseller who murdered his 22 year old wife, and his mother-in-law, Mrs Margaret Sloan, in the latter's home at Gallowgate, Glasgow, on 1 March.

    Barr was a widower when he remarried, but had an unhappy second marriage; they had been separated seventeen times because of his brutality.

    On the last occasion he followed his heavily pregnant wife to her mother's house and, when Mrs Sloan tried to prevent him entering, he beat her to death before rushing in and attacking his wife. She died in hospital after giving birth to a still born child.

    Barr was captured eleven days later in Aberdeenshire, trying to find work on a farm, but in the intervening period over forty tramps were taken into custody on suspicion of being the wanted man.

    He was taken back to Glasgow and convicted; hanged by Marwood.

1876

July 26th: John WILLIAMS (37)   **Durham**

On 26 June, Williams, a Welsh born miner, had quarrelled with his wife over money and she had left and sought refuge at her mother's home. Later, when her two brothers came home from work, they went to her house at Edmonsley, near Durham, to try and pacify her husband.

As they approached the house, Williams pointed a rifle from the window and threatened to shoot the first to come near. No sooner had he made the threat than the rifle went off hitting the younger brother, John Wales, in the chest, fatally wounding him.

The other brother alerted Williams's wife and she easily disarmed her shocked husband, and he was dragged to the local police station.

Hanged by Marwood.

August 1st: James PARRIS (27)   **Maidstone**

A labourer from Offham, convicted of the murder of William Crouch (6), whom he beat to death with an iron bar in a barn at Ryarsh on 11 June. He had committed the crime in a rage after the child's mother had failed to keep an appointment with him. After carrying out the murder he walked to the local police station and confessed.

Hanged by Marwood.

August 14th: William FISH (26)   **Liverpool**

At just after 4pm on the afternoon of 27 March, Emily Holland (7), disappeared as she walked down Birley Street, Blackburn, after telling a friend she was going to fetch some tobacco for an adult. After a search lasting several days, the child's dismembered body was uncovered in a trunk, wrapped in a copy of the Preston Herald. The autopsy revealed she had been raped and had her throat cut prior to the dismemberment.

Fish, a father of three, who ran a barber shop in Moss Street, was arrested and immediately confessed to the crime which had horrified the whole town.

(Birley Street was to feature again in Blackburn's dark history over seventy years later, when child killer Peter Griffiths was arrested outside his house on the same street).

1876

August 14th: Richard THOMPSON (22)   Liverpool

Thompson, a labourer, had been courting a young girl who lived in the house of John Blundell, a miller. For some unexplained reason Blundell forbade the couple to use his house for their courtship, which led to ill feeling between the two men. They had previously been the best of friends and only four months earlier Thompson had been the best man at the other's wedding.

On 15 April, Blundell and a friend were walking home when Thompson, in a drunken rage, rushed up and stabbed him over a dozen times.

Sentenced to death by Mr Justice Lindsay on 28 July after his defence of manslaughter was dismissed.

Hanged alongside **FISH** [above] by Marwood, Fish having a drop of six feet, Thompson seven feet.

August 21st: Steven McKEOWN   Armagh

Sentenced to death by Mr Justice Fitzgerald, for the murder of Mary McShane (18), at Forkhill on Sunday 23 April.

Several years earlier her father had also been murdered and McKeown was suspected of being responsible for that crime, but had fled to America before he could be arrested.

Soon after McKeown returned to Armagh from America, Miss McShane took him to court after he had made repeated threats when she spurned his advances. He was bound over to keep the peace and ordered to stay away from her.

On Sunday 23 April, he followed her into a field and brutally beat her about the head with a large stone. He was immediately arrested.

Hanged by Marwood.

August 25th: Christos Emanuel BAUMBOS   Cork

A Greek seaman convicted at his second trial for the murder of the captain during a mutiny aboard the ship 'Caswell'.

Baumbos was one of the crew that mutinied off the coast of Buenos Aries on 4 January. Baumbos claimed he wasn't an instigator in the assault, which left several of the crew dead, and had been bullied into carrying out a small part in the attack in fear for his life. Witnesses claimed they saw Baumbos stab the captain to death.

1876

August 25th: Thomas CROWE (63)   Cork

Found guilty of the murder of John Hyland, a driver who worked for a land agent called Nat Buckely, in Tipperary.

Buckely was returning after collecting a large amount of money when the cart he was travelling in was ambushed as he passed a wood. The police who were escorting the agent caught one of the men, but he was left unattended when two others opened fire at the cart. During the fight, someone shot Hyland. When Crowe was arrested, he contested he was innocent and that he was the first man they had detained.

Hanged beside **BAUMBOS** [above], by Marwood.

August 29th: John EBLETHRIFT   Newgate

Eblethrift, a ground labourer, and his wife Emma (45), were both heavy drinkers who frequently quarrelled. She had three children from her first marriage and when her husband died, he left her a small boat business and a great deal of money which she soon squandered on drink.

Shortly before 10pm on 24 June, Mrs Eblethrift was talking to neighbours outside her home on Clarendon Street, Paddington. John Eblethrift emerged from the house and headed for the local pub, returning at 11.15pm muttering threats against his wife.

Being used to his violence, Mrs Eblethrift usually locked him out of their bedroom when he returned home drunk, but that evening a neighbour advised her not to stay at home and offered her a bed for the night, but she refused.

Later that night, a fellow lodger heard Mrs Eblethrift cry out and found her dead on the floor.

John Eblethrift was tried at the Old Bailey and pleaded not guilty to murder but guilty to manslaughter, saying he stabbed her out of jealousy.

He was convicted of murder and hanged by Marwood, who gave him a drop of five feet six inches.

December 11th: Charles O'DONNELL (57)   Newgate

On Sunday 30 October, O'Donnell, a labourer and former asylum inmate, visited some friends alone, and during dinner he made certain statements that made them suspicious as to why his wife Elizabeth hadn't accompanied him to their house.

They knew that the couple, who had been married for two years, had been separated since he was released from the asylum and had only recently got back together and moved into a room in Chelsea.

Next morning they notified the police who called at the room and found Mrs O'Donnell dead in bed. She had been battered to death with a pair of tongs that lay bloodstained on the floor. A neighbour in the flats told police that earlier in the week Mrs O'Donnell had given her some money to keep safe as her husband wanted to take it off her.

Hanged by Marwood.

December 14th: Robert BROWNING (25) **Cambridge**

A tailor and former soldier, sentenced to death at Norwich Assizes on 24 November for the murder of Emma Relfe (15).

Despite her age the victim earned her living as a prostitute, and had been living in a brothel for several weeks before the murder. Browning had met her in August, and whilst drinking with her on a common, he caught her stealing some money from him. After cutting her throat, he went off in search of more drink. Her body was later found with her head almost severed.

He was recommended for mercy on account of his age, but was hanged by Marwood.

December 19th: Silas BARLOW **Horsemonger Lane**

Aka Silas Smyth, found guilty of the double murder of his former sweetheart Ellen Soper (27), and their young child, at Battersea on 11 September.

They had lived together until she had left him and moved to lodgings. He visited her twice at her new address and each time she felt sick after he left. Eventually she died, and the next day he took custody of the child saying that his cousin would look after it, but it was later found floating in a Battersea reservoir. The body was identified and, when examined, found to have been poisoned with strychnine.

Barlow was arrested and charged with murder after a search of his home produced bottles of the poison. The contents of Miss Soper's

stomach were then analysed and also found to contain poison. Barlow denied killing the woman but later admitted that he had killed the child.
Hanged by Marwood.

December 19th: James DALGLEISH (27) Carlisle

Dalgleish had moved to Penrith in 1870 and had held several good jobs in the town. Early in 1876, he was sacked from his last position and took to drink.
   On the evening of 24 September, he entered the parlour being shared by his landlady, Sarah Wright, and her cousin. They were awoken, and the cousin saw him whisper something to Mrs Wright, who followed him from the room, returning immediately.
   Later that night, the cousin woke and saw a figure leave the room. She turned up the gas and found Mrs Wright lying beaten to death on the bed. Her screams alerted the other lodgers and Dalgleish was seen entering his room covered in blood. A bloodstained billhook was found in his room and he later confessed.
   Sentenced to death by Mr Justice Lopes at Manchester Assizes on 31 November. No motive was ever established for the crime although witnesses testified that they had frequently quarrelled over rent money.
   Hanged by Askern.

December 20th: John GREEN (41) Leicester

A painter who shot his wife, Emma, dead at their home at Leicester on 21 August.
   They had lived unhappily together due to Green being an alcoholic. On the day of the murder, he told a colleague as they clocked off work that this would be his last day. Immediately after arriving home he walked into the house and shot his wife in the neck. She died in hospital later that night, leaving a family of nine children.
   The prosecution easily proved that it was premeditated murder and he was convicted; hanged by Marwood.

December 21st: William FLANAGAN (35)   Manchester

Aka William Robinson. A drifter and layabout, he was dismissed from his job as a sheriff's officer because he was considered insane.

On 8 September, Flanagan and his common-law wife Margaret Dockerty, went out drinking, and returned to their bedsit later after both getting drunk, where they continued drinking with several other lodgers.

Next morning he accused her of stealing some money from him and then killed her by cutting her throat, the body being discovered by their landlady who had entered the room to retrieve a saucepan.

Flanagan was later arrested in possession of the murder weapon and charged. His defence was that he was insane, and evidence was shown that he had made several attempts to commit suicide, in one instance while he was awaiting trial.

After conviction, he was hanged by Marwood, on his first visit to Manchester.

1877

Cases where no executioner is recorded are multiple executions, and readers are asked to refer to the entries before or after for details of the hangman.

1877

January 2nd: Isaac MARKS (23) Horsemonger Lane

In the spring of 1874, Isaac Marks, a Jewish antique dealer, began to court Caroline Bernard, and later, as the relationship flourished, he proposed marriage. Frederick Bernard, father of thirteen and a fellow Jew, checked out his prospective son-in-law and gave his blessing to their engagement.

All was well until the summer of 1876, when Marks' house was destroyed by fire. Bernard helped Marks to make the insurance claim, and later presented him with a hefty bill for his services. Marks was so angry at being asked to pay what he considered an unreasonable amount, that he broke off the engagement. This caused great animosity between the two men.

On the afternoon of 24 October, Marks waited outside a shop in Lambeth and as Bernard emerged he fired seven shots at him, killing him instantly. He was immediately detained by a member of the public and held until the police arrived.

A shopkeeper testified that he had sold a gun to Marks only an hour before the crime, effectively ruining the defence of non-premeditated murder. Marks's counsel claimed that he was insane; he was known in his family as 'Mad Marks', and both his parents had died in an asylum.

Marks was hanged by Marwood with the dubious distinction of being the first Jew to be hanged in Great Britain for over two hundred years.

March 12th: Francis TIDBURY (27) Reading
            Henry TIDBURY (24)

Shortly after midnight on 11 December 1876, Police Constable Tom Golby was patrolling a turnpike road in Hungerford, Wiltshire, expecting to rendezvous with an Inspector Drewatt at the entrance to some woods, a police conference point. As PC Golby approached the meeting place he came across the body of another police officer, PC Shorter, lying in the road. Golby rushed back to the station to notify his colleagues, after first attracting the attention of a gamekeeper whom he ordered to keep watch for anyone leaving the woods. Reinforcements soon arrived on the scene and began a search for Inspector Drewatt, who had failed to report back. Within the hour his body was discovered in a nearby lane.

The gamekeeper was able to report that he had seen two men, William Day and William Tidbury, leaving the woods. Recognising Day as the leader of a gang of poachers, the police soon had four men in custody, three of whom were brothers. All four were charged with the double murder as there was ample evidence to link them to the crime. There were traces of blood on their clothing; imprints from their boots matched those found at the scene; most damning of all, a cap belonging to one of the brothers, Henry Tidbury, had been found underneath the body of the Inspector.

The four poachers stood trial at Berkshire Assizes, before Mr Justice Lindsay on 19 February 1877. Henry Tidbury confessed that he and Francis carried out the killings and that the other two were out of the woods when the shooting took place. He admitted that while returning home with two pheasants, they were stopped by the Inspector who had recognised them, and fearing arrest they had shot him down. When they saw the other officer, PC Shorter, they had no alternative but to shoot him down. Henry Tidbury told the packed courtroom how the policeman had dodged the first bullet and made a desperate bid for survival, but as he ran down a country lane, he, Henry, aimed his rifle and shot him. The brothers then walked over to the stricken men and beat them with a walking stick to make sure they were dead.

William Day and William Tidbury were sent to prison; Francis and Henry Tidbury were sentenced to death and later hanged by Marwood. Francis Tidbury celebrated his birthday on the day of his execution.

March 26th: William CLARK   Lincoln

Aka William Slener, sentenced to death at Lincoln Assizes on 8 March, for the murder of Henry Walker, a gamekeeper at Norton Disney, in February.

He was arrested at Lowestoft, and at the trial two colleagues testified that they had been with him when he shot Walker dead.

Hanged by Marwood.

March 27th: John McKENNA (25)   Manchester

A Rochdale plasterer convicted of the murder of his wife, in what the prosecution claimed were pure unmitigated brutal circumstances.

Annie McKenna was the same age as her husband; they had been married for several years and had two children. They did not have a happy marriage on on account of his drunkenness, which often ended in violence against his pretty wife.

On 24 February, McKenna and his heavily pregnant wife visited their neighbour, Mrs Higgins. John McKenna sent his wife out on more than one occasion to fetch ale, before they went home in the evening. Later, Annie McKenna returned to Mrs Higgins to seek refuge from her husband's threatening behaviour.

McKenna who had become more drunk, went over to the Higgins house and demanded to see his wife. Mrs Higgins, who was quite used to shielding the unfortunate wife, told McKenna to go away and offered to buy him a quart of ale. McKenna refused, pushed his way inside and dragged his wife home by the hair.

Fearing for her safety, Mrs Higgins rushed over to the McKenna house and saw through a window that McKenna was beating and kicking his wife. She watched him repeatedly bang her head against the floor before calling for another neighbour, Henry Dunn, to intervene. Dunn and McKenna quarrelled and fought outside the house whilst a mortally wounded Annie McKenna was treated inside. After twenty minutes of trading punches with Dunn, McKenna forced his way back into his house, lifted his wife's head off the pillow and started punching her about the face.

She died soon after, by which time McKenna had fled. He was soon located in Liverpool, brought back to Manchester and convicted.

Hanged by Marwood.

April 2nd: James BANNISTER **Chester**

Convicted of the brutal and unprovoked murder of his wife at their home on Russell Street, Hyde, Manchester.

Early in the morning of 15 December 1876, a Mr and Mrs Grayson, who lodged in the same house as Bannister and his wife, were awakened by moaning coming from across the corridor. They saw a light on and heard the sound of a blow being struck. Grayson ran into the room and found Mrs Bannister lying on the bed with her head bashed in. Her husband was lying beside her with a self-inflicted throat wound.

They were both taken to hospital where she died the next day. Bannister recovered and was later sentenced to death by Mr Justice Lush at Chester Assizes in March.

He was hanged on a scaffold that had to be reached by walking down a steep incline which reporters noted would incur caution at any time. Bannister never faltered in his step and on reaching the drop, Marwood gave the little man a drop of six feet two inches.

1877

April 3rd: John Henry JOHNSON (37) Leeds

During the evening of 26 December 1876, Johnson and his paramour, Amelia Sewell, visited several Bradford pubs. When they entered the Bedford Arms they met Amos White, an old acquaintance.

Later, as Sewell walked across a yard to the toilets she was accosted by White and screamed for Johnson to help. The two men squared up and traded a few blows before being separated. Johnson then staggered home, returning later with a gun with which he shot White dead. A friend of the victim helped detain Johnson who was immediately arrested.

He was convicted before Mr Justice Lopes and hanged by Askern who badly botched the execution. Firstly the rope snapped and when a new one was secured, the drop wasn't sufficient to cause instant death, leaving Johnson slowly choking on the end of the rope.

April 17th: Frederick Edwin BAKER Warwick

Mrs Maria Saunders and her second husband ran a public house at Ambridge, until she was widowed in autumn 1876. Fred Baker had been a barman at the pub and was very fond of his employer. The fondness was probably mutual, for when Mrs Saunders relinquished the pub she took Baker in as a lodger.

Soon this arrangement became strained, for whatever affection she might have had for her lodger, it did not stop her seeing other men, which made Baker increasingly jealous.

Matters came to a head on 17 January when she returned home from a night out with a man called Silvers. Neighbours heard a fierce row and the next morning Mrs Saunders was found dead, with her throat cut from ear to ear.

Baker was arrested after police surrounded a house in Stafford the following day. Mrs Saunders' children told police they pleaded with Baker not to kill their mother; he blamed Silvers for the murder, asking at the remand hearing: 'Let me have five minutes with Silvers, then you can hang me.'

Hanged by Marwood.

1877

July 31st: Henry ROGERS (27)   Stafford

A Wolverhampton bricklayer and thief, who confessed to the murder of his wife Sarah (22), on 5 July. After being informed of the crime, officers went to a nearby field and found the woman with horrific throat injuries.

Rogers admitted that he had planned to kill his wife after he discovered that she had been unfaithful, and had failed in a first attempt the previous day.

At the remand court he accused every witness who testified against him, including his aged father, of having an affair with his wife.

Hanged by George Incher.

July 31st: John Henry STARKEY (28)   Leicester

A coachman and habitual criminal, with a string of convictions under a number of aliases, convicted of the murder of his wife.

He married her at the beginning of the year but within weeks had started seeing another woman. On 4 April she taxed him about the affair which angered him so much that he attacked her, her screams waking up the neighbours.

At 5am next morning, he went to work and told a friend that he feared his wife had committed suicide. By 9am the body had been discovered, with the head almost severed.

Starkey was arrested and although there were blood stains on his clothes he claimed he was innocent and that their lodger had killed his wife. He later confessed before he was hanged by Marwood.

August 13th: Henry LEIGH (23)   Chester

A Macclesfield carpet weaver sentenced to death at Chester Assizes for the murder of Alice Halton (8), on 24 March.

On the previous evening, the girl's mother had called at Leigh's house to gossip with his mother. Leigh overheard Mrs Halton telling his mother she planned to send her young daughter to collect her wages from the mill where she worked because she was too poorly to go herself.

Next morning Leigh sent a young boy with a note to collect the woman's money, but the mill manager was suspicious and refused to hand it over. Alice later arrived and picked up the money; soon after she was found dead in a nearby canal. She had been beaten and robbed.

Acting on information received, police visited Leigh but he fled before he could be detained. As more evidence was amassed, police stepped up the hunt and Leigh was found hiding in a shed and arrested.

Hanged by Marwood.

August 14th: Caleb SMITH (38) Horsemonger Lane

On 14 April, at their home in Croydon, Smith and his common-law wife, Emma Elizabeth Osbourne had another in a long series of drunken quarrels during which she slapped him across the face. In a rage he pulled out his razor and cut her throat before turning the blade on himself.

He was tried at the Central Criminal Court on 24 July, and pleaded manslaughter through provocation, but the jury found him guilty and he was sentenced to death. While in the condemned cell he expressed surprise when told of how soon the execution would be carried out after conviction. He went to the gallows wearing a scarf which Marwood removed as they reached the drop.

August 21st: John GOLDING Liverpool

John Golding and Daniel Lord were friends and lived within a few streets of each other at Edge Hill.

On 16 July they had a quarrel which ended with Golding beating Lord about the head with a poker. Lord died from his injuries three days later.

Sentenced to death by Mr Justice Hawkins at Liverpool Assizes, although the jury recommended him to mercy.

August 21st: Patrick McGOVERN Liverpool

A labourer convicted of the murder of John Campbell on 23 July. Campbell was a Liverpool butcher who happened to be passing by when McGovern and his wife were having an argument on their doorstep.

At a request from Mrs McGovern, Campbell tried to persuade McGovern to let his wife into the house. McGovern responded by stabbing Campbell to death with a carving knife.

Hanged by Marwood alongside **GOLDING** [above].

1877

October 15th: John LYNCH (26)   Newgate

Lynch, a journeyman tailor, had become very upset at the death of his child in June and had taken to drink. He had been married to his wife Bridget (20), for five years and they had four children.

On 5 August they visited several public houses in Islington with some relatives when he suddenly pulled out his razor and cut her throat.

He pleaded guilty before Mr Justice Hawkins at the Central Criminal Court on 30 September, and wrote a full confession in the condemned cell.

Hanged by Marwood.

November 12th: Thomas Benjamin PRATT   Newgate

Sentenced to death at the Central Criminal Court on 25 October, for the murder of Eliza Francis Rockington, with whom he lived.

She had threatened to leave if he didn't curb his violent habits and although he repeatedly vowed he would, he failed to keep his promise. She eventually left him but he tracked her down and stabbed her to death.

Whilst in the condemned cell he asked for some tobacco but was told that it wasn't allowed. When he stated that he had no wish to smoke but merely to chew it, the request was granted.

Hanged by Marwood.

November 19th: William HASSELL   Exeter

On 8 October, Hassell, a Barnstable butcher returned home drunk and stabbed his wife three times with a pig-knife while she breast fed their baby. They had repeatedly quarrelled and he had become dismayed at their unhappy life.

He refused legal aid and pleaded guilty at his trial, although a petition for a reprieve was organised on the strength that he was drunk when he committed the crime.

Hassell walked to the scaffold with a firm step but cried bitterly before he was hanged by Marwood.

1877

November 20th: Henry MARSH (50)   Norwich

Henry Marsh and Henry Bidwell worked together in a forge owned by Thomas Mays (76), at Wymondham, Norfolk and during the summer both men learned that they were to lose their jobs as Mays was retiring and selling the business.

Marsh was particularly upset as he had been employed at the forge for thirty seven years, and while out on an errand he called at a pub and had several drinks. When he returned to work he got into a row with Bidwell and in a rage beat him to death with a heavy iron bar.

A servant girl at the house saw the attack and rushed to tell the elderly owner. When Mays entered the forge, Marsh turned on him and declared: 'Might as well swing for two as for one,' and beat the old man to death as well.

Hanged at Norwich Castle prison by Marwood.

November 21st: Thomas GREY   Nottingham

Sentenced to death by Mr Justice Hawkins on 31 October at Nottinghamshire Assizes for the murder of Ann Mellor at Carcolston in August.

Ann lived with her mother and brother in a village shop and was engaged to a man from Middlesbrough named Holt, who at the time of the crime was staying with them.

Early in the morning of 20 August, Grey entered the shop. He had repeatedly tried to court Ann but she had shown no interest in him, and the appearance of Holt had fuelled him with a jealous passion. Finding her alone in the shop, he tried to force his advances on her; when she pushed him away he cut her throat repeatedly.

Hanged by Marwood.

November 23rd: Cadwaller JONES (25)   Dolgelly

Sentenced to death for the murder of Sarah Hughes (36) in June.

They began an affair when Jones fell out of love with his prim and proper wife. Hughes disappeared on 2 June and no trace of her was found until parts of her body were washed up from a river. Police ascertained the body was Sarah Hughes and investigations led them to Jones.

He confessed that he had killed her, by striking her with a large stone, after she told him she was pregnant and began to pester him for money.

Hanged by Marwood on a scaffold borrowed from Chester Prison.

November 27th: John SWIFT (19)   **Leicester**
                   John UPTON (32)
                   James SATCHELL (28)

Swift and Satchell, both colliers, and Upton a banker, were drinking in a public house in Coalville on 1 September, when they were joined by Joseph Tugby, an old pedlar.

At closing time the four left together carrying a bottle of whisky, and were last seen heading for a railway bridge. Soon after midnight Tugby was found dead. It was later discovered that he had been kicked so savagely that all his teeth had been knocked out as well as suffering other horrific head wounds.

Next day Upton was drinking in a pub when he boasted that he had killed the old man: he was soon arrested. Satchell asked a friend to swap hats in an attempt to disguise himself and his friend remarked: 'If they hang you, you won't haunt me cause I'm wearing your cap?' but this poor attempt at evading capture was unsuccessful. The last man, Swift, was found hiding in his mother's loft and arrested.

They were sentenced to death by Mr Justice Hawkins and hanged by Marwood.

1878

Cases where no executioner is recorded are multiple executions, and readers are asked to refer to the entries before or after for details of the hangman.

1878

February 4th: George PIGGOTT (29)   Manchester

In 1876 Piggott, a married man with two of small children, left his wife after seducing Florence Galloway, a young domestic servant, and set up home with his lover in Birmingham.

After living together for eighteen months Florence became pregnant but left Piggott because of his brutality and returned to her family. He moved back in with his wife, who forgave him for the affair, and took a job as a tram driver.

On 24 November 1877, Florence Galloway's mother saw Piggott near her house and told him to stay away. On 5 December he forged a letter to Florence arranging a meeting to discuss a job. Only days after she had given birth to his child, she arrived for the meeting whereupon he shot her dead.

Hanged by Marwood.

February 11th: James CAFFYN   Winchester

An illiterate labourer charged with the murder of Maria Barber at Ryde on the Isle of Wight.

They had been living together in a house they shared with her father and his paramour, when, on Monday 27 November, a neighbour heard screams and saw Maria flee from the house covered in blood. Another neighbour went inside to remonstrate with Caffyn and saw him put down an axe. Later that day Maria was found hacked to death.

Caffyn fled to Portsmouth but was arrested on the Tuesday. He claimed that the motive for the crime was her threat to leave him.

Hanged by Marwood.

February 12th: James TRICKETT   Liverpool

Trickett, a bird catcher, kept a pet shop in Hopewood Street, Liverpool and occupied a flat above. After a drunken row on Boxing Day, he kicked his wife to death. The crime was discovered when a neighbour called the police after hearing a disturbance.

When taken into custody Trickett claimed that his wife had been permanently drunk for the last thirty-one weeks and that she had fallen down and banged her head on a box. He admitted later that he had thrown

her down but the injuries were more consistent with being kicked to death and he was convicted and sentenced to death at Liverpool Assizes.
Hanged by Marwood.

February 13th: John BROOKS   **Nottingham**

Brooks was employed as a lace maker when he met Caroline Woodhead, who was separated from her husband. He left his job and together they travelled extensively across England, and also lived for a while in Calais, France.

They returned to Nottingham, and following a quarrel in the autumn of 1877, Caroline Woodhead decided to return to her mother's house. On the night of 11 December, Brooks called at the house, in Lenton, and during another quarrel with Woodhead, he pulled out a razor and slit her throat. He tried to hide the body in a hedgerow at the bottom of the garden but it was soon discovered.

Sentenced to death on 24 January, and hanged by Marwood, who was carrying out his third execution in three days.

April 1st: Henry ROWLES (26)   **Oxford**

On 15 December, Rowles, the son of a wealthy farmer, went to visit his fiancee, Mary Hannah Allen, at her grandfather's house. They had a quarrel over him being a troublemaker when drunk, and she told him she wished to end the relationship and for him to go away and leave her alone.

He contacted her later that afternoon asking if she would see him in the evening to talk over their problems and she agreed. When they met up he shot her. She died the following week by which time he was already in custody.

Hanged by Marwood on a scaffold in the grounds of the county gaol below the castle.

April 15th: Vincent Knowles WALKER (48) York

A ship's carpenter, sentenced to death by Mr Justice Pole at York Assizes, for the murder of Mrs Lydia Wills White, the wife of a fishing smack owner.

Walker and his wife had split up and she had gone to live with Mrs White. He was jealous of his wife's adultery and blamed Mrs White for her misconduct.

On 18 February he went to see his wife and when Mrs White answered the door he stabbed her over thirty times, causing instant death. His wife fled through the back door and Walker was soon arrested. He admitted the crime and claimed he intended to give his wife the same treatment.

Hanged by Marwood, who had now become the chief executioner for Yorkshire, following the death of Thomas Askern. It was noted however that Marwood botched the execution and Walker died hard.

May 31st: Eugene Marie CHANTRELLE (44) Edinburgh

A French born school teacher from Edinburgh who poisoned his wife Elizabeth by inserting opium into her food.

He had taken out an insurance policy the previous year for one thousand pounds which included a clause for accidental death. He tried to disguise the poisoning by making the death look as if it was the result of a broken gas main in the bedroom. Traces of opium were found in vomit stains on his wife's nightgown and Chantrelle was arrested and charged.

Hanged at Calton Prison by Marwood after a jury had returned a unanimous guilty verdict.

July 29th: Charles Joseph REVELL (25) Chelmsford

A gardener sentenced to death by Lord Justice Thesiger at Essex Assizes for the murder of his wife, Hester (23), in Epping Forest.

Following lunch with her parents on Sunday 10 June, Revell went out to fetch some ale for them all to share. When he returned home over an hour later, he was drunk.

Revell and his wife began to quarrel over money when she grabbed him by the lapels and struck him. He knocked her to the ground and fled from the house. Against advice from her family she followed him into the forest where her body was discovered the next day, her throat cut from ear to ear.

Hanged by Marwood.

July 30th: Robert VEST   **Durham**

A ship's steward convicted of the murder of William John Wallace, a pilot on the barge 'William Leckie', at Sunderland.

The captain of the boat had cautioned Vest for being drunk on duty and Wallace had sided with the captain. Shortly afterwards, Wallace went to a closet where he was surprised by Vest who stabbed him in the throat and abdomen.

Vest was detained on ship until the police could take him into custody. Sentenced to death by Mr Justice Bagalley on 14 July, after a plea of insanity had failed, although the jury did recommend him to mercy.

Hanged by Marwood.

August 12th: Thomas CHOLERTON   **Nottingham**

Thomas Cholerton and Jane Smith had lived together as man and wife until the end of May when she left him because of his ill-treatment of her and went to stay with a family called Lynch.

At 7pm on 6 June, Cholerton went to the Lynch house and later he and Smith left together. At around 10pm that night, an old man heard screaming and when he went to investigate he found Jane Smith on the ground with Cholerton kneeling over her, cutting her throat. The old man dragged him off and almost at once a police officer arrived at the scene. Before she died in the street, Jane Smith pointed weakly at Cholerton, who then attempted cut his own throat, pleading with the officer: 'Let me kill myself.'

He was convicted at Nottinghamshire Assizes, before Mr Justice Hawkins on 28 July, and hanged by Marwood.

August 15th: Selina WADGE — Bodmin

A young domestic servant convicted on 28 July, for the murder of her illegitimate son.

She had met a man called Westood who promised to marry her if she rid herself of the youngest of her two children. While travelling from Stretton to Launceston she entered a field and, in the presence of the elder child, threw her son down a well.

When she arrived at her family home in Launceton she was asked where her young son was; she replied that he had died from a throat disease. Suspicions were aroused and after questioning she confessed to the crime.

Sentenced to death by Mr Justice Denman at Cornwall Assizes, he told her she had no hope of a reprieve. She made a painful scene on the scaffold and was hanged by Marwood who gave her a drop of eight feet.

October 3rd: William McDONALD — Cupar

A fisherman from St Andrews convicted at Perth Court and sentenced to death on 7 September for the murder of his wife, whom he shot dead on 13 June.

McDonald had failed in an attempt to take his own life, and pleaded that he was innocent because his wife had died as part of a suicide pact. Despite a strong recommendation for mercy he was hanged by Marwood on a scaffold erected in the garden of the prison above a ventilator shaft.

October 8th: Thomas SMITHERS (31) — Wandsworth

Thomas Smithers and Amy Judge lived together at Battersea, where on 22 July he stabbed her to death in a jealous rage.

He fainted in the dock at the Old Bailey as sentence was being passed by Mr Justice Denman on 18 September, and had to be carried from the court. He admitted his guilt and expressed his sorrow at the crime.

Hanged by Marwood.

1878

November 12th: Patrick John BYRNE (38) Northampton

Byrne, a Staff Sergeant with the Northampton & Rutland Militia, and a father of five children, had twelve years service in the army when during the summer of 1878 he received a number of warnings about his drinking, and about being slow to pay certain debts.

Matters came to a head when he was reported to his superiors and as a result was demoted to a lower rank and evicted from his quarters.

On 3 September he was ordered to clear his room by 10am but as the deadline approached he was seen loitering in the barracks. He entered a reading room where he was met by Quartermaster Sergeant Griffiths and Paymaster Sergeant Brooks. Griffiths told him that he had left his room in a state and had better tend to it.

Twenty minutes later Griffiths went to check on Byrne's progress and was shot in the head. Brooks, who was close by, was shot in the heart. Byrne was soon overpowered but not before one of his captors received a severe arm wound. He was detained until police arrived when he was charged with murder.

He later said he held the two men responsible for his demotion.

Hanged by Marwood.

November 18th: Joseph GARCIA (21) Usk

On the morning of Wednesday 17 July, a young farm worker called at the house of William Watkins (40), at Llangilly, near Newport, to find out why he had failed to report for work. As he approached he noticed smoke coming from an upstairs window and entering the house he discovered the bodies of Watkins, his wife Elizabeth (44), and their three children: Charlotte (8), Frederick (5), and Alice (4).

Mr and Mrs Watkins had been stabbed to death while the children had been hacked to death with an axe as they lay asleep. Their bed was then set alight.

On the previous morning, a Spanish sailor named Joseph Garcia had been released from Usk Prison after serving a nine month sentence for house breaking. On the Wednesday night a mail cart driver witnessed him walking towards Newport, and offered him a lift, which Garcia refused. When the driver reached the town he read about the murder and reported the suspicious traveller to the police who set up observation points around the town.

Garcia was spotted as he entered the town and police noticed that he had cuts, bruises, bloodstains and other obvious signs of a struggle. When searched he had in his pockets some items he hadn't been in possession of when released from prison. He spoke little English and protested his innocence through a Spanish counsel.

Hanged by Marwood who received a heroes welcome when he reached the town, and after carrying out the sentence he was cheered all the way to his train. He thanked the crowd for their reception and said he 'Hoped to have occasion to come this way again.'

November 19th: James McGOWAN (55)   Manchester

As a result of being a heavy drinker, McGowan, a Salford bleach worker, began to suffer delusions and became convinced that his nephew, whom he had taken a sudden and unexpected dislike to, was attempting to break into his house.

He told his wife of the break in and, knowing it to be all in his head, she refused to help him. This caused him to grow angry and as a result he threw her to the ground. She climbed to her feet and they began to struggle, during which he hacked away at her throat with a pocket knife. She died and he collapsed in a drunken heap. When he recovered his senses he reported the crime to the police.

His execution was scheduled for 18 November but he was granted a one day stay when Marwood replied that he couldn't officiate until the 19th as he was engaged at Usk.

November 25th: Henry GILBERT (30)   Huntingdon

An agricultural labourer sentenced to death by Mr Justice Hawkins at Cambridge Assizes on 6 November for the murder of his illegitimate child.

Gilbert lived with a woman called Colbert at Wailweston, near Huntingdon, and evidence showed that he had been repeatedly cruel to the child and at various times had kicked and beaten it. The child died as a result of being struck about the head as it lay in bed.

Gilbert, who admitted the crime but claimed he never intended to commit murder, was recommended for mercy by the jury but later hanged by Marwood.

1879

Cases where no executioner is recorded are multiple executions, and readers are asked to refer to the entries before or after for details of the hangman.

1879

January 10th: Thomas CUNCEEN   **Limerick**

Sentenced to death at Cork Assizes on Friday 13 December 1878 for the murder of Hannah Hogan, with whom he lived, and their child, at Singland.

Cunceen had led the woman and child to a lonely spot, then battered them to death and concealed their bodies beneath a heap of manure.

Hanged by Marwood.

February 4th: Stephen GAMBRILL (28)   **Maidstone**

A farm labourer sentenced to death at Kent Assizes on 14 January for the murder of Arthur Gillow (24), the son of a gentleman farmer.

The farm had been suffering from vandalism and as a result Arthur had volunteered to stay up through the night to keep guard. On the morning of 5 December his body was discovered beaten to death in the grounds.

Gambrill was suspected of the crime and charged when enough evidence was collected against him. He confessed in the condemned cell but maintained that he had only killed in self-defence.

Hanged by Marwood.

February 10th: Enoch WHISTON (21)   **Worcester**

On 5 December, Alfred Meredith, a clerk at an ironworks, was returning to Dudley after drawing over three hundred pounds from a bank to pay the wages of the workforce. He was followed to a quiet spot on a road between Dudley and Woodside where he was shot in the face and robbed. Whiston, a labourer and horse driver, was arrested along with his sweetheart at her house where he had shared out some of the money.

He was initially charged with robbery and attempted murder and confessed that he knew the routine of the victim and also that he had hidden some of the money in a nearby river, which the police retrieved.

Alfred Meredith died from his injuries over a week later and the charge was changed to one of murder. He was sentenced to death by Baron Huddleston at Worcester Assizes.

Hanged by Marwood.

1879

February 11th: William McGUINESS (40) Lancaster

On Friday 19 October, McGuiness returned to his home at Barrow from his job as a labourer on a building site at Carnforth railway station. He had made a threat to a workmate that he'd commit murder before leaving Barrow for his native Ireland.

Later that night a neighbour heard a disturbance at the house but paid no heed to it. A week later the next door neighbour, while hanging out washing, climbed onto a fence and looked through Mrs Ann McGuiness's window and saw her body on the floor. When the body was examined, it was discovered she had been kicked to death.

McGuiness was traced to Dublin after a magazine carried a description of the crime and wanted man; he was arrested and brought back to face trial.

Sentenced to death by Mr Justice Thesiger at Lancaster Assizes, and hanged by Marwood.

February 25th: Charles Frederick PEACE (46) Leeds

The notorious cat burglar and murderer who evaded arrest for over twenty years.

Peace was a master of disguise due to his almost rubber like features, and often carried his housebreaking tools inside an old violin case, an instrument on which he was very proficient. In 1877, while living at Banner Cross Terrace, Sheffield, he began an affair with a neighbour, Mrs Katherine Dyson. Although she was a willing instigator of the relationship, she soon decided that she wanted no further part of it and tried fruitlessly to be rid of him. Eventually Peace took the hint and left the area.

Around this time, Peace shot dead a policeman, PC Nicholas Cock, in Manchester but the crime was attributed to a young Irishman, William Habron, who was convicted and sentenced to death, which was later commuted to life imprisonment on account of his young age.

During the summer, Peace returned to Sheffield where he again chased after Mrs Dyson. One night her husband caught him as he pestered her and Peace shot him dead. He fled to London and set up with a new name but was soon in trouble again, and while robbing a house in Blackheath he attempted to shoot a police officer. Peace was arrested and gave his name as John Ward.

He was tried for the attempted murder of a police officer and sentenced to life imprisonment but no sooner had he begun his sentence, than he was recognised as being wanted for the murder of Katherine Dyson's husband at Banner Cross, and he was returned to the north to face trial.

On the journey, he attempted to escape from the train by throwing himself through a window but was thwarted in his bid.

Convicted at Leeds Assizes, he was hanged by Marwood after confessing to the murder of PC Cock at Manchester, which resulted in the release from prison and also compensation for William Habron.

March 24th: James SIMMS (43)   **Newgate**

A former American seaman sentenced to death by Mr Justice Hawkins at the Central Criminal Court on 5 March, for the murder of a prostitute.

On the afternoon of Sunday 9 February, Simms, now a pitman, was drinking with Lucy Graham (23) in the White Hart at Shadwell, in London's east end. Witnesses saw them quarrel over money, and Miss Graham was then overheard asking a William James to join them. James refused and went back to the bar, but as he looked over his shoulder, he saw Simms draw out a razor and run it across Graham's throat.

Simms later claimed that he had killed her after she had stolen his wages on a previous meeting.

Hanged by Marwood.

May 12th: Edwin SMART (35)   **Gloucester**

On 2 April, a commercial traveller, Charles Cox, was on his way towards Thornsby when he approached a pit pool and saw Smart with the body of a woman, Lucy Derrick, lying at his feet. He told Cox that he had just committed murder, so Cox hurried to the next town and raised the alarm.

Smart was taken into custody and admitted the crime, claiming that he'd 'done it out of devilment,' and that the poor woman was a total stranger that he had chanced upon. In his pockets police found a razor and pocket knife, both covered in blood.

Sentenced to death by Mr Justice Hawkins at Worcester Assizes on 25 April. Despite the nature of the crime, the jury recommended him to mercy but it was ignored and he was hanged by Marwood. He was seen to breathe for several minutes on the end of the rope.

May 20th: William COOPER (42)   **Manchester**

A former Bolton soldier convicted at Manchester Assizes of the murder of Ellen Mather.

Cooper and Mather had been courting many years earlier but had split up after a petty quarrel. As a result Cooper had joined the army and left the country, returning just two days after she had married another man.

In 1878, Ellen and her husband split up and she began working as a barmaid at the Albert Inn on Derby Street. When Cooper learned of this he became a regular and although she still liked him she had no wish to get involved in a serious relationship.

On St Patrick's night, Ellen was asked if she would like to earn extra money by waiting on a dance at a local hall, so after her shift at the pub she set off on the two mile walk. As she neared a railway station, she was waylaid by Cooper who tried to prevent her from going to the dance. After a short argument, he cut her throat.

Cooper was immediately arrested and charged with her murder. He was one of two sentenced to death at that sitting of the Assizes, but the only one to hang when the other, a Nantwich man, was reprieved. The local press reported that there seemed no reason why one should be reprieved and not the other when both crimes were of a similar nature, and put it down to Cooper having a received 'a bad number from the Home Office lottery.'

Hanged by Marwood, who gave him a drop of 10 feet.

May 26th: Catherine CHURCHILL (55)   **Taunton**

On Tuesday evening 4 March, a witness saw Mrs Churchill dragging an object towards a fire outside her isolated cottage two miles from Ilminster. On Wednesday morning, her eighty year old husband failed to turn up for an appointment with a neighbour who later called at the house and found him dead. He had been beaten to death with a billhook and badly charred about the head and shoulders.

Mrs Churchill was soon arrested and could supply no reasonable motive for a callous crime. She was convicted at Taunton Assizes.

Hanged by Marwood.

1879

May 27th: John D'ARCY (22) York

A clock cleaner convicted at York Assizes on 7 May, for the murder of William Metcalfe (85), a gamekeeper from Oulton, near Leeds.

On 4 March two women heard a cry of murder coming from a cottage on an estate, and saw a man robbing the elderly gamekeeper. Also in the vicinity were a father and son named Mosely, the younger of whom grabbed the cottage door handle to prevent the man escaping while his father rushed for assistance. Before the police could arrive, the robber pulled out his gun and threatened that this would be 'another Peace case' if the door was not released [see **PEACE** above]. Mosely sensibly complied and the man fled, leaving Metcalfe dead on the floor. He had been battered to death.

Metcalfe's niece told police she had seen John D'Arcy at the cottage earlier and he was arrested in his lodgings at Hunslet, Leeds. Upon identification by witnesses, he was charged.

Hanged by Marwood.

May 28th: Thomas JOHNSON (20) Liverpool

On 23 March, Johnson and Eliza Parton (21), visited a house of ill repute at Liverpool and after spending an hour or so drinking, they went upstairs to a room.

Soon afterwards Eliza came downstairs with scratches on her face. Moments later Johnson followed and without a word, stabbed her in the neck and then rushed out. He was arrested soon after and could offer no defence, claiming that he had done it through cruelty.

The determined looking and powerfully built man broke down as the sentence of death was passed and had to be carried in tears from the dock.

Hanged by Marwood.

July 29th: Catherine WEBSTER (30) Wandsworth

A twice married Irish domestic worker and petty thief, sentenced to death at the Old Bailey for the murder of her employer, Mrs Julia Thomas, whom she hacked to death with an axe.

On 5 March a workman found a wooden box on the banks of the River Thames at Hammersmith, and after opening it was horrified to find the remains of a woman's body. Police later ascertained that the victim was

Julia Thomas, a widow from Richmond. Enquiries at the house found that the domestic help was missing, and later traced her to her native Ireland, where she was brought back to London to stand trial.

After being convicted she confessed that she had killed her employer after being given the sack, and then dismembered the body and boiled the remains, which were found by the witness, although the head was never located. It was later claimed that she had posed as Mrs Thomas before leaving the country and had sold jars of human dripping in a local public house.

Hanged by Marwood.

August 11th: Annie TOOKE   **Exeter**

A middle aged baby farmer convicted of the murder of a child, Reginald Hide, whom she battered to death with a blunt instrument on 18 May. She then dismembered the body and dumped it in a mill pond. The infant was the eight month old illegitimate child of a Mary Hoskings.

Sentenced to death on 22 July, she was hanged by Marwood on a scaffold erected in the prison hospital, after being visited in the condemned cell by her four children.

August 25th: James DILLEY (41)   **Newgate**

A picture framer of Shefford, Bedfordshire, convicted along with his paramour Mary Rainbow (29), a domestic worker, for the murder of their three month old illegitimate child.

Dilley, a married man, also worked part-time as a letter carrier for the post office and through this job he met Miss Rainbow who worked six miles away at Baldock, Herts. On 22 April she gave birth to the child. On 10 May, Dilley called at her home and after spending the night together, they set off for London. They then deposited a parcel at St Pancras station, and were seen drinking together later that afternoon.

Next day a workman at the station opened the parcel and discovered the remains of the child, which had been beaten to death and poisoned.

They were tried together on 8 August and both convicted. Miss Rainbow was reprieved on Saturday 23 August, while he was hanged by Marwood.

1879

August 25th: Joseph PRISTORIA   **Cork**

Aka Francisco Moschera, a Sicilian sailor, convicted at Cork Assizes for his part in the 'Caswell' mutiny and murder of 1876, when five Greek and Italian crewmen stabbed to death the captain and several officers. (See also **1876, August 25th: Christos Emanuel BAUMBOS**)

    While the ship was on Argentina's River Plate, Pristoria and his brother escaped in a boat, and when the 'Caswell' landed at Queenstown in May 1876, the mutineers who had remained on board were charged with murder.

    Christos Baumbos was hanged in August that year, while another mutineer died from his injuries. While Pristoria was working on a wharf at Montevideo he was recognised by a crewman who had survived the mutiny. He was arrested and brought back to Ireland to face trial.

    He was hanged on the same scaffold as Baumbos exactly three years later. His executioner was a man named Stanhouse who had travelled from Gainsborough, England, to carry out the sentence.

August 26th: John RALPH (28)   **Warwick**

Ralph lived in Birmingham and began an affair with Sarah Alice Vernon, the wife of a wealthy jeweller.

    Eventually tiring of her, he cut her throat with a razor and threw her into a canal. She crawled from the water begging for mercy and declaring her love for him, but he coldy pushed her back and she drowned.

    Sentenced to death by Mr Justice Thesiger on 6 August and told he had no hope of being reprieved. He was visited in the death cell by his wife who offered her forgiveness.

    Hanged by Marwood.

December 3rd: Henry BEDINGFIELD (46)   **Ipswich**

Bedingfield, a pavior, was a married man who began courting an Eliza Rodden, a laundress. During May, a witness overheard him declare that he would kill her before he would allow another man to come between them.

    On the night of 7 July, they had one of their frequent quarrels and early next morning he called at her house. No sooner had he entered than she fled from the house bleeding from a horrific neck wound, which proved fatal.

Bedingfield tried to cut his own throat before he was detained. When searched at the station he was found to be carrying two razors, but told the police that she had slit her own throat after trying to kill him.

He maintained throughout his trial that he was telling the truth but the judge declared that the evidence wasn't consistent with his defence and he was found guilty of murder.

Hanged by Marwood.

1880

Cases where no executioner is recorded are multiple executions, and readers are asked to refer to the entries before or after for details of the hangman.

1880

January 5th: Charles SURETY (29)   Newgate

A bricklayer sentenced to death by Mr Justice Lindlay at the Central Criminal Court, for the murder of a two year old girl, the daughter of his girlfriend Mary Ann Pepper (32).

Evidence showed that Surety had brutally ill-treated the unfortunate child: on one occassion he bashed it against a door; he also expressed a wish to lay the child on the floor and thrash her till she couldn't move; and to starve her. The actual cause of death was probably a beating with the fists.

His execution caused a controversy when, as Marwood completed his preparations and Surety had only a matter of minutes to live, an express letter arrived carrying a reprieve. The Governor, after a conference with other officials, decided that the letter was a forgery and the execution went ahead as planned. It was later discovered that the letter was written, for no apparent reason, by a London doctor who received a prison sentence and heavy fine for attempting to obstruct the course of justice.

January 16th: Martin McHUGO   Galway

Convicted at his third trial, after the first two ended with the jury failing to agree on a verdict, of the murder of Michael Brehaney. He had become incensed at Brehaney who was taking out proceedings against him for defamation of character.

On Christmas Eve 1879, he followed Brehaney down a quiet lane at Woodford, County Galway, and battered him to death with a large stone.

He pleaded an alibi but the presence of a piece of cloth in the dead man's hand which matched perfectly with a piece torn from McHugo's raincoat was enough to convince the jury of his guilt and he was convicted.

Hanged by Marwood.

1880

February 17th: William CASSIDY — Manchester

Cassidy and his wife had been married for many unhappy years and after a series of rows, he decided to be rid of her. He joked with a friend in a pub that he intended to kill his wife and that he would swing for her. One night in November 1879, he crept into her room as she slept and after soaking the bed in paraffin he set it alight. She awoke engulfed in flames and died in great agony from her burns.

Hanged by Marwood who gave him a very long drop of almost ten feet, and as a result his head was almost pulled off.

March 2nd: Hugh BURNS / Patrick KEARNS — Liverpool

Jointly convicted at Liverpool Assizes by Lord Coleridge for the murder of Patrick Tracey. The two men lodged with Tracey, a labourer, and his wife at Widnes, Cheshire.

Shortly after midnight one night in October 1879, Tracey was shot dead as he lay in bed. Mrs Tracey gave evidence to the police that they had been robbed of a box containing over fifteen pounds. Despite a thorough investigation police could find no evidence of a break-in and as a result the two lodgers were charged with the crime.

Later as the police continued with their enquiries, Mrs Tracey was also charged. The motive for the crime was to claim the insurance money on Tracey, which was an extraordinarily large amount considering his circumstances.

All three were sentenced to death. Mrs Tracey was reprieved because she was pregnant; the two lodgers were hanged by Marwood.

March 22nd: John WINGFIELD (34) — Newgate

Wingfield and his wife Margaret had separated, and she refused his repeated pleas to come back. On 27 January, he saw her walking down a street. When she spotted him, she turned and walked the other way, whereupon he ran across the road. He punched her and then stabbed her seventeen times.

After a plea of insanity was rejected, he was hanged by Marwood.

1880

April 14th: Peter CONWAY   Omagh

Sentenced to death by Mr Justice Harrison for the murder of James Miller, his brother-in-law, at Pomeroy in July 1879.

The Conway family were struggling to pay for the upkeep of their smallholding and had to mortgage the land to pay the bills. Through abject poverty, Peter Conway killed Miller on 14 July, then robbed him of some money. Witnesses saw Miller call at the Conways after he had spent the day fishing; he was never seen alive again.

When his body was found battered to death a few miles away the next day, Conway and his father were arrested. Conway senior was acquitted at the trial but his son was later hanged by Marwood.

May 10th: William DUMBLETON   Aylesbury

On 3 February, John Edmunds called at a public house at Ludgershall Buckinghamshire, offering a selection of watches for sale. After doing some business he left the pub and Dumbleton was seen to follow him. In a field the next morning, Edmunds' body was found with horrific throat injuries, and Dumbleton was arrested later that day.

He was convicted at Northampton Assizes on 20 April and despite the jury's recommendation for mercy on the grounds that he had a defective upbringing, he was hanged by Marwood.

May 11th: John Henry WOOD   York

Sentenced to death by Mr Justice Stephens at York Assizes for the murder of John Coe.

On the evening of 15 February, Wood met Coe in the Chequers Inn at Whiston, near Rotherham. They drank together, and visited several other pubs, before ending up in a house of ill repute.

They were later seen together in the High Street and Westgate areas of Rotherham. The next morning, Coe's dead body was found; he had been battered about the head with a bloodstained stake. Beside the body was a stripped piece of branch that witnesses had seen Wood carrying.

He was arrested on suspicion after he tried to sell the dead man's watch and when it became known that he had told a friend about Coe being killed before the body had been discovered, he was charged with murder.

Hanged by Marwood.

1880

July 27th: Thomas BERRY (37)   **Maidstone**

A powerfully built Irish born carpenter who set up home with a Caroline Adams at Erith, after she had parted from her seafaring husband. Berry and Adams' relationship wasn't a happy one as he frequently ill-treated her, and after eighteen months together she left him. It was the beginning of May 1880.

On 15 June, Caroline and her sister were having tea at the Leather Bottle Tea Gardens, Belvedere. At 3pm that afternoon, Berry, who had been drinking for two hours, approached the sisters and asked Caroline if she had decided to return to live with him. She told him she had no intention of returning and he struck her. As she tried to leave he pulled out a large carpenter's chisel and plunged it repeatedly into her chest. Customers followed him when he left and one saw him throw the chisel into some bushes, from where it was later recovered.

Berry was soon arrested and confessed that it had been a 'good job.' He also added that he had intended to kill the sister, whom he blamed for the separation.

He was tried at Kent Summer Assizes, before Baron Pollock, on 6 July and pleaded not guilty. The defence claimed he was not responsible for his actions at the time, but the prosecution had a strong case and it was only a short trial which ended with his conviction.

He was hanged by Marwood who gave him a drop of eight feet. The rope hanging from the beam was a little short and when the hangman knotted it tightly around his neck, Berry was standing on tip-toes before the drop fell.

August 16th: John WAKEFIELD (28)   **Derby**

Convicted of the callous, motiveless murder of Eliza Wilkinson (9). Miss Wilkinson and her elder sister were in the area trying to sell comb boxes. On 26 April she entered a court where Wakefield lived with his elderly widowed mother, and on the pretence of buying something, he invited the girl into his home.

When she failed to meet up with her sister a search was launched but in the meantime Wakefield gave himself up. Police visited his home and found the young hawker dead in a pool of blood from four cuts to the

1880

neck. When arrested his only excuse was that he was tired of life and wanted to hang.

He pleaded insanity but was convicted, and hanged by Marwood.

November 16th: William BROWNLESS (22)   Durham

On 15 August, despite repeated rejection, casual farmworker William Brownless called at the home of Elizabeth Holmes (25) and asked her to go out with him. Her father answered the door and told him to go away. The family disapproved of Brownless because they thought him to be a rough, good for nothing drunken layabout.

Three days later two bodies were found lying side by side near the field where Elizabeth worked. A witness thought that they were asleep but on closer inspection saw that they both had their throats cut. Elizabeth was dead but Brownless later recovered in hospital.

Sentenced to death by Mr Justice Field on 5 November, and hanged by Marwood who gave him a drop of eight feet six inches.

November 26th: Thomas WHEELER   St Albans

Early in the morning of 22 August, Wheeler and two other members of his family called at Marshall's Wick farm in St Albans and shouted at the window for the owner, Edward Anstree, to open up.

Anstree obliged and was promptly blasted in the head with a shotgun, dying instantly. The three men then entered the house and ransacked it, while the dead man's wife locked herself in the bedroom in sheer terror.

No motive was clearly established but the Wheeler family were immediately arrested on suspicion and it was noticed that Tom Wheeler had blood stains on his trousers and boots.

Hanged by Marwood.

Wheeler's daughter Mary, who was fourteen when her father was executed, was herself hanged ten years later. (See **1890, December 23rd: Mary Eleanor WHEELER**)

1880

November 27th: William Joseph DISTON (35) — Bristol

On 27 August, Eliza Daniels, a widow who lived with Diston as his wife, stormed into the local public house and dragged him home for his dinner. They were joined by a friend of Diston's and sat down for supper apparently on good terms.

Soon after the friend left, Mrs Daniels, bleeding from a wound to the shoulder, staggered into their landlady's room, where she collapsed and died.

Diston was recommended to mercy at the trial on the grounds that the crime wasn't premeditated but he was hanged by Marwood.

December 13th: William HERBERT (44) — Newgate

An Australian immigrant who had left his poverty stricken family back home to make a vain attempt to claim on an inheritance, worth sixteen thousand pounds per annum.

During the summer he persuaded his sister-in-law, Jane Messenger, to leave her husband and set up home with him. On 22 October they were together in Finsbury Park when a witness saw him draw a pistol and fire two shots at her before turning the gun on himself.

He claimed he had become disheartened at his financial state and decided they should both die together.

December 13th: George PAVEY (29) — Newgate

Sentenced to death by Mr Justice Hawkins at the Old Bailey for the murder of Ada Shepherd (10).

The young girl's father had left her alone in the house with Pavey while he went out. When he returned he found the child dead on the bed with her throat cut. She had also been violently raped.

Pavey disappeared but was later arrested in a Hendon workhouse wearing bloodstained clothing.

His plea of not guilty was unsuccessful and he was hanged by Marwood in a double execution with **HERBERT** [above].

1881

Cases where no executioner is recorded are multiple executions, and readers are asked to refer to the entries before or after for details of the hangman.

1881

February 21st: William STANWAY — Chester

A native of Newcastle-under-Lyme, who earned a living as a broom maker and hawker, convicted at Chester Assizes of the murder of Ann Mellor at Macclesfield, where they lived with their nine year old daughter. Both were addicted to drink and frequently quarrelled, which usually ended with him giving her a beating. Shortly after Christmas 1880, they went out drinking one afternoon and later when they returned home, he beat her up.

Stanway went out again that evening, leaving her in bed; when he returned he called for her to come and fix him some supper. She at first refused to come down but he eventually persuaded her. When she reached the foot of the stairs he stabbed her in the chest with a red hot poker. He didn't call a doctor for two days, during which time she lay in extreme agony and by the time help arrived, she had died.

His defence that the crime was not premeditated was rejected and he was hanged by Marwood.

February 22nd: James WILLIAMS (24) — Stafford

On 28 December 1880, Williams, a tailor, escorted his sweetheart, Edith Bagnal to the Stafford Servants Christmas Fair. They set off for home together later that night, and walked down a secluded path beside a canal.

Williams arrived home alone in a highly excited state and claimed he had pushed Edith into the canal. When charged with the murder he claimed that he had killed her because she wanted to saddle him with an illegitimate child.

Hanged by George Incher.

February 28th: Albert ROBINSON (20) — Derby

Robinson's wife and a neighbour went out drinking during the afternoon of 2 October 1880, and returned home drunk. Robinson, a weaver from Hadfield near Glossop, waited until the neighbour went home before he turned on his wife and cursed her for being drunk.

The Robinsons' lodger, a young girl named Campbell, told police that she saw him reach into a drawer, pull out a knife and chase his wife into the street, stabbing her repeatedly as she fled in terror. Robinson then returned to the house and attempted to cut his own throat.

Hanged by Marwood.

1881

May 17th: Albert MOORE (23)   **Maidstone**

A soldier sentenced to death at Kent Assizes for the murder of Mary Ann Marsh (74).

On 15 February, she was left in charge of 'The Woodlands', the residence of a Lieutenant Scriven of the 52nd Regiment, at Gravesend, during his temporary absence. On his return he found her dead inside the house. Her throat had been cut from ear to ear.

Moore, a private in the Regiment, who worked as the Lieutenant's batman, was identified as the man seen leaving the house shortly before the murder was discovered.

Hanged by Marwood.

May 23rd: James HALL (53)   **Leeds**

A Sheffield cutler who killed his licentious wife, Polly, by splitting her head in two with an axe.

Shortly before midnight on 26 March, Hall's daughter and her boyfriend walked home from the pub and found they were unable to gain entry into the house. Looking through the window, she saw her father standing over her mother holding a hatchet.

After repeatedly knocking on the window, Hall eventually opened the door and as the young couple entered, Hall struck his daughter in the face with the weapon. Her boyfriend managed to overpower Hall, while a neighbour who had been attracted by the commotion, called the police.

Once in custody, Hall confessed to the murder and explained his motive. He claimed that three years earlier he had come home from work unexpectedly and found his wife with another man. He later forgave her but warned that if she was ever unfaithful again he would kill her.

At 11pm on the night of the crime, he came home from the pub sooner than usual and found his wife on the sofa with a neighbour, William Londe. Mrs Hall grappled with her husband while the man made his escape. Then, in a violent, drunken rage, Hall picked up a hatchet and attacked her.

His daughter denied that her mother was an adultress, as did Londe, who claimed he was nowhere near the house on the night in question.

Sentenced to death at Leeds Assizes and hanged by Marwood.

1881

May 31st: Joseph Patrick McENTIRE (42)   Liverpool

McEntire, a Liverpool born tailor, had been married to his wife Ellen for twenty four years, but they had spent the last two decades unhappy.

On 4 April he got very drunk in a local pub. His wife was later found lying in a pool of blood on the bedroom floor; she had been beaten to death with a broom handle.

McEntire was arrested on 7 April trying to find lodgings in nearby Garston.

Hanged by Marwood.

August 15th: Thomas BROWN   Nottingham

A shoemaker who lived with his mistress, Eliza Caldwell, in the Meadows district of Nottingham. After a drunken quarrel on Monday 20 May, he slashed her throat with so much force that her head was almost severed.

Hanged by Marwood, who gave him a long drop of nine feet four inches.

August 23rd: George DURLING (36)   Maidstone

Convicted at the Old Bailey on 5 August, of the murder of Fanny Mussow, aka Francis Vincent (25), with whom he lived in lodgings at Woolwich.

Both were heavy drinkers and as a result had frequent drunken quarrels. On 20 July they had a fight in the street, during which Durling threw bricks at her and threatened to kill her before the night was through. They made up and walked home together, but on reaching the garden adjacent to their lodgings, the quarrel started up again. This time he picked up an iron carpet beater, swung it around and smashed it into her head with such force that it penetrated her skull to a depth of four inches.

She died at once, and realising what he had done, Durling fell to his knees and began kissing her and begging her forgiveness. He was arrested and immediately confessed.

Hanged by Marwood.

1881

November 24th: Alfred GOUGH (34)   Derby

On 20 August, a group of young children were picking blackberries in a field at Brimington, near Chesterfield. At around 9.30am Gough, a hawker, passed by the group with his barrow, and soon after one of the children, six year old Eleanor Wendle, told her friends that she was going to follow him and ask for a toy from his barrow.

Gough was later seen with the young girl in Johnsons Lane, and soon after she was found dead. She had been raped and strangled. He was arrested on suspicion after he told a friend that he knew something about the crime, and later witnesses testified that they had seen a bundle on his barrow around the time the girl vanished.

He was convicted at Leicester Assizes on 2 November and confessed in the condemned cell. Hanged by Marwood.

November 28th: John Aspinall SIMPSON (23)   Manchester

Simpson, an unemployed clerk from Preston, had been courting Annie Radcliffe (16), for over eighteen months, although her parents didn't approve of the relationship.

Later, when she became pregnant, her father, a Preston publican, forbade Simpson to see his daughter. Early in the morning of 3 August, Simpson called to see Annie at the pub and while her father was upstairs, he cut her throat.

Hanged by Marwood.

November 29th: Percy LEFROY (22)   Lewes

Aka Percy Mapleton, a vain, romantic, distinctive looking, unsuccessful poet, who earned a meagre wage as a clerk. To finance the standard of living he yearned, he decided to commit a robbery.

On 27 June he collected a gun from a pawn shop and purchased a railway ticket to London Bridge. From there he boarded a train bound for Brighton, and selected a carriage whose only occupant was a dealer in foreign coins, Mr Isaac Gold (64).

When the train pulled into Preston Park station, on the outskirts of Brighton, a guard noticed a passenger covered in blood and looking very distressed. The man gave his name as Lefroy and claimed he had been beaten up by two passengers during the journey, fallen unconscious, and awoken to find his two mystery assailants had vanished.

Lefroy asked for a policeman to be called and when he was helped from the carriage someone noticed a watch-chain protruding from his sock. He explained that he had hidden it there during the struggle. He was taken to hospital and discharged later that afternoon.

Meanwhile, workers on the railway line reported the finding of several items of clothing and while Lefroy was being taken home he overheard an officer report that a body had been found. When he reached his house he asked to be allowed to get a change of clothes before being taken to the station to help with enquiries. While the officers waited he fled through the back door.

The body found was that of Isaac Gold; he had been stabbed, shot, and also fallen from a moving train.

Lefroy was at liberty for several weeks during which time the case against him was firmly established. He was caught after sending a telegram to an old girlfriend asking for help. She informed the police and he was arrested.

Tried at Maidstone Assizes, he pleaded not guilty and told a warder that he hoped he wouldn't be mobbed when he was acquitted. He was found guilty, sentenced to death, and hanged by Marwood.

Lefroy wrote a full confession to a friend shortly before his execution.

1882

Cases where no executioner is recorded are multiple executions, and readers are asked to refer to the entries before or after for details of the hangman.

1882

January 31st: Charles GERRISH (70) — Devizes

On Thursday 24 November 1881, two old paupers were sitting in front of a fire at a Devizes workhouse. The two men began to quarrel after Gerrish told the other man, Stephen Coleman, that it was his turn to get warm, but when Coleman refused to move, Gerrish withdrew a red hot poker from between the bars on the grate and thrust it into his neck.

Coleman died instantly and Gerrish was charged with his murder. After being convicted, he was hanged by Marwood who was reported to have given him the unlikely drop of twelve feet.

February 13th: Richard TEMPLETON (36) — Manchester

Templeton, a machine printer, lodged at a house in Burnley. He was very fond of his landlady, Mrs Betty Scott, who looked after her four children from an earlier marriage, and her crippled brother.

On Monday evening 2 June, Templeton crept into her bedroom, which she shared with her brother, and when she awoke she told him to get out. They had a brief struggle which ended when he returned to his room. The young children were awoken by the commotion but Mrs Scott reassured them everything was fine and they went back to bed.

Early next morning Mrs Scott was found dead in bed with her throat cut. Templeton was arrested but denied any knowledge of the crime. He was tried at Manchester Assizes on 26 January and sentenced to death by Mr Justice Chitty.

Hanged by Marwood.

April 28th: George Henry LAMSON (29) — Wandsworth

In 1880, Doctor Lamson bought a practice at Bournemouth with money left to his wife after the mysterious death of her brother the previous year. He was unable to make a success of the practice and often had to pawn his surgical instruments to pay for a drug habit he had acquired whilst working in Europe.

Lamson had a crippled brother-in-law, Percy John Malcolm, who was resident at a Wimbledon special school. On 3 December 1881, Dr Lamson visited the school and had lunch with the headmaster. After the meal he gave the teacher some cake and administered some tablets to the sick boy. He concluded his visit saying he had to catch a train to France, and within ten minutes of his departure Percy Malcolm was dead.

Detectives waited for Dr Lamson to return from Paris, then arrested him. He was tried at the Old Bailey in March and the prosecution alleged that he had killed his young relative with aconitine poison, which he was known to have purchased at the end of November.

Lamson was found guilty of the murder, sentenced to death and hanged by Marwood. He confessed to the chaplain shortly before his execution.

May 16th: Thomas FURY   **Durham**

On 19 February, 1869, Maria Fitzsimmons, a prostitute who worked the docks at Sunderland, was seen drinking in the company of a sailor. Early next morning her body was found in her room; she had been stabbed ten times, nine of which had pierced her heart.

A sailor called Anderson was arrested next day but later that week a note was found which was signed by 'A monster in human form.' The note claimed that Anderson was innocent and that its author was the real killer and on his way to America. With no real evidence against Anderson, he was released and the case left unsolved, despite someone offering one hundred pounds to catch the killer.

Twenty years later, in the spring of 1879, Thomas Fury, aka Wright, also a sailor, was arrested on a charge of burglary and attempted murder at Norwich. Soon after his arrest, he enquired whether the reward offered for information on the killing of Maria Fitzsimmons could still be claimed, as he said he could identify the killer. When told it wasn't, he said no more about it.

He was tried for the attempted murder and sentenced to fifteen years at Pentonville, but no sooner had he started his sentence than he asked to see a police inspector and confessed he had murdered Fitzsimmons. Fury said he'd awoken after spending the night with her to find her attempting to strangle him with a cord. He knocked her down, pulled out his knife and stabbed her.

He was taken back to Durham, convicted at the summer Assizes entirely on his own testimony, and hanged by Marwood. He confided to a guard that he had confessed in order to escape the torture of prison.

1882

May 22nd: William George ABIGAIL (19) — Norwich

At 6am on Tuesday 25 April, Jane Plunkett (22) was found shot dead in the room she shared with William Abigail.

Abigail worked as a waiter at the Star Hotel, Norwich, where he had first met Plunkett who was employed there as a chambermaid. She didn't tell him she was already married, and later they went through a form of marriage and moved in with his half-brother at New Catton.

It was his brother's son who reported hearing the shots, and Jane Plunkett was discovered blasted in the head and chest. Abigail confessed he had killed her when he found out she was already married.

Abigail was an unstable character and it was reported that he had tried to commit suicide four years earlier by swallowing rat poison.

He was convicted, and hanged by Marwood.

May 23rd: Osmond Otto BRAND (27) — Leeds

William Pepper was an apprentice from Hull who was serving aboard a fishing smack on the high seas.

Osmond Brand was the skipper of the boat and a brutal bully to the young Pepper, often kicking and beating him if he thought his work was not up to scratch. On 29 December, the apprentice did something to anger the captain to the extent that he beat him up and threw him overboard. The crew testified against him when the boat landed and he was convicted.

Hanged by Marwood.

August 21st: William TURNER — Liverpool

Sentenced to death by Mr Justice North at Liverpool Assizes, for the murder of his wife Ellen, whom he kicked to death at Skelmersdale on 23 June.

Turner, a collier, and his crippled wife, were drinking in a public house when she told him she felt unwell and wanted to go home. Turner at first refused to listen to her but when it became obvious that she was ill, customers in the pub organised a cart and she was taken home.

As they got inside the house, she collapsed to the ground and in a drunken temper he declared: 'I'll hang for thee!', then brutally kicked her to death and stole her purse.

Hanged by Marwood.

1882

August 22nd: Thomas HAYNES (40) — Cork

A farmer from Inneshannon, County Cork, convicted of the murder of his wife Ellen on 25 March.

During a drunken quarrel he stabbed her several times, and as she lay bleeding on the ground he proceeded to kick her to death.

Haynes made a vain attempt to cheat the gallows by trying to cut his own throat before he was hanged by two local men. Their identities were kept secret, and they were offered the appointment after Marwood failed to arrive at the prison.

September 11th: Francis HYNES — Limerick

A young man from a wealthy family, sentenced to death by Mr Justice Lawson on 12 August, for the murder of John Doloughty, an old shepherd.

Doloughty was a father of seven who was employed as a herdsman on an evicted farm at Moyresik, two miles from Ennis, County Clare. On 9 July Doloughty went into Ennis to attend lunchtime mass and as he walked home he was ambushed and shot in the chest and head. The shot had blown away both his eyes.

A passer-by discovered the body and as he looked around for any clues he heard a rustle in the bushes and recognised Hynes, who fired at him but only managed to inflict minor wounds. Other passers-by managed to detain the gunman until police arrived.

It was thought the crime was committed because Doloughty worked on the evicted farm and that Hynes was sympathetic to the evicted man's plight. He had been one of a gang who had recently destroyed some property on the land.

Hanged by Marwood, who was accompanied to the gaol by six English and two Irish detectives, following threats made to him about coming back to Ireland.

September 22nd: Patrick WALSH — Galway

On 24 April 1881, a party of men went to a house occupied by the Lyden family at Letterfrack, Co Galway. Martin Lyden and his father were dragged from their beds and taken outside where they were shot. The old man died instantly, his son lingered for several weeks before he too died, after first identifying Walsh as the ringleader of the gang.

Walsh was later arrested and it was proved in court that he had shot the men as the result of a vendetta caused when they had taken over the running of a farm from which Walsh's father had been evicted. The murder weapon was found hidden at Walsh's house, and the sale of the fatal bullets was traced to him.

Sentenced to death by Mr Justice Lawson and hanged by Marwood.

November 13th: William Meager BARTLETT — Bodmin

Bartlett was a Cornish mining manager, and the father of eight children. While his wife was pregnant with their last child, he seduced the nurse who was attending her. Later when the nurse gave birth to a daughter, he persuaded her to hand it over with a promise that he would care for it.

He then strangled the sixteen day old illegitimate child and threw it down a deserted mine shaft at Laulivery, Cornwall.

He later confessed to the murder and was convicted on his own testimony. It was reported that his jet black hair turned grey while in the condemned cell. Hanged by Marwood.

On the morning of the execution the prison officials allowed no information to be leaked to the press - an unusual occurrence at the time.

November 28th: Edward WHEATFALL — York

Wheatfall was the second hand on the fishing smack 'Gleamor'. On 24 February, while on the high seas, Wheatfall went below deck and entered the cabin of deck hand Peter Hughes (16). He dragged him from his bunk and ordered him up on deck to see to some mooring ropes.

As Hughes attended to his work, other crew members heard him plead 'Don't hit me.' Later on he was again overheard, this time talking to Wheatfall; soon after this, Hughes vanished from the ship, probably thrown overboard by his tormentor.

Wheatfall, who had a terrible police record, was arrested in port and convicted.

Hanged by Marwood.

1882

December 4th: Bernard MULLARKEY (19)   Liverpool

Convicted of the murder of a Tom Cruise at Maghull, Liverpool, in September.

Mullarkey, Cruise, and another man, Tom Jordan, were three labourers employed on a farm owned by a John Sumner, where they were allowed to sleep in a hay loft. During the summer, Mullarkey was heard to make repeated threats to Cruise, and one witness reported hearing him say that he would 'Burn the place down and hang for Cruise.'

On Monday 25 September, a serious fire destroyed the hay loft and when it had burnt itself out, police found Cruise's body among the remains. They ascertained that the victim had been killed by a blow to the head before the fire started. Mullarkey was immediately under suspicion, and was later charged with murder.

Hanged by Marwood.

December 12th: Charles TAYLOR   Wandsworth

Convicted of the murder of his wife who was found dead in their home on the Old Kent Road. She had died from a cut throat; Taylor had also cut his own throat in a suicide bid but was nursed back to health and hanged.

Marwood carried out the execution and gave him a relatively long drop which resulted in the wound opening up and almost severing the head.

The hangman was due to visit Ireland later that week and because of fears of an assassination attempt, detectives escorted him from the prison.

December 15th: Pat CASEY   Galway
Miles JOYCE
Pat JOYCE

Convicted together for the massacre of John Joyce (45), a distant relative of two of the men, and his family at Maamtrasna, Galway.

On the morning of Friday 18 August, a neighbour called at the John Joyce farm intending to borrow some farming equipment. As he approached the farmhouse he was surprised to find no signs of activity, which was most unusual. Entering the house, he was shocked to find the bodies of John Joyce, his wife Bridget (40), his mother Peggy (85), his daughter Peggy (17), and two sons Michael (17) and Patrick (12). John had been shot in the chest and beaten around the head, the rest battered to death except for Patrick who had survived the assault.

1882

The boy identified the attackers as locals from the village, and later ten men were arrested. It was thought Joyce was murdered because he was suspected of giving information which had led to the arrest of **Patrick HIGGINS (see 1883, 15th January), and Michael FLYNN and Thomas HIGGINS (see 1883, 17th January)**, for the murder of two bailiffs and were still awaiting trial.

At the trial in November, three of the ten were convicted of murder, while the other seven were sentenced to various terms of imprisonment at Mountjoy Prison, Dublin, for their part in the crime.

The three were hanged together by Marwood. Casey and Miles Joyce were both in their forties, Patrick Joyce was in his thirties. It was noted that Pat Casey and Pat Joyce died at once from a broken neck, but Miles Joyce went after a violent struggle.

A witness claimed Marwood stood over the drop with his foot pressing down hard on Miles Joyce's shoulder in an attempt to speed up his death. An inquest found that his neck wasn't broken and he had died from strangulation.

1883

Cases where no executioner is recorded are multiple executions, and readers are asked to refer to the entries before or after for details of the hangman.

1883

January 2nd: Louisa Jane TAYLOR (37) — Maidstone

Mrs Taylor was an attractive dark haired widow, whose seventy year old husband had died in March 1882 leaving her a small pension. In August she visited William Tregillis (85), a friend of her husband, who lived with his wife in a two roomed cottage at Plumstead.

The Tregillis' were enchanted by the young widow and asked her to stay with them; she agreed, and shared a room with Mary Tregillis while William slept in the other. Within a few days though, Tregillis began to doubt the wisdom of his hospitality. Firstly he noticed small items had vanished from the house; then he was none too pleased when Mrs Taylor invited her new lover to stay the night.

In September, Tregillis became worried about his wife's state of health but when he mentioned his fears to Louisa she responded with a request for him to elope with her! On 23 October, Mrs Tregillis passed away and the family doctor arranged for an autopsy which revealed traces of lead poison. Taylor was arrested later that day, charged with murder and convicted at Maidstone Assizes.

Hanged by Marwood.

January 15th: Patrick HIGGINS (55) — Galway

Convicted of the murder of Joseph and John Huddy at Clougbrack, Lough Mask, on 3 January 1882. The two men were bailiffs employed by Lord Ardilaun. They were requested to evict Higgins and his family from a farm they rented on the Lord's land when they fell behind with the payments.

As the bailiffs called at the farm, Patrick Higgins and his two accomplices attacked the men. Patrick Higgins attacked Joseph Huddy with a stone and knocked him down, while Thomas Higgins shot dead the younger Huddy. The three accused then forced witnesses at gunpoint to assist them in tying up the two men and carry the bodies to Lough Mask. The bodies were later found chained together under a spur near the Lough.

Hanged by Marwood.

1883

January 17th: Michael FLYNN   **Galway**
             Thomas HIGGINS

Convicted along with **Patrick HIGGINS** [above], at a special sitting of the Dublin Special Commission, of the murder of the Huddys.

    Hanged by Marwood, who had hanged Patrick Higgins on the same scaffold three days earlier.

January 23rd: Sylvester POFF   **Tralee**
             James BARRETT

Convicted of the murder of Thomas Brown who was shot dead in broad daylight at Castleisland, Co Kerry.

    A witness testified that at 5pm on 3 October 1882, she saw the two men enter a field where Brown was working, and after an exchange of words, they shot him dead.

    At his trial, Poff, who was described in court as a sober, thrifty, religious peasant who had never committed a crime in his life, declared that he was totally innocent of murder. Barrett, the young son of a well-to-do farmer, also contested his innocence but the prosecution was able to show there was a long standing dispute between the men, and the jury found them guilty of murder.

    Hanged together by Marwood.

February 12th: Abraham THOMAS (24)   **Manchester**

Abraham Thomas and Mrs Christina Leigh (39), were both employed by a Captain Ansell who kept a large house at Kearsley Moor, outside Bolton. Thomas served as the butler, Mrs Leigh worked as housekeeper. The captain was frequently away from the house and on such occassions Mrs Leigh was left in charge, and often when Ansell returned she reported Thomas for his bad behaviour.

    On 22 December 1882 Captain Ansell went away for a holiday, again leaving the housekeeper in charge. He returned on 3 January and at once Mrs Leigh reported Thomas. The Captain told the butler that he wasn't to return to work until he had seen him in his office; Thomas still turned up the following day but was refused the keys.

    He then hid in the grounds until Mrs Leigh arrived and was seen by the gardener. Soon after, a shot was heard and the housekeeper was found dead. Thomas was immediately arrested and charged.

Sentenced to death by Mr Justice Key at Manchester Assizes and hanged by Marwood.

February 19th: James ANDERSON (50) Lincoln

A Lincolnshire coal miner sentenced to death by Mr Justice Cave at Lincoln Assizes for the murder of his wife at Gainsborough on 6 December 1882.

Anderson cut her throat, and then his own after a quarrel. He expressed deep regret for the crime and despite a petition signed by thousands of local people, he was hanged by Marwood.

April 30th: Timothy O'KEEFE (20) Cork

Convicted at his second trial of the murder of his uncle, John O'Keefe, who was shot dead at Kingwilliamstown on Sunday 30 April 1882.

At the first trial the jury had failed to agree, but at the second, the prosecution claimed there was evidence that proved the prisoner's guilt. They alleged that Timothy's father had financial difficulties and had to sell their farm. The uncle bought the farm and evicted his brother when he couldn't pay his debts.

The execution was originally scheduled for the 26th April but had to be put back as Marwood was otherwise enagaged. When he eventually carried out the job, he gave O'Keefe a drop of nine feet.

May 7th: Thomas GARRY Lincoln

Alias Irish Joe, a labourer convicted of the murder of John Newton (74), a farmer, residing at Great Hale Fen, Sleaford.

Newton had lived alone on his farm since the death of his wife in the summer of 1882. Garry worked for him as a casual labourer and slept at the house. At the beginning of 1883, he took to drink with the result that his work became sloppy and he was warned by the old man that if he didn't shape up he would have to move on.

On 2 February, Newton was found dead on the kitchen floor at the farmhouse. He had been blasted in the chest with his own shotgun which lay nearby. Police found a bloostained footprint which matched markings on Garry's boots; further examination revealed bloodstains on his clothing. Convicted at Lincolnshire Assizes and hanged by Marwood.

May 8th: Patrick CAREY   Chester

Samuel Carlam and his common-law wife Mary Mohan, kept a lodging house at Smallwood, a village just outside Congleton, Cheshire.
    On 9 February they were found battered to death at the house, which had also been robbed. A hammer was found beside the bodies. The police soon learned that a tramp had been seen in the area carrying a large bundle shortly after the robbery was discovered.
    Police arrested Patrick Carey who was a father of four, and also known as John White. He was convicted at Chester Assizes, and hanged by Marwood.

May 14th: Joseph BRADY (22)   Dublin

The chief executioner of the Irish Invincibles sentenced to death on 2 May by Mr Justice O'Brien for his part in the murder of Harry Burke, the Permanent Under-Secretary for Ireland, and Lord Frederick Cavendish, the Chief Secretary, in Phoenix Park, Dublin.
    The gang of Invincibles laid in wait for Burke as he strolled through the park with Lord Cavendish on 6 May 1882. During the attack, Brady was alleged to have driven a long knife into Burke's back, and then stabbed Lord Cavendish who tried in vain to fend off the attack with his umbrella.
    Following intensive police work, twenty three men were rounded up, and later three of them turned informer.
    Brady was the first of five condemned; he was hanged at Kilmainham gaol by Marwood.

May 18th: Daniel CURLEY (31)   Dublin

A Superintendent with the Invincibles who was alleged to have masterminded the Phoenix Park murders. He had been a Fenian for 18 years and held a high rank in the organisation.
    Hanged by Marwood.

1883

May 21st: Joseph WEDLAKE   **Taunton**

Wedlake was very jealous of a young man called Thatcher who was dating his cousin Emma Pearce at Winford, near Bristol.

On 7 January he lay in wait for Thatcher with the intention of killing him with an axe. Mark Cox, a total stranger passing by, was mistakenly attacked by Wedlake and died from his injuries. Wedlake's brother was first arrested on suspicion but he was able to convince the police of his innocence, while at the same time condemning his brother. Joe Wedlake was taken into custody and confessed.

May 21st: George WHITE   **Taunton**

Pleaded guilty at Taunton Assizes to the murder of his wife at Henstridge, near Wincanton, Somerset.

They had been married for less than a year when he deliberately kicked her to death on 28 March. He gave himself up at once and never showed any remorse for the crime.

He was hanged alongside **WEDLAKE** [above] on a scaffold constructed at the end of a corridor. Marwood executed them both as a crowd of over two hundred gathered outside.

May 23rd: Henry MULLEN   **Glasgow**
          Martin SCOTT

In February 1883, a farmer's wife taking a short cut home through a field at Port Glasgow, discovered the bodies of two gamekeepers. They had been shot dead at such close range that there were powder burns on their faces. Many local poachers were questioned before one, a man named Kyle, turned informer. On his evidence Henry Mullen and Martin Scott were soon arrested and charged.

They were convicted at Glasgow Circuit Court on 25 April, and sentenced to be hanged on 17 May. The executions had to be put back until 23 May because Marwood had an engagement in Dublin with the Phoenix Park murderers. They were the first men to be hanged at Duke Street prison.

1883

May 28th: Michael FAGAN   Dublin

A brawny young blacksmith, hanged by Marwood for his part in the Phoenix Park murders. (See **1883, May 14th: Joseph BRADY**).

June 2nd: Thomas CAFFREY   Dublin

Pleaded not guilty to the Phoenix Park murders. He claimed in the dock that the real killers were Joseph **BRADY** [above] and Timothy **KELLY** [below] and that he had entered the park under threat of death.
    Hanged by Marwood.

June 9th: Timothy KELLY   Dublin

The last of the Invincibles to go to the gallows when he was hanged by Marwood. Kelly was alleged to have slit the throat of Harry Burke as he lay wounded on the ground.

August 6th: James BURTON (33)   Durham

Convicted of the murder of his wife Elizabeth (18) at Tunstally, near Sunderland, on 8 May. Burton, the son of a police sergeant, and his young wife were on their way to her father's house when they began quarreling. Elizabeth Burton had threatened to tell her father about some deed her husband had perpetrated. During the argument Burton struck her and she replied by stabbing him with her umbrella. This prompted him into a rage whereupon he picked up a large stone and beat her to death, ignoring her pleas for mercy. Seeing that she was dead, he concealed her body by burying it under a large pile of stones, although it was soon discovered.
    He was convicted at Durham Assizes and maintained his innocence until two days before the execution when, with all hope gone, he broke down and confessed. He was hanged by William Marwood, officiating at his last execution, who gave him a drop of seven feet ten inches.
    Marwood, who was noted for the humane innovation of instantaneous death, signed off with a dreadfully botched execution.
    On the stroke of eight he pushed the lever, the trap opened, and Burton plunged down. Witnesses noted that as he fell, the rope swung violently and they watched in horror as Marwood swung down in an effort

to free the slack rope which had become entangled with the culprit's arms. With the assistance of a warder, Marwood hoisted the condemned man into the air and drew up the slack rope; he then repositioned the cap which had worked free, and bodily threw him back into the pit! He threw Burton down with such force that the rope swung violently across the yawning hole and had to be steadied by the hangman. A warder claimed that Burton had pleaded 'Oh, Lord help me.'

Marwood claimed in his report that he had speeded up the execution because he sensed that Burton was about to collapse on the drop. He added that a similar occurrence would be avoided if planks were placed across the trap for officers to support the prisoner. This last suggestion was his final legacy to British execution procedure and became standard practice until abolition.

November 6th: Henry POWELL (24)   Wandsworth

On 27 September, Powell, a bricklayer employed by a Balham building firm, collected his wages but was unhappy at the amount he had received for his last job.

He confronted John Briton, the son of the owner, and during a quarrel he beat him about the head with a heavy chisel.

Hanged by Bartholomew Binns, officiating at his first execution.

November 13th: Thomas Lyons DAY (31)   Ipswich

In 1877, Day became acquainted with Caroline Meek. They began a relationship and in 1879 a child was born. Soon afterwards, they split up and she later married another man.

When Day, a former Coldstream Guard from Oldbury, Staffordshire, discovered this he went to Ipswich and tracked her down.

They met up and after he cursed her for her unfaithfulness, he took his child, sat it on his knee and cut its throat.

Sentenced to death at Norwich Assizes, he protested his innocence to the end.

Hanged by Binns.

1883

November 19th: Peter BRAY (32)   Durham

A Durham pitman and returned convict, sentenced to death for the murder of Thomas Pyle, a plate layer, in April 1882.

Bray was among a gang of men who got into a quarrel with Pyle, and when he threatened to attack the man he asked for assistance but they all refused to help him. Bray then picked up a hedge stake, battered the man to death, and fled.

Police failed to locate him and it was over 18 months before he was arrested.

He was convicted at Durham Assizes and wrote out a full confession before he was hanged by Binns.

November 26th: Thomas RILEY (55)   Manchester

Mrs Elizabeth Alston was separated from her husband and lived alone at Preston. She was acquainted with Thomas Riley, a stone mason who lived nearby, and they often went drinking together.

On 27 September, following a visit to a local pub, a neighbour heard them singing in Mrs Alston's house. Shortly before closing time Riley went back to the pub in a very excited, drunken state and asked for another drink. The landlord refused to serve him and noticed that he had blood on his hands. Riley hurried out and a few people from the pub followed him; at Elizabeth Alston's house, they found her body lying in a pool of blood on the floor. She had been hacked to death with a shovel.

Riley was convicted before Mr Justice Hawkins at Manchester Assizes on 8 November. A petition of over 7,000 names was presented to the Home Secretary in the hope of securing a reprieve, but to no avail.

Hanged by Binns.

December 3rd: Henry DUTTON (22)   Liverpool

Dutton, an iron moulder, lived in a house on Atholl Street, Liverpool, with his wife, whom he had only recently married, and her grandmother Hannah Henshaw (71). He was very jealous of his wife, and while out on the evening of 6 October they had a row which resulted in Mrs Dutton going to stay with a friend.

Dutton was heard to say he would do for her or her grandmother, and later that night cries were heard coming from his house. A neighbour gained entry and found Mrs Henshaw dying from a throat wound, and also suffering from several other horrific head wounds.

Dutton was arrested at a friend's house but denied the crime. He was sentenced to death by Mr Justice Denman at Liverpool Assizes on 17 November and hanged by Binns.

It was the first of Binns' botched executions; the Governor was informed that the hangman was drunk and didn't know how to carry out an execution properly.

December 17th: Patrick O'DONNELL (28)   Newgate

An Irishman convicted at the Central Criminal Court in November for the murder of James Carey.

The murdered man was an informer whose testimony had sent five men to the gallows in Dublin for the Phoenix Park Murders. (See **1883, May 14th: Joseph BRADY** and subsequent executions).

Carey was being escorted from Capetown to Port Elizabeth on board the ship 'Melrose'. O'Donnell had boarded the vessel and shot the informer while at sea on 30 July.

Hanged by Binns and Alfred Archer.

December 18th: Joseph POOLE (28)   Dublin

A tailor and prominent member of the Stephenite Fenian society, convicted of the murder of John Kenny, an informer, who was shot dead in July 1882.

Kenny had offered to reveal to the British Government information regarding various activities involving the society, including information on the unsolved murder of a police officer.

Joseph Poole went to a house in Seville Place where Kenny was staying and shot him dead in front of several witnesses, none of whom would testify against him.

He later called on his dead wife's brother and told him of the crime, and it was on his evidence that Poole was convicted.

He was hanged at Richmond Prison by a man named Jones, who had volunteered to carry out the execution. It was reported that Poole's feet touched the ground when he fell through the trap and that the rope had to be pulled up to allow him to die.

1884

Cases where no executioner is recorded are multiple executions, and readers are asked to refer to the entries before or after for details of the hangman.

1884

January 15th: Peter WADE   Dublin

Sentenced to death by Mr Justice May for the murder of Patrick Quinn, an old gardener from Rathfarnham, near Dublin, whom he was alleged to have beaten to death.

    Wade, a young and respectable man, fell out with the old man after he was accused of trying to stop Quinn getting a job for a friend.

    One night in November 1883, he waited outside Quinn's house for him to return home. When he did so, Wade persuaded a colleague to lure him outside on the pretext of meeting an old friend. Shortly afterwards, screams were heard and Quinn was found with horrific head wounds. Wade was later arrested when bloodstains were found on his clothing.

    Hanged by Binns.

February 25th: Charles KITE   Taunton

On Wednesday 2 January, two young labourers, Charles Kite and Albert Miles, started to quarrel in a Bath public house. As the row escalated they decided to go outside to settle their differences. Once outside they had a further exchange of words before returning inside.

    As they re-entered the bar, Kite asked Miles to make friends and unusually offered his left hand. Momentarily confused, Miles pulled away and as he did so, Kite stabbed him with a knife he had been holding in his right. Miles fell to the ground dead and Kite fled but was arrested within the hour hiding at his mother's house.

    Sentenced to death on 6 February and hanged by Binns.

March 5th: Catherine FLANAGAN (55)   Liverpool
Margaret HIGGINS (41)

Margaret Higgins had insured her husband Thomas with five different insurance companies over a twelve month period, during which time she had been gradually poisoning him with small doses of arsenic, so at to make it appear he was terminally ill.

    At the end of September 1883, Thomas Higgins died. Police learned that a lodger had also died at the house earlier in the year, and an autopsy was ordered on Mr Higgins which revealed traces of poison. The body of the lodger, Mary Jennings, was later exhumed and also found to contain arsenic.

1884

Margaret Higgins was charged along with her elder sister, after it was alleged that they had acted together in planning the murders. Police believed they were also responsible for many other killings. They were sentenced to death by Mr Justice Butt at Liverpool Assizes on 16 February. Mrs Flanagan confessed after sentencing.

They were hanged by two executioners. Bartholomew Binns escorted Mrs Flanagan up the twenty two stone steps to the gallows, while Samuel Heath led Mrs Higgins. With both women noosed, the hangmen stepped back and each pulled a lever.

March 10th: Michael McLEAN (18)   **Liverpool**

McLean was one of a gang of Liverpool street corner hooligans who set upon two Spanish sailors as they made their way back to their ship at Liverpool docks on 5 January.

One made it back unharmed, but when the other, Jose Jimenez, failed to return, a search party was set up. Police had already discovered the body and soon had the four youths in custody. Jimenez's companion was able to testify that McLean was the ringleader and the other three were released.

McLean was hanged by Binns, who had arrived at the prison drunk. The Governor had taken the precaution of contacting Samuel Heath, who waited on stand-by. Despite Heath's presence, and Binn's drunken state, he still carried out the execution, botching it so badly that McLean took twenty minutes to die through strangulation.

Following a complaint filed by the Governor, Binns was dismissed.

March 31st: William INNES   **Edinburgh**
        Robert Flockheart VICKERS

The two men were miners from Gorebridge who were caught poaching on 15 December 1883 on land owned by Lord Rosebery. The gamekeeper, James Grosset, and his assistants John Fortune and John McDiarmid, spotted the men in the woods and challenged them to come out. The two poachers each selected a victim, opened fire, and Fortune and McDiarmid fell dead, while Grosset escaped with his life. He was able to identify the two killers and they were later taken into custody.

1884

Sentenced to death by Lord Young at the Edinburgh High Court on 10 March. They were hanged by James Berry who was carrying out his first execution, and his assistant Richard Chester.

May 26th: Mary LEFLEY   **Lincoln**

Convicted of poisoning her husband at Wrangle, near Burton, on 9 February, by putting arsenic into his rice pudding. No motive was ever established for the crime.

She claimed she was innocent, and was hysterical with terror on the morning of the execution, and had to be dragged screaming to the gallows where she was hanged by Berry and Chester.

Mary Lefley had been a friend of Priscilla Biggadyke, who was hanged on the same scaffold sixteen years earlier. (See **1868, December 28th**).

A confession appeared in the local press many years later from a man on his deathbed, claiming that he had sneaked into the house while Mrs Lefley was talking to a neighbour, and administered the poison.

May 27th: Joseph LAWSON (25)   **Durham**

In February 1884, three young miners, James Hodgson (20), William Siddle (22), and Joseph Lawson, attended a pigeon shooting handicap at Butterknowle, and then spent the evening in a local pub. As they left they spotted Police Sergeant William Smith standing across the road watching them.

After walking a short way, the three men turned back and began antagonising Smith. When the Sergeant walked off, they were seen to follow him. Soon after, Smith's body was found beaten to death in a field. The miners were arrested on suspicion and police found traces of blood on their clothing.

All three stood trial together before Mr Justice Hawkins at Durham Assizes. James Hodgson was acquitted, the other two convicted and sentenced to death despite claims that the evidence was fabricated by the police.

William Siddle was granted a reprieve a few days before the scheduled execution, while Joseph Lawson, who weighed over sixteen stone, was hanged by James Berry.

1884

August 19th: Peter CASSIDY (54) Liverpool

Cassidy was a tinsmith who lived with his wife at Bootle on Merseyside. On 25 June he returned home after a drunken binge to find his wife in a similar inebriated state. They began to argue, but Cassidy - although very mild mannered when sober - became so enraged that he picked up a cleaver and wooden mallet and smashed his wife's head in.

Sentenced to death by Mr Justice Day at Liverpool Assizes on 31 July and hanged by Berry.

August 24th: James TOBIN Wexford

On 19 May 1884, an old farmer named Moore left his farm at Rathlow, Wicklow, on business. He returned one hour later and found that his wife Elizabeth (80), was missing. A search of the land found her beaten to death in a field. She had been attacked with a broken shovel which lay covered in blood at her side. The motive for the crime was thought to be robbery as several items were missing from the house.

Tobin, a tramp seen lurking nearby, was the immediate suspect, and was arrested after selling some of the stolen property later that day.

Convicted of murder and hanged by Berry.

August 26th: Joseph LAYCOCK (34) Leeds

At 6pm on 10 July, Laycock spotted a policeman and complained to him about his wife, Maria, drinking with another man. The officer told the man, who was sober, that there was nothing he could do about it, so Laycock went home.

At 10pm, with their four children asleep in bed, Laycock and his wife sat down to supper. He offered her a drink and when she refused he warned her that she may as well have a drink while she had a chance.

Later that night neighbours were alerted by screams coming from the house and found the bodies of Mrs Laycock and the four children, all with their throats cut. Laycock also had a neck wound and pleaded with neighbours to let him die.

He was tried at Leeds Assizes and pleaded insanity. Evidence was brought into court that there was a history of insanity in the family but Laycock was found guilty and sentenced to death.

Hanged by James Billington, officiating at his first execution.

October 6th: Thomas Henry ORROCK — Newgate

A Dalston born criminal from a respectable religious family, who purchased a revolver from the 'Exchange & Mart' and used it to murder a policeman.

On 1 December 1882, he set off alone to commit a burglary, armed with a selection of chisels and his gun. On that night, London was immersed in a thick fog and Orrock took the opportunity of this natural cover to carry out his first job, and therefore earn the respect of the criminal fraternity he had recently started mixing with.

He selected the local chapel as his target but as he carried out his reconnaissance, he was seen by two police officers, one of whom, a Sergeant Cobb, knew him well. Orrock acted naturally and the two officers walked past and out of sight. A few minutes later, as he was trying to force one of the chapel's windows, Orrock was seized by another police officer, PC Cole, and dropped his chisel during the struggle before Cole took a firm hold of his arm and escorted him to the station.

Fearing that the arrest and probable subsequent imprisonment would make him a laughing stock among his new friends, Orrock decided to pull out the gun with his free hand and frighten the officer into releasing him. PC Cole merely responded to the threat by taking a tighter grip and so Orrock pointed the gun and fired four shots at the constable, fatally wounding him. The gunman then fled into the fog and escaped.

Two women who had witnessed the shooting gave a description to Sergeant Cobb who, remembering seeing Orrock, quickly had a suspect. The chisel dropped by Orrock when he was apprehended by Cole was found and had the letters R-O-C-K scratched on the side.

Orrock was brought in and placed on an identity parade but the two women witnesses failed to recognise him and when he was released, he quickly disappeared from the area.

It was over a year later when Sergeant Cobb, who had vowed to bring his colleague's killer to justice, learned that Orrock had been practising shooting his gun on some marshes just before the murder. He was taken to a tree and was able to find several bullets which later were discovered to match those removed from the murdered officer.

A search eventually located Orrock in Coldbath Prison, where he was serving a stretch for burglary. He was arrested for PC Cole's murder and as more evidence against him was amassed, he was charged. Sergeant Cobb even managed to find the person who had scratched the name on the chisel when Orrock took it to him to be sharpened.

He was convicted at the Old Bailey on 17 September and sentenced to death.

October 6th: Thomas HARRIS (48)   Newgate

A respectable looking market gardener and father of eleven, sentenced to death at the Old Bailey for the murder of his wife at Kilburn on 9 August.

Harris was alleged to have cut her throat with a razor but pleaded insanity and claimed to have no recollection of the events on the night of her death.

Hanged alongside **ORROCK** [above] by James Berry and Richard Chester.

November 24th: Kay HOWARTH (25)   Manchester

On 3 October, Richard Dugdale (37), a commercial traveller from Wakefield, arrived in Bolton to do business with many of the town centre publicans. While in one pub he met up with Robert Hall, an old business friend, who invited Dugdale to join him for a drink. As they sat in the bar they were joined by Kay Howarth, who was well known to Hall as a local layabout and thief, and despite Hall's attempts to rid them of Howarth's presence, the three men visited a number of local bars as Dugdale carried out some business.

At one pub, Dugdale returned to the table brandishing a large cheque which he put in his bag along with the rest of the money he had collected. At 6.15pm, Hall had to return home. Anxious that his now very drunk friend should not be left to walk the unfamiliar streets alone with so much money, he asked Howarth to escort him back to his hotel.

Later that night a man stumbled over the body of Dugdale in a secluded street. He had head and throat wounds and the horrific gash in his neck left the man in no doubt that he was dead. A suicide note left beside the body was soon dismissed as a fake by the police, and investigations soon led them to Robert Hall. He told detectives he had left Dugdale in the company of Howarth, and a visit to the latter's room uncovered some of the dead man's possessions and money; they also found large traces of blood on Howarth's clothing.

Howarth was tried before Mr Justice Smith at Manchester Assizes, convicted of murder and sentenced to death.

November 24th: Harry Hammond SWINDELLS (50) Manchester

In 1877, Swindells, a book-keeper at an Oldham foundry met Mrs Suzannah Wild, a wealthy widow and mother of two and after a short courtship the couple married. Mrs Wild had been left a successful yeast business and a healthy annual income.

After the wedding Swindells left his job at the foundry and began working for his wife's business. Very soon, he began pestering her for the money which he knew she had, and when she eventually relented, he quickly frittered a large sum away on drinking and womanising.

Mrs Swindells seemed to tolerate her husband's behaviour for a while but when a friend informed her he was responsible for another woman's pregnancy, she threw him out of the house.

Swindells used some of his wife's money to emigrate to America, only to return home when it had run out and attempt to win his wife, and her wealth, back. Despite his constant attempts, Mrs Swindells, with the backing of her children, refused his pleas.

In July 1884, Swindells called at the house and made a scene, and his step-daughter was sent to fetch her Uncle Jim who lived nearby. James Wild (59), hurried to the house and told Swindells to leave, a request which quickly erupted into a fierce quarrel. The step-daughter was again sent to find assistance, this time a policeman. Before help could arrive, Wild was shot dead.

Swindells fled the scene and a thorough search failed to find him. It was assumed he had managed to return to America and the hunt cooled, but a few weeks later he was spotted dressed as a tramp near Oldham, and taken into custody. Sentenced to death at the same Assizes as **HOWARTH** [above], the two men were hanged together by Berry and Chester.

1884

December 8th: Ernest EWERSTADT (23) Liverpool

A Russian sailor sentenced to death by Mr Justice Day at Liverpool Assizes on 22 November, for the murder of his former paramour.

Ewerstadt had been living with Elizabeth Hamblin for many months until she left him during the summer of 1884 because he was reluctant to give her any housekeeping money. They parted but remained on friendly terms.

On 19 September he asked a friend to visit Elizabeth with a request to meet him that night. The friend later returned with the news that not only did she have no wish to meet him, but that she was also in the company of two black sailors who were plying her with drink. Ewerstadt told his friend that when he received his wages, he would buy a gun and shoot her.

The next day he bought a dagger instead, and went to find Elizabeth. He caught up with her in a bar and told her that unless she agreed to come back with him, there would be a 'bloody deed done that night.' She took no notice and together they visited a friend's house where she left after he again threatened to kill her. He followed her home, and after a quarrel on the doorstep, stabbed her to death. He fled, but later bumped into a friend to whom he said: 'Me kill my Lizzie, me die too!'

December 8th: Arthur SHAW (31) Liverpool

On Monday 3 November, a police constable called at a house in Collyhurst, Manchester, and found the body of Ellen Shaw dead on the floor. After a short investigation, her husband was arrested and charged with murder.

At his trial, it was alleged that Mrs Shaw, a drunkard, was chatting to a neighbour in the back garden when her young daughter came out and delivered the request that her husband wanted to see her. She went in, and soon after, Shaw came into the garden and told the neighbour that his wife had fallen and hurt herself.

Throughout the trial Shaw, a tailor, maintained that he was innocent and that her death was accidental, but he was convicted when evidence proved that she had been strangled.

Hanged alongside **EWERSTADT** [above] by Berry and a new assistant called Speight. Ewerstadt was given a drop of seven feet; Shaw, being a lighter man received seven feet six inches. When the trap fell, it was noticed that Shaw took over two minutes to die. An investigation found that the trap door had swung back and displaced the rope and its 'knot', causing him to be slowly strangled.

William Calcraft (Hulton Deutsch)

William Marwood   (Hulton Deutsch)

James Berry   (Hulton Deutsch)

Bartholomew Binns

James Billington

Newgate exterior: the execution chamber is to the right (HM Prison Service Museum)

Newgate interior: execution chamber (HM Prison Service Museum)

This excellent picture from the mid-1890's shows the gallows in the yard at Barrack Square prison, Gloucester, before an execution chamber was constructed on a level floor. Note the lever clearly visible in the background. (HM Prison Service Museum)

1885

Cases where no executioner is recorded are multiple executions, and readers are asked to refer to the entries before or after for details of the hangman.

1885

January 13th: Horace Robert JAY (23)   **Wandsworth**

At Christmas 1883, Jay (aka Thorpe) met Florence Kemp, then just sixteen, and they immediately fell in love. They lived together until July 1884 when she left him and went back to live with her parents.

On 15 November, at his invitation, they had tea together at his lodgings. He asked her if she would move in with him again and when she answered by saying she had met another man, jealousy got the better of him and in a rage he cut her throat, and then his own.

He was tried before Mr Justice Hawkins at the Central Criminal Court on 22 December. His defence that he was insane and drunk failed, and he was hanged by Berry.

January 16th: Michael DOWNEY   **Galway**

Convicted of the murder of a John Moylan (or Molsh) at Clonbooland on 19 December 1883.

Moylan was a farmer who had recently returned from America to take up a tenancy on an evicted farm at Clonbooland, seven miles from Galway. On Wednesday 19 December, he and his wife were strolling down a country lane when they were approached by a man who asked if Moylan was 'Burke?' Moylan made no reply and was immediately shot by the stranger. His wife dived across his prostrate body in an attempt to shield him from further shots, but the assailant merely dragged her off and fired again before fleeing.

It was first thought the crime may have been committed in consequence of Moylan taking over at the farm, and the previous tenants were questioned, all of whom satisfied the police of their innocence.

Acting on information received, police later arrested Mrs Moylan and Downey, with whom she had been having an affair. It was alleged that Downey had killed her husband so that they could be together. Charges against her were later dropped; Downey was hanged by Berry and Chester after leaving a note confessing his guilt.

1885

January 20th: Thomas PARRY   **Galway**

A steward from Kings County who travelled 112 miles to commit a murder.

Parry had broken up with his fiancee, a Miss Burns, and after spending the night in an expensive hotel he called to see her at her sister's house where she had been staying. Parry asked her if she meant what she wrote in her last letter, and that she had really ended their relationship. When she replied that they were finished, he said 'We'll see,' pulled out his revolver and shot her dead. He then turned the gun on himself but only succeeded in inflicting a minor wound.

Hanged by Berry and Chester after he was sentenced to death by Mr Justice Lawson. Parry left a full written confession in his cell.

March 17th: Henry KIMBERLEY   **Birmingham**

Henry Kimberley and Harriet Stewart lived together for seventeen years until Christmas 1884, when they agreed to separate. They consulted solicitors and it was agreed that she would keep the house while he got twenty pounds and a piano. They signed forms but almost at once Kimberley wanted it cancelled and for her to come back to him.

On 27 December he saw Harriet and a friend, Mrs Emma Palmer, and followed her to a public house that was run by Mrs Palmer's husband. Kimberley entered and asked Harriet to come back to him, but she again refused. He turned to Emma Palmer and asked her to persuade Harriet to come back with him, and when she refused he pulled out a gun and shot them both. Harriet Stewart was only wounded but Emma Palmer received a fatal wound and fell dead on the floor. A barman tried to arrest the gunman and was fired at, but with the aid of other customers he managed to detain Kimberley until the police arrived.

He was hanged on the scaffold at Winson Green Prison by James Berry. It was the first execution in the city for over eighty years.

1885

May 18th: James LEE (45)   **Chelmsford**

On 20 January, an Inspector Simmons and PC Morden from the Essex Constabulary were walking through a field near Romford. They had been called out to investigate a burglary and were on the lookout for three men. Heading towards a railway line, they spotted three men carrying suspicious packages and decided to challenge them. As the officers approached them, two of the men pulled out pistols, and minutes later Inspector Simmons fell mortally wounded on the grass.

All three men fled but James Lee was soon arrested and convicted at the Old Bailey; he was hanged by Berry. Another was later detained but was able to make a successful plea of mistaken identity and was acquitted.

The third man, James Martin, remained at large for nearly a year, until he was involved in robbing Netherby Hall, near Gretna, and the murder of another policeman whilst trying to evade capture. (See **1886, February 8th**).

May 25th: Moses SHRIMPTON (65)   **Worcester**

Shrimpton was first sent to prison for poaching in 1848, and from then on was seldom at liberty for more than a few weeks.

On the morning of 28 February 1885, a PC Davies stationed at Beoley, a small rural Worcestershire village barely a dozen miles from Birmingham, failed to return to the station after his night beat. When it was learned he had also failed to rendezvous with a sergeant at 4am, a search was organised of the nearby countryside. Later that morning, Davies was found dead in a field, with over forty stab wounds to his upper body. The pool of blood in which the body lay yielded a clear set of footprints.

A search of the surrounding area revealed a number of dead chickens which had been poached from a nearby farm. Police knew that most local poachers worked only in the woods and fields, and that only one was known to steal from farm buildings. Moses Shrimpton was down on their records as a notorious thief and hen stealer, and he was made the number one suspect.

On 4 March, detectives tracked him down to a squalid Birmingham back street lodging house and after breaking down the door, Shrimpton was taken into custody. A search of his room revealed blood stained clothing, and a knife that fitted the wounds on the dead policeman. But most damning of all was a pair of boots with an identical print to those found at the murder scene. In another room at the lodging house, the policeman's watch and chain was found, the owner of which claimed he had bought it off Shrimpton.

He was tried before Baron Huddlestone at Worcester Assizes on 6 May and although the evidence against him was circumstantial, the jury took only a short time to find him guilty.

Berry calculated a drop of nine feet after taking into account the man's weight, but he didn't allow for the weakness of the neck muscles. When the drop fell the force ripped Shrimpton's head clean from his shoulders.

July 13th: Henry ALT (31)   Newgate

A German journeyman baker convicted of the murder of Charles Howard, whom he stabbed to death in a jealous quarrel over a woman.

Alt had been paying his attentions to a middle-aged woman and proposed marriage to her. She turned him down and later announced to Alt that she was going to marry Howard. As they were drinking in a pub, Alt stabbed Howard to death then wounded the woman and himself.

He was convicted at the Old Bailey in June, and after a plea for a reprieve by the German Embassy failed, he was hanged by Berry. As the hangman placed the noose around his neck, Alt cried out 'This is all through an evil deceitful woman.'

August 3rd: Joseph TUCKER (37)   Nottingham

Tucker, a shoemaker, had lived with Elizabeth Williams (32) as man and wife for nine years. Both were addicted to drink and often quarrelled violently when drunk.

On 9 May they returned home drunk and began to row, during which Tucker kicked her to the ground, and as she lay stunned he poured a bottle of paraffin over her and set her alight. Her screams alerted neighbours who tried in vain to extinguish the fire as Tucker stood by shouting:

'Let the bitch burn!' When she died five days later, he was charged with her murder.

Sentenced to death at Nottingham Assizes by Baron Pollock, and hanged by Berry.

August 17th: Thomas BOULTON (47) — Stafford

A labourer convicted of the murder of his niece Elizabeth Bunting (15), at Handsworth, Birmingham.

On the evening of Tuesday 20 April, Boulton, an army pensioner, returned home from his casual gardening job at a local gentleman's house. He was lodging with his married sister and her family, and after eating his tea he went to a local pub, returning home around 9.45pm.

At 10pm, with her husband still at work, Elizabeth's mother went to bed leaving her daughter reading to her uncle. A few minutes later, a piercing scream caused her to hurry downstairs where she found her brother standing over the body of Elizabeth, who lay battered to death on the carpet. Boulton then dropped the hammer and fled, but was soon captured.

When he stood trial in July, the only motive offered by the prosecution was that he disliked her boyfriend. The defence pleaded for a verdict of insanity and claimed that Boulton had suffered sunstroke while serving in India but the jury convicted him and he was hanged by Berry.

October 5th: Henry NORMAN (31) — Newgate

A painter convicted for the murder of his adulterous wife.

Norman was jealous of the landlord where he and his wife lived and after discovering she had been unfaithful he stabbed her to death.

He had told his mother that he had forgiven her for a number of previous indiscretions but after discovering she had been with the landlord he stabbed her through the heart as she slept.

Norman claimed he had no recollection of committing the crime, but after listening to the evidence against him, the jury didn't even need to retire before finding him guilty. He was sentenced to death by Mr Justice Hawkins at the Old Bailey on 17 September, and hanged by Berry.

1885

November 23rd: John HILL   Hereford
                John WILLIAMS

Hill, alias 'Sailor Jack', and Williams, known as 'Irish Jack', were convicted of the murder of Anne Dickinson at Weobley. Hill admitted that he had attempted to make the assault but Williams had come up and hit her on the head with a large stick, whereupon Hill ran off.

    Hanged by Berry.

November 30th: Robert GOODALE   Norwich

Condemned to death for the murder of his unfaithful wife at Walsoken, Norfolk. Goodale was a fifteen stone giant of a man who worked as a market gardener and farmer. Each day after work, he and his wife would travel into Wisbech where they would spend the night.

    On 16 September he returned to the town alone and his manner caused some suspicion among his friends. When a search of Goodale's farm was carried out, his wife's body was discovered at the bottom of a well - her skull had been smashed with a sharp instrument.

    He was hanged by Berry at Norwich Castle. The hangman, who already had had two unnerving scenes that year with the failure to execute John Lee at Exeter in February [see chapter on biographies], and the decapitation of **SHRIMPTON** [above], was to have another unfortunate experience.

    He calculated a drop of seven feet eight inches but on observing the condemned man's build, he decided on a shorter drop of five feet nine inches. He selected the same rope he had used to hang **WILLIAMS** [above] the week before, and made his usual preparations. Goodale was in a state of terror when Berry entered his cell and had to be half carried to the gallows. When the drop fell, officials were horrified to find that his head had been torn clean from his shoulders.

December 7th: Daniel MINAHAN (28)   Newgate

A labourer from Bromley, Kent, sentenced to death by Mr Justice Smith at the Old Bailey on 17 November, for the murder of his wife Bridget, whom he beat to death.

    They lived happily together with their two children until an incident at home on the morning of 28 October when Minahan was woken up late for work. In a mad rage, he picked up a hammer and battered his wife to death, inflicting over a dozen head wounds and massive chest injuries.

He pleaded guilty to manslaughter caused by great provocation but was convicted, and hanged by Berry.

December 9th: George THOMAS   **Liverpool**

On Wednesday 9 September, Thomas, a coloured sailor, visited a public house in the Toxteth district of Liverpool with his paramour of eight years Mary Askins, a former prostitute.

When he had returned to port two days earlier, she had told him that she no longer wanted to live with him. They ordered their drinks and after the bar tender left the room to fetch them, Thomas pulled out a gun and shot her in the head. As she fell dead on the ground, he put the weapon to his own head and fired, but miraculously suffered only a slight injury.

At his trial at Liverpool Assizes it was shown that on the day before the murder he had pawned his watch and purchased the gun, thereby showing that the crime was premeditated.

Hanged by Berry.

1886

Cases where no executioner is recorded are multiple executions, and readers are asked to refer to the entries before or after for details of the hangman.

1886

January 12th: John CRONIN   **Mullingar**

Convicted at Sligo Winter Assizes on Saturday 12 December 1885, of the murder of his father, Thomas Cronin, at Longford after a family quarrel in October.
    Hanged by James Berry.

January 20th: William SHEEHAN   **Cork**

Convicted at Cork Assizes of the murder of his mother, brother and sister, at Castletown Roche in 1877.
    The victims were about to leave their farm and settle elsewhere when Sheehan systematically killed them after they had objected to his impending marriage. He first beat to death his brother, Thomas, by attacking him with a plough after a quarrel in the stable. When his sister Hannah came to find out what was delaying her brother, he seized her by the throat and choked her to death. Finally, when his mother Christine came to find the others, Sheehan also choked her.
    He disposed of their bodies by throwing them down a well, where they lay hidden for eight years. Because they had been due to leave the town, their disappearance wasn't noticed. Later that year, Sheehan emigrated to New Zealand.
    In 1885, when the bodies of the Sheehans were discovered by a new tenant on the farm, William Sheehan was traced and bought back to Ireland to face trial, and after being sentenced to death, was hanged by Berry. Sheehan's brother-in-law who was also arrested was acquitted at the trial.

February 1st: John HORTON (36)   **Devizes**

John Horton shared a house at Bradford-on-Avon with his aged father, who was having a relationship with their housekeeper, Charlotte Lindsay.
    On 21 November 1885, Horton and his father had a fierce quarrel over the woman while out walking and they squared up. Horton beat his father to death, inflicting terrible injuries. He then went back to the house and attacked Miss Lindsay with a razor; she died on the following morning.
    Horton was convicted at Wiltshire Assizes on 13 January. In his defence he claimed that he hadn't intended to kill them and that many of the witnesses at the trial had falsely testified against him.
    He was hanged by James Berry who gave him a drop of six feet.

1886

February 8th: Anthony Ben RUDGE   Carlisle
James BAKER
James MARTIN

Anthony Rudge was the leader of a gang of London villains, and a seasoned housebreaker. Among his gang, who specialised in robbing country houses, was James Martin, wanted for his part in the shooting of a police inspector at Romford the previous year, [see **1885, May 18th**].

    The gang decided to travel to Glasgow and caught a train up north. Alighting at Crookston, just outside Glasgow, they celebrated their arrival by stealing the station safe. Later, they tried to pinch a second safe, again from a railway station, and only just escaped by shooting at a pursuing policeman.

    On 28 October they carried out a daring robbery from Netherby House, near Gretna, stealing a large amount of jewellery while the house was occupied. The police were notified to be on the lookout for the gang and later that evening they were spotted by two officers. As they approached the thieves, James Martin fired, wounding them both in the upper body. They managed to slip through a police cordon by beating up a constable, and the following morning they entered a small surburban railway station and asked for tickets for a London train. The station master was suspicious of the men and alerted the police.

    The gang was next seen leaving a public house by two police officers. When they challenged them, Martin pulled out his gun which discharged during the ensuing struggle, and one of the officers, PC Byrne, fell dead. The gang escaped by jumping onto a southbound train but were captured near Crewe and charged with murder.

    After conviction, they were hanged by Berry and his assistant Charles Maldon, in reality one Sir Claude de Cespigny, an Essex magistrate who paid Berry for the privilege of assisting him.

February 9th: John BAINS   Lancaster

Bains, a Barrow fish hawker, and his wife had been quarrelling repeatedly for many months, during which time he made several threats on her life. On Christmas Day 1885, they had such a fierce argument that she left and went to stay with a friend. Bains picked up a sharpened butcher's knife, followed her to the house, and when she opened the door he stabbed her four times.

    Hanged by Berry.

February 10th: John THURSTON (20)   Norwich

Convicted on circumstantial evidence at Norwich Assizes of the murder of Harry Springhall, who was found robbed and battered to death beside a road in Norfolk. Thurston, a labourer, had borrowed a sovereign off the old man and told a friend he intended to get more.

When Thurston was questioned, the police noticed blood stains on his clothing; when they checked his pockets they found a number of sovereigns that he had not been in possession of earlier in the day.

Hanged by Berry.

February 16th: George SAUNDERS (29)   Ipswich

A Lowestoft fisherman convicted of the murder of his wife. They were having a drunken quarrel at their home on Christmas Eve when he lost control and cut her throat with his razor. She died at once and the shocked husband hurried to the police and reported the crime.

Sentenced to death at Ipswich Assizes on 29 January and hanged by Berry.

February 22nd: Owen McGILL (39)   Knutsford

Early in the morning of 31 October 1885, Owen McGill, an Irish farm labourer, drove a cart of corn into Birkenhead from his home at nearby Lincarton. He was accompanied on the journey by his wife, and on the way back they called at a couple of public houses but both were sober when they returned home. Later that afternoon, his wife Mary stopped him getting into a fight with a couple of farm hands, calming him down and preparing his tea.

In the evening a neighbour saw Mary McGill run screaming from the house, and soon afterwards, another neighbour saw Owen standing over his wife and telling her to get up. The next morning, he visited his cousin and asked her to come quickly as his wife was ill, but when she arrived she found Mrs McGill dead. McGill told the police that she had fallen off the cart the previous day but his story didn't tie in with what witnesses had reported, and as it was apparent that she had received a vicious beating, McGill was was arrested and charged with murder.

Sentenced to death by Lord Chief Justice Coleridge on 3 February, he became the first man to be hanged at Knutsford prison which had taken over from Chester Castle as the execution prison in Cheshire.

Hanged by Berry.

March 1st: Thomas NASH   **Cardiff**

A labourer employed by Swansea Corporation, and convicted at Cardiff Assizes on 9 February for the murder of his six year old daughter, whom he killed by throwing her off a pier into the sea. He was visited in the condemned cell by his other daughter but his wife refused to see him.

Hanged by Berry.

March 2nd: David ROBERTS   **Swansea**

On 30 October 1885, travelling salesman David Thomas left a pub in Cowbridge in the company of two men, and at 2am the next morning he was found dead; he had been beaten to death with a hedge stick found nearby. Acting on information, the police soon had two men in custody: David Roberts, a labourer, and his father.

It was alleged that Thomas had joined the two men for a drink and at closing time Roberts walked home with his father and then sneaked out, followed Thomas, then robbed and killed him. Police found some of the dead man's papers in the Roberts' fireplace.

Roberts and his father were jointly tried at Cardiff Assizes but, as the case against Roberts senior was weak, he was soon acquitted. After a fair trial, David Roberts was convicted and sentenced to death.

He was hanged by Berry, who calculated a drop of three feet seven inches, adding that the expected stretch of the rope would give a true drop of four feet two inches; the thought of a repeat of the Goodale execution [see **1885, November 30th**] led Berry to give shorter and shorter drops.

In 1888 a memorandum was issued stating that drops of less than five feet were forbidden.

May 31st: Albert Edward BROWN   **Winchester**

On 8 April, two sailors, Brown, a native of Greenwich, and James Stanley Parker sailed from Millwall to Southampton on a coasting voyage. On arriving at Southampton the two set off to walk to Winchester, and the next morning Parker was found dead in a field with a cut throat. Brown was located, and arrested when police found bloodstains on his clothing.

Convicted at Winchester Assizes on 11 May, he later admitted that he had killed his colleague by hitting him with a hammer, then cutting his throat with a razor. The motive was to rob Parker of the four shillings Brown knew he was carrying.

May 31st: James WHELAN   **Winchester**

Whelan was a seaman aboard the Nova Scotian brigatine 'Emma J Shore', sailing under a British flag from New York to the River Plate. The vessel had a mixed crew but was comprised mostly of Scandinavians.

While on the high seas, the second mate, George Richardson, found fault with Whelan's work and threatened to 'kick him out of the rigging.' He also warned Whelan to take care as he would beat his brains out on a dark night. Whelan laughed off the threat and replied that if he saw Richardson again during the voyage he would kill him.

For several days the men avoided seeing each other but on 15 March their paths crossed. Spying Richardson approaching, Whelan jumped on him and punched him about the head before hurling him overboard. He was immediately seized by members of the crew and put in irons, after telling them that Richardson was now 'stoking coals for the devil.'

He was shipped back to England to stand trial, and on 8 May stood before Mr Justice Day at Winchester Assizes. His defence was manslaughter through self-defence, but he was convicted and hanged by Berry alongside **BROWN** [above]. He left a note in his cell confessing to the murder of two other men on previous occasions.

1886

June 15th: Edward HEWITT (34)   Gloucester

Times were hard for Edward Hewitt and his wife Sarah (43), as he, like thousands of other men, was unable to find regular work. He visited neighbouring towns to find work, and after securing a week's employment in Sharpness, he returned to Gloucester with his wages. He handed the money to his wife to buy food, keeping a little for himself to enjoy some ale. Returning from a public house drunk, he demanded more money from his wife; when she refused, he kicked her to death in a rage.

Sentenced to death after a short trial and hanged by Berry. At the inquest after the execution, it was revealed that when the doctor had made his way down into the pit immediately after the drop to examine the body, he found the heart still beating and when he lifted the white hood, he noted that the man's features exhibited traces of extreme agony: the eyes stared from their sockets, and his tongue which he had bitten through, protruded from his mouth.

July 27th: William SAMUELS   Shrewsbury

A grocer's assistant convicted on circumstantial evidence at Newton Assizes, North Wales, by Mr Justice Groves on 9 July, of the murder of William Mabbots at Welshpool.

Mabbots died after drinking a glass of stout, which was later found to be laced with strychnine. Samuels was arrested on suspicion and admitted that he had offered Mabbots the drink but denied that he knew it was poisoned.

He was hanged by Berry after the jury took just twenty-five minutes to find him guilty of murder. He left a full written confession in the condemned cell.

August 9th: Mary Ann BRITLAND (39)   Manchester

When Mary Ann Britland, a factory operator, suddenly lost her daughter and then her husband, a friend, Mary Dixon, invited her to move into her home at Ashton, near Manchester. Mrs Dixon took pity on the widow and helped to feed and cloth her until her own sudden death on 13 May.

Police were immediately suspicious at the mysterious death and ordered an autopsy on Mrs Dixon which revealed traces of poison, and Mary Ann Britland was taken into custody. Police then ordered the bodies of her husband and daughter to be exhumed and again traces of poison were found. She confessed that she had poisoned Mrs Dixon and her own family so she could be free to marry Mrs Dixon's husband, and on this testimony he too was arrested and charged.

At their trial at Manchester Assizes it was soon clear that Mr Dixon was in no way guilty of the crime, or even of offering the slightest encouragement, and he was acquitted. Mrs Britland was convicted and broke down as sentence was passed.

She lost all composure in the death cell and had to be carried screaming to the gallows where she was hanged by Berry.

November 16th: Patrick JUDGE (47)   Newcastle

A former soldier sentenced to death at Newcastle Assizes for the murder of his wife, Jane.

They lived unhappily together at Walker-on-Tyne, and on Saturday 9 July, they had a disagreement that ended with Judge pulling out a revolver and shooting her twice in the head.

Hanged by James Berry and an unnamed assistant.

November 29th: James MURPHY   York

In March, Murphy, a collier from Dudsworth near Barnsley, was arrested by a PC Austwick on a charge of drunkenness. He received a summons and later a fine, and as a result he bore a grudge against the officer and swore revenge.

On 31 July, a neighbour reported a disturbance at Murphy's house, and as a result PC Austwick went to investigate. Murphy recognised him at once and shouted: 'Oh, it's you I want, wait here!' Murphy then rushed off, returned shortly with a gun and shot the officer dead; the shot was heard by the PC's wife at their home nearby. Murphy fled and was at liberty for many weeks. A reward was offered for information but it was still some time before he was finally taken into custody.

He was convicted at York Assizes and remained calm to the end. Introduced to Berry on the eve of his execution, Murphy, who was eating at the time, said in a letter to his family that despite the meeting, he consumed his meal none the worse for it.

On the morning of the execution as Berry adjusted the noose, Murphy said to him: 'Put it right old boy and don't be nervous.'

1886

November 30th: James BARTON (27) — Leicester

One afternoon in August, two Leicestershire labourers were caught poaching by a policeman and as a result had their nets confiscated. They retired to a nearby pub and several drinks later they decided to retrieve their property from the police station.

As they left the pub, they saw a PC Barrett and began to insult and pick a fight with him. One of the labourers, James Barton, started grappling with Barrett and they tumbled down an embankment, where he picked up a stick and beat the officer to death.

Later that night Barton staggered down a street brandishing the murder weapon and shouting 'I killed a bobby.' Next morning the body was found and when Barton bragged to a workmate that he had killed someone, word reached police and he was arrested. His friend who had witnessed the crime was not charged as he was able to convince the police that he played no part in the murder.

Hanged by Berry.

December 13th: George HARMER (28) — Norwich

On 14 August, Harmer, a plasterer and petty thief, was released from gaol and went to visit a friend. As they sat down to breakfast, Harmer mentioned that he intended to rob a wealthy recluse, Henry Last, a carpenter who lived nearby.

On 20 August, Harmer approached the old man with a drawing which he asked to be made into a model, and later that day Last was found battered to death in his bed. Harmer was seen to be flash with money and was able to redeem some of his clothes that he'd had to pawn only the day before.

He was soon arrested and made a full confession. Hanged by Berry.

1887

Cases where no executioner is recorded are multiple executions, and readers are asked to refer to the entries before or after for details of the hangman.

1887

February 14th: Thomas BLOXHAM (62) — Leicester

A framework knitter sentenced to death at Leicester Assizes for the murder of his wife in November 1886 by first stabbing her five times in the chest and then cutting her throat.

He remained very callous in the condemned cell until a last visit by relatives and friends, whereupon he became resigned to his fate and met his death calmly in the hands of Berry.

February 15th: Thomas LEATHERBARROW (47) — Manchester

In the months leading up to Christmas 1886, Leatherbarrow and Mrs Kate Quinn, a married woman separated from her husband, occupied an apartment in a small cottage at Pendleton. As a consequence of him being out of work he was unable to supply Mrs Quinn with money, resulting in a series of quarrels which culminated in murder.

On New Year's Eve 1886, they had a drunken row and when he awoke on the following morning he shouted at her to 'get up or I'll knock your brains out.' Next day he told her he had found a job and for the next week he left home first thing in the morning. On Saturday 8 January, he left the house as usual but when he returned home, they got into a fierce row during which he kicked her to death. He then went drinking in a Salford pub where he was arrested, and later charged with murder.

He pleaded guilty at his trial at Manchester Assizes before Mr Justice Smith who sentenced him to death. Hanged by Berry.

February 17th: Edward PRITCHARD (20) — Gloucester

On 31 December 1886, factory clerk Henry Allen (14), called at the local bank to collect over one hundred pounds in wages. Edward Pritchard and a friend called Noyes had watched the young lad make the journey on several other occasions, and when he left the bank they followed him down a quiet street on a hired pony and trap.

Later that day the boy's body was found battered to death and evidence soon led the police to Pritchard. The pony and trap was traced and police found bloodstains upon it. Witnesses also testified that they had heard the two men planning the robbery earlier in the day, and that Noyes was seen in the area before the murder.

Noyes was tried as an accessory to murder and for robbery. Pritchard was tried for murder, convicted, and hanged by Berry.

February 21st: Richard INSOLE (24)   Lincoln

A Grimsby fisherman sentenced to death by Mr Justice Field at Nottinghamshire Assizes on 1 February for the murder of his wife.

They lived apart and when she refused to come home, Insole became very jealous and shot her five times with a revolver; more than one of the bullets had been fired as she lay dead on the ground.

Hanged by Berry.

February 22nd: Benjamin TERRY (29)   Nottingham

Terry and his wife of twelve years lived unhappily on account of his groundless suspicion of her infidelity. On the morning of 29 December 1887, he called on some neighbours and asked them to look after his children, adding that he had just killed his wife and was going to fetch a policeman.

Two officers accompanied him back to the house and found Mrs Terry dead on the bedroom floor. He admitted that he had intended to murder her the previous night but had fallen asleep after drinking gin, and when he had awoken in the morning, he'd picked up a poker and beaten her to death.

Sentenced to death by Mr Justice Field after his plea of insanity was rejected. A request for a reprieve also failed and he was hanged by Berry.

March 14th: Elizabeth BERRY (31)   Liverpool

Convicted of the murder of her daughter Edith (11), whom she killed by putting creosote in her tea, in order to collect the insurance money.

Mrs Berry was a nurse at Oldham Infirmary, and was also rumoured to have murdered her husband and mother in a similar fashion.

Convicted at Liverpool Assizes after her plea of insanity failed, she was the first person to be hanged at Walton Prison.

James Berry carried out the sentence; he was an old acquaintance but no relation.

March 21st: Joseph KING (41)   Newgate

King was a bricklayer, who shared a lodging house with several people, including one Annie Sutton and her young son Henry. Both King and Sutton were single and he asked her many times for a date but she repeatedly refused him. On 20 January he discovered that she had accepted a date from another lodger and during a jealous quarrel, he killed her and her son by cutting their throats with such force that he almost severed their heads.

Tried before Mr Justice Hawkins at the Old Bailey, his defence was insanity based on the fact that he had suffered a severe head injury many years earlier. The jury found him guilty but recommended him to mercy. None was granted and he was hanged by Berry.

April 18th: Thomas William CURRELL (31)   Newgate

Thomas Currell had been courting Lydia Green (31) for over ten years and although they were in a serious relationship they still lived apart, with Miss Green occupying a room in a Hoxton boarding house, upstairs from her mother. After a night out, Currell would usually call at her room and leave in the early hours.

Early in the morning of 5 February, Lydia's mother heard a bang from upstairs. After dressing, she went to investigate and discovered her daughter shot dead. When police went to interview Currell, he had disappeared.

Currell had fled to a guest house across London under an assumed name. He would have escaped detection much longer if he had not been arrested for stealing another lodger's coat. He was identified as being wanted for the Hoxton murder and was charged.

It was later revealed that he had gone to Scotland Yard to confess, but had been thrown out by the two officers manning the desk as they thought he was having them on!

Hanged by Berry.

1887

May 9th: Charles SMITH (63)   Oxford

Smith was a gypsy living at Cowley, Oxfordshire, and for many years had been mistreating his wife, more than once severely beating her with a stick. At the time of the murder they were living in abject poverty, in a tent, and were very miserable.
    On the night of 19 February, Smith and his wife, and their two children went to bed. Almost at once he began to attack his wife beside the sleeping children. One awoke and saw Smith brandishing a hammer; as Mrs Smith cried out, the other child awoke and went to fetch help. Mrs Smith crawled from the tent, then collapsed and died.
    Convicted at Reading Assizes by Baron Huddlestone after a plea of manslaughter was rejected. There was no motive suggested for the brutal murder. Smith remained callous in the condemned cell and told Berry not to put the straps on when he came to pinion him, but as he was led to the gallows he collapsed in a faint and had to be supported until the drop fell.

May 16th: Henry William YOUNG (27)   Dorchester

A one legged shoemaker sentenced to death at Dorset Assizes by Mr Justice Denman on 28 April for the murder of Percival John Ings, his wife's one month old illegitimate child.
    Young and his wife lived together at Poole and after she gave birth to the child he showed no affection towards it, even though his wife told him he was the father. On 8 February, the doctor was summoned when the child began to suffer from a stomach upset, and remained in the physician's care for the next four days until he deemed that the illness was past.
    The next day, Young was left alone with the child and when his wife returned home he informed her that the baby had suffered a relapse and died. The doctor was called and issued a death certificate without further examination. Later that night, Young was heard to boast that he had tried to poison the child by administering caustic soda and water. The doctor was informed and a post mortem revealed that the cause of death was strangulation and severe chest injuries.
    He made a full confession in which he claimed his wife had been unfaithful and that he wasn't the father of the child. Despite strong attempts to secure a reprieve, Young was hanged by Berry.
    The hangman recalled that before his appointment at the gaol, he stayed in a temperance hotel in Bournemouth, and that during the evening

he became involved in a conversation with the landlady who was discussing the pending execution with other guests.

Unaware that her new guest was the hangman, she said that Berry was not fit to mix with normal people, and was a man without a soul. Berry smiled amiably and passed his own opinions on the subject before retiring to bed. When the woman brought him his night light, he handed her his business card, almost causing her to faint.

May 30th: Walter WOOD (35)   **Manchester**

Wood and his wife Emma lived happily together at Darwen, where he was employed as a machine fitter, until he lost his job. From then on the marriage deteriorated and eventually they split up. He moved to Bolton and she took their daughter back to her native Bury where she reverted to her maiden name.

Several times he made unsuccessful attempts to get her back but eventually went to Bury to make a last desperate plea. He called at her house, told her he had found a job, and suggested they go for a walk and try to sort out their marriage. While in a field, he cut her throat. He was arrested soon after the body was discovered and police had to save him from being lynched by an angry mob.

Convicted at Manchester Assizes and hanged by James Berry. Berry was reported to have been at school with Wood at Wrea Green, near Blackpool, and sat with him for a few hours on the eve of the execution.

August 1st: Alfred SOWERY (24)   **Lancaster**

Convicted of the murder of his sweetheart, Annie Kelly, whom he shot dead at Preston. He failed in his attempt to shoot himself after the crime.

Hanged by Berry who claimed later that it was one of the worst cases he ever had to deal with as Sowery was half-dead with fear on the morning of the execution. During the time between sentence being passed and it being carried out, Sowery had made himself seriously ill through terror. He had to be half pushed and carried down the corridor to the scaffold, and his groans and cries could be heard all over the gaol. His teeth chattered and his face kept turning from deathly white to a livid red. Berry claimed that every inch of ground to the drop was violently contested, and as he placed the rope around Sowery's neck he received a kick in the shin, and carried the scar until the day he died. The bullet from Sowery's suicide attempt was still lodged in his head and after he was hanged, Berry removed the bullet and kept it as a souvenir.

August 16th: Thomas Henry BEVAN (20)   **Knutsford**

On 26 March, Bevan, an apprentice ironmoulder from Crewe, called at the house of his aunt, Mrs Sarah Griffiths, then beat her to death, stealing the contents of her purse. The robbery yielded just seventeen shillings and sixpence and when he was spotted by his half-sister Mary Jones (11), he attacked her as well, leaving the girl for dead. Fortunately she survived and was able to testify against him.

He was tried before Mr Justice Denman at Chester Assizes on 28 July, and after conviction, confessed that he had initially tried to strangle his aunt but when she had slipped onto the floor, he finished her off by jumping up and down on her until she died.

Hanged by Berry.

August 22nd: Henry HOBSON (54)   **Leeds**

On 23 July, Mrs Ada Stodhart, the wife of a Sheffield engineer, was having a morning drink with her maid in the kitchen, when she was surprised to see Hobson call at the house. She recognised him as a former employee of her mother's who had been recently dismissed for drunkeness, but she opened the door and asked him what he wanted.

Hobson said he was passing and could he have a drink of water. He was given the drink and left, only to return fifteen minutes later and ask for a piece of rope. While Mrs Stodhart went to fetch some from the cellar, Hobson took out a knife and attacked the maid. Her screams attracted the attention of Mrs Stodhart who came running to investigate, only to be attacked by Hobson when she came into the kitchen. The maid rushed into the street screaming 'Murder!' Hobson took to his heels but was arrested later that day.

At his trial at Leeds Assizes, he admitted that he had cut Mrs Stodhart's throat as revenge for being dismissed from his job, and that he had since been unable to find suitable employment.

Hanged by Billington.

1887

August 22nd: Israel LIPSKI (22) — Newgate

Israel Lipski was a Polish immigrant who occupied the attic room in a house at Whitechapel. The room immediately below was shared by Isaac and Miriam Angel, a young married couple, and on the morning of 28 June Isaac Angel left home for work as usual. Miriam (22), usually had breakfast with her mother who lived just around the corner, but when she failed to appear her mother went to her house. She was unable to get any answer by knocking at the door so she called for help and the door was forced. Inside, she found the body of her daughter on the bed, and on the floor beside was Israel Lipski. Both had been poisoned with nitric acid.

Lipski recovered in hospital and told police that he had been passing Mrs Angel's door when he heard a disturbance. He entered to offer assistance and saw two men robbing and assaulting the woman. Lipski claimed that after poisoning Mrs Angel, they turned on him before fleeing. Although the police thought that only a madman would poison himself with acid, the evidence seemed to suggest that Lipski wasn't telling the truth and after further invesitgations he was charged with murder.

Lipski was tried at the Old Bailey, and despite some detectives having doubts as to the strength of the prosecution's case, the jury took only eight minutes to return a guilty verdict. While Lipski was in the cell awaiting execution, a huge campaign was mounted to get the sentence quashed, because many thought the conviction unsafe. As a result, the sentence was deferred for a week. Lipski was about to make a statement but then heard about the stay of execution. However, he wrote a full confession when told the execution was going ahead as scheduled.

Hanged by Berry, who was reported to have miscalculated the drop, giving nearly nine feet instead of a more realistic six; as a result Lipski's head was very nearly pulled off.

August 29th: William WILTON — Lewes

Convicted of the murder of his wife, Sarah, at Brighton on 9 July.

She was found dead in bed, her throat cut, in a room in a poor area of the town. She and Wilton, her second husband, shared the room with a third party who told the police that when he had left to go out to work, the couple were both asleep.

A search was instigated successfully for Wilton, and when arrested he confessed.

Hanged by Berry.

November 14th: William HUNTER (32)   Carlisle

A native of Glasgow, working as a blacksmith in Manchester, Hunter had been 'tramping' from Wigton to Carlisle with Mary Steele and her daughter Isabella. Hunter had a wife back in Manchester but had been with Steele for the last three months. On 8 September while approaching Carlisle Isabella told Hunter she was tired. He called her to come to him and when she refused, he walked up to her, grabbed her by the throat then kicked her, as the girl's mother screamed that he had better not have hurt her 'we-un.'

Hunter then carried Isabella into a field where he said he would revive her with water. The girl's body was later found dead. Hunter had cut her throat with a pocket knife then turned the weapon on himself.

He was tried before Mr Justice Day at Carlisle Assizes and as the judge passed sentence, Hunter's wife, who had made the journey up from Manchester to offer her support, collapsed in the court. She was carried outside and later discovered that someone had picked her pocket and stolen the money her friends had clubbed together for her expenses.

Hanged by Berry.

November 15th: Joseph WALKER   Oxford

On Friday 23 September, Walker, a saddler from Chipping Norton, had been drinking all afternoon following a quarrel with his wife Henrietta earlier in the day. He told a friend in the pub that he would 'do for her when he got home', and when he left the pub he was very drunk indeed.

He first put his children to bed then followed his wife upstairs to their own bedroom. The children then heard a fierce row erupt, and when one of them opened the bedroom door, they saw their father rip a knife from their mother's neck.

Walker was sentenced to death by Mr Justice Hawkins, and when he heard the jury add a recommendation for mercy he told the court he could see no reason why Walker should receive mercy as the crime he had committed was cruel, wicked and merciless, and he implored Walker to look upon the world no more.

Hanged by Berry.

November 21st: Joseph MORLEY (17) Chelmsford

Convicted on overwhelming evidence at Chelmsford Assizes on 10 November for the murder of a young married woman with whom he lodged at Dagenham. After sentence was passed, he confessed that he had killed the woman, a Mrs Rogers, by cutting her throat with a razor he had found in her bedroom, but denied that when he had entered the room he had intended to kill her.
    Hanged by Berry.

November 28th: Enoch WADELY (27) Gloucester

A former private in the 2nd Gloucestershire Regiment who had been dismissed as unfit for service after a stay in an asylum while serving in India. He returned to his family at Kempley and made acquaintance with Elizabeth Hannah Evans (18), with whom he worked at a local farm. He had often tried to establish a more intimate relationship with her but she had refused him, although they still went out together. Wadely told his sister that it was hard to love and not be loved in return.
    On 18 June, the couple were working in the fields together and at the end of the day he walked her home. Along a lonely stretch of path, he made amorous advances towards Evans. She pushed him away and it drove him into a frenzy whereupon he raped her, then stabbed her over forty times with his knife, and then ran off. The girl's faint cries were heard by a passing farmer and she was able to say who her assailant was before she died. The police, meanwhile, already had Wadely in custody on a public nuisance charge: he had been dancing around the streets in a highly excited state and had given Evans' purse to a stranger.
    Wadely was tried at Gloucester Assizes and his defence was insanity. The jury at his first trial was unable to agree and they were dismissed, with a new trial being ordered for the next Assizes. This time he was convicted, sentenced to death, and hanged by Berry.

December 6th: Thomas PAYNE Warwick

A labourer who pleaded guilty to the murder of his sister-in-law, Charlotte Taylor.
    Charlotte Taylor shared a house in Coventry with her sister and brother-in-law, Thomas Payne. She and Payne were having a clandestine

1887

affair, and he was obsessed with her. When he learned that she was also seeing a Salvation Army officer, Payne became insanely jealous and threatened to kill her if she carried on seeing him.

One afternoon in August, he saw them together and when she returned home later, he cut her throat, then surrended himself at the local police station.

He stood trial in November at Warwick Assizes before Baron Huddlestone, and insisted on pleading guilty. Many women in the packed courtroom were in tears when the judge passed the death sentence.

Hanged by James Berry.

1888

Cases where no executioner is recorded are multiple executions, and readers are asked to refer to the entries before or after for details of the hangman.

1888

January 10th: Phillip Henry Eustace CROSS (63)   **Cork**

Dr Cross was a retired army surgeon from a good family, who lived at Dipsey, Co Cork, with his wealthy young wife and their five children, two of whom suffered from epilepsy.

In the summer of 1886, they employed Effie Skinner (20), as a governess for the children, and soon she began an affair with the old doctor. When Mrs Cross found out, she ordered that Effie be dismissed. Dr Cross immediately terminated the girl's employment and she left for Dublin.

Within a week of her leaving, Cross told his wife he had to go away on business and spent five days with Effie in a Dublin hotel. Mrs Cross suddenly became ill and when her husband examined her, he diagnosed typhoid. Her condition deteriorated and in June 1887, Mrs Cross died. Dr Cross himself signed her death certificate.

He may have got away with murder if he had not been hasty in marrying and installing Effie as the new mistress in the family home. Local gossip spread to the extent that police ordered an exhumation of the dead woman and traces of arsenic were discovered in the body.

Cross was found guilty despite protesting his innocence and claimed that his wife had self-administered arsenic to aid her complexion. He was hanged by Berry after telling his guards that he did not fear death as he had faced it many times on the battlefield.

March 13th: David REES (25)   **Carmarthen**

On 12 November 1887, Thomas Davies was travelling from Llanelly to a tin plate works at Dafen, carrying wages for the work force, when he was ambushed by Rees and an unnamed accomplice. The two men beat Davies to death and robbed him of the money.

Rees was caught, convicted, and on 24 February was sentenced to death. He confessed in the condemned cell and blamed his actions on drink.

He was hanged by Berry; Rees's accomplice was never caught.

1888

March 20th: James JONES   Hereford
Alfred SCANDRETT

On 19 October 1887, the two men broke into a house belonging to an old man by the name of Phillip Ballard, at Tapsley, Hereford, and attacked him with an axe. They were soon arrested and Jones claimed that Scandrett had delivered the fatal blow while he had been a mere bystander.

The two men tried to blame each other for the crime, and on being sentenced to death, Scandrett tried to strangle Jones in the dock as he believed that he was responsible for his fate.

Hanged by Berry.

March 27th: George CLARKE (42)   Winchester

A former tailor and discharged army pensioner, who ran a public house at Aldershot after retiring from the army.

Clarke ran the bar with his wife and children, including his stepdaughter Annie Vaughan (18). Two years earlier, Clarke and Annie had had an affair but they stopped for fear of his wife finding out.

On 5 February, Annie spoke to her father about a man whom she wished to marry. Clarke told her that he disapproved of her intended, but she told him she was adamant. The next morning, one of the children saw him leaving Annie's bedroom. When someone tried to rouse Annie, she was found dead with her throat cut so savagely that the head was almost severed.

Sentenced to death at Winchester Assizes by Mr Justice Field and hanged by Berry.

March 28th: William ARROWSMITH   Shrewsbury

On 11 November 1887, Arrowsmith, a labourer from Denton, visited his elderly uncle George Pickerill (80), who lived in a lonely cottage near Whitchurch. He brutally killed him by beating his brains out then cutting his throat, before stealing some property and a small sum of money he knew to be in the house.

He was arrested when he was seen selling some of the stolen goods, and charged with murder when police matched his footprints with those found at the scene.

Hanged by Berry.

1888

April 29th: Daniel HAYES   **Tralee**
              Daniel MORIARTY

Convicted together for the murder of James Fitzsimmons, an elderly farmer from Liscnaw, who was shot dead in front of his daughter on a public road close to his home on 31 January.

    Moriarty, a labourer who had recently married, and Hayes a journeyman shoemaker with a chronic drink problem, both protested their innocence before they were hanged by Berry.

May 7th: James KIRBY (35)   **Tralee**

Kirby, nicknamed 'The Fox', was convicted of the murder of Patrick Quirke (80), at Liscahere on 8 November 1887.

    Quirke, whose daughter was a cousin of Kirby's, evicted him from his land after he failed to keep up with the rent. He was alleged to have shot the man dead in revenge.

    He protested his innocence but was hanged by Berry.

May 15th: John Alfred GELL (32)   **Manchester**

Gell lodged with Mrs Mary Miller (46) at Moston, Manchester, and for a time they had been on intimate terms. During the winter he was unemployed, and as a kindness his landlady and sometime lover allowed him to stay without paying until he found work.

    As spring neared, it seemed that Gell was making no efforts to seek employment, and eventually Mrs Miller tired of this and told him to find either a job or other lodgings.

    On 1 March he left the house first thing in the morning but returned at noon and attacked Mrs Miller with an axe. Her daughter, Isabella, called for assistance as Gell turned his attack on her. A nearby police officer was attracted to the house by the commotion and gave chase as Gell fled, arresting him a few minutes later.

    Mary Miller died, but Gell admitted he had intended to kill Isabella Miller as well, and then himself. He was convicted at Manchester on 27 April and hanged by Berry. As the drop fell, he called out 'Isabella Miller, I hope you have had your revenge!'

1888

May 22nd: James William RICHARDSON (23)   Leeds

Richardson was a labourer employed by a brick maker at Barnsley. On 21 March, he went to work as normal but soon after he clocked on, he was seen talking angrily to his foreman, William Berridge. He later threw down his tools and stormed out.

Some hours later, he returned to the factory and waited outside an office until Berridge came out. The foreman had only gone a few yards when Richardson began shooting at him, before making an attempt to flee. He was detained, and when arrested claimed that the foreman had accused him of breaking a sweeping brush on purpose. The foreman died a week later from his wounds and Richardson was charged with murder.

He was tried before Mr Justice Matthew at Leeds Assizes on 3 May and despite a spirited defence by his counsel, the judge summed up in favour of the prosecution and the jury returned a guilty verdict.

The spring sitting of Leeds Assizes was one of the busiest for years, finishing with four people being sentenced to death. One was reprieved immediately on account of a flaw in the judge's summing up. In the meantime Billington was requested to carry out the remaining three executions at the prison. A woman called Mary Holloway was to be hanged on Monday 21 May; a Doctor Burke from Barnsley, who had committed a murder at Monk Bretton was due to be hanged alongside Richardson on the Tuesday. When the hangman arrived at the prison, he learned that both Holloway and Burke had been granted reprieves, again on account of the judge's summing up. The people of Barnsley vigorously campaigned for a respite but Richardson was hanged as scheduled.

He left a touching farewell note to his wife, pledging his love for her with a promise that he would await her on the other side.

July 17th: Robert UPTON (61)   Oxford

On 23 May, after finishing his day's work as a builder's labourer, Upton turned to a workmate and told him there would be a 'rum-do' presently, and without explaining any further, Upton went home.

Soon after he arrived at his cottage at Milton-under-Witchwood, Oxfordshire, neighbours heard his wife scream. One of the neighbours, a man called Miles, hurried to see what was going on and Upton told him he was going to kill his wife. Miles then watched as Upton chased his wife out of their cottage and before he could do anything, Upton beat her to death with a large iron bar. Miles grabbed the weapon from him and called for help.

Upton was hanged by Berry at Oxford Castle, with a drop of five feet. When the body was taken down after hanging for the regulation one hour, the neck had stretched almost twelve inches.

July 18th: Thomas WYRE (30)   **Worcester**

Wyre was an agricultural labourer who lived with his wife and two children at Wolverly, near Kidderminster. The marriage wasn't a happy one and after a series of rows, his wife told him they should part.

On 3 March, she packed her bags and told Wyre that she would care for the elder of their children and that he could look after the youngest, a boy of four. Wyre told his wife he would take the boy to his parents but the child wasn't seen alive again.

On 2 June, workmen at Castle Hill, Wolverly, found the body of a child in a well and although the features were unrecognisable, the clothing was identified as being made by the child's aunt, and Wyre was arrested.

Convicted at Worcester Assizes on 31 June and sentenced to death by Mr Justice Denman; hanged by Berry.

August 7th: John JACKSON (33)   **Manchester**

Also known as Charles Wood Firth, Jackson was serving a six month sentence at Strangeways Prison, Manchester, after being convicted on a burglary charge in April.

Due to his apprenticeship as a plumber, he was asked to fix some gas pipes in the house of the matron. He agreed to the work and on 22 May was taken to the house and accompanied by a warder, Ralph Webb (45), with whom he got on well. At 4pm that afternoon, the matron heard a noise in the bedroom and when she went to investigate, she found the door locked. She called for help and three warders arrived and forced the door open to find Webb beaten to death on the floor, and a hole in the ceiling from which Jackson had made his escape.

He was at large for several weeks while a massive manhunt went on.

He was eventually arrested at Bradford, after he had been caught breaking into a house. Back at the station, he was identified as Jackson and taken to Manchester on a murder charge.

Tried by Mr Justice Grantham at Manchester Assizes on Friday 13 July, the jury needed just six minutes to find him guilty. He was hanged by Berry, who had become friendly with the murdered warder when they had shared a room together on a previous visit.

August 10th: Arthur James DELANEY (31)   **Derby**

Delaney, from Chesterfield, and his wife had been married for four years but had recently been on bad terms due to his drinking. In the spring of 1888, he attacked her while drunk and as a result she took out a separation order on him. Delaney was also fined by the court and when he repeated the attack, she again went back to the courts and Delaney received another fine. Upon leaving the court, he rushed over to her and assaulted her so viciously that she died from her injuries.

Hanged by Berry.

August 15th: George SARGENT   **Chelmsford**

Sargent, a railway labourer and sometime poacher from Copford, had been married to his wife, Annie (21), for just a year when she left him and returned to her mother's at Wakes Colne, near Colchester. She had become increasingly fed up with his drunken moods, and eventually packed her bags when he smashed all their furniture.

On 17 July, Sargent called at her mother's house and pleaded with her to come home, adding that he would stop drinking and would work overtime to replace the furniture. She refused to listen to him, and in a rage he grabbed her by the hair, and locking her head between his knees he cut her from ear to ear with a clasp knife, almost severing her head. He ran away after the crime but was caught hiding in fields near the house.

Hanged by Berry.

August 28th: George Nathaniel DANIELS (34)   Birmingham

Widower Daniels, a printer, was in the habit of visiting Emma Hastings, the daughter of a Birmingham publican with whom he was having an on-off relationship. At closing time on 14 April he called at the back door of the pub, and after kissing her he shot her twice with a revolver. One bullet hit her in the chest, the other blew her brains out. His defence of insanity failed.

August 28th: Harry Benjamin JONES   Birmingham

A gasworker who from time to time lodged with the family of Richard Harris at Aston. The two men had met three years earlier when they worked together, and when Jones became homeless his friend offered him a room. When he discovered that Jones was having an affair with his wife, he asked him to leave but was unable to get him to go. In desperation, Harris uprooted his family and moved to Gloucester. Soon afterwards, Jones tracked them down, and while Harris was out at work he went to see Mrs Harris, got into a row with her, then shot her. The wound wasn't serious but it was enough to land Jones in prison, and while he was safely locked up, the family took the opportunity to move back to Birmingham.

Following his release from prison, an undaunted Jones also moved back to Birmingham, and again found the Harris'. With Richard Harris away working, Mrs Harris invited him to stay, and the affair began again. Rumours spread that he was the father of her youngest child.

On 11 June, Harris returned home from working in Wales and told Jones to get out. This time he managed to evict the unwanted guest but three days later Jones returned to the house in a drunken rage and shot the family. All were wounded but a daughter, Florence, succumbed to her injuries.

He was sentenced to death by Mr Justice Wills at the same Assizes as **DANIELS** [above], and the two were hanged together by Berry. It was noted that Jones took a very long time to die, while in Daniels' case death was instant.

November 13th: Leir Richard BARTLETT (66)   Newgate

Bartlett was a stevedore who lived with his wife Elizabeth at Poplar. While he worked at the docks, his wife ran a small general store. On 18 August he returned to the shop after a drinking spree and demanded more money, which was refused. Later that night, while his wife was asleep, he beat her to death with a coal hammer, then cut his own throat.
    Hanged by Berry.

December 11th: Samuel CROWTHER (71)   Worcester

An aged shoemaker convicted of the murder of John Willis, a gardener, at Dudderhill, near Droitwich.
    Early on the morning of 1 August, Willis spotted Crowther stealing fruit from some tress on his property. He challenged the elderly thief who responded by pulling out a knife and stabbing Willis three times, leaving him for dead. Willis was able to crawl into his house and tell his wife that Crowther had stabbed him before he collapsed and died. Crowther was arrested later that morning.
    He was convicted at Worcester Assizes in November. The frail old man had no visitors while awaiting execution as his only living relative, a daughter, had testified against him in court.
    Crowther was lame and walked to the drop with the aid of a stick. He was hanged by James Berry who gave him a short drop of three feet six inches.

December 18th: William WADDELL (22)   Durham

Sentenced to death at Durham Assizes for the murder of Jane Beetmore (28).
    On the evening of Saturday the 22 September, Miss Beetmore, who had recently been discharged from a local hospital, set out to buy some sweets to take with her prescribed medicine. When she failed to return home that night, her parents organised a search at dawn and later that morning her body was discovered. She had been stabbed three times in the chest.
    The newspapers were full of the Jack the Ripper outrages in London and police at first thought it might be the work of the same man as the

method was similar. However, when they questioned Miss Beetmore's friends, they soon found a likely suspect.

Waddell, a Gateshead iron-worker, had been known to have tried for many years to force his attentions on Jane and she repeatedly had to fend off his unwelcome advances. No one had seen him in the area on the night of the murder but when police went to interview him and learned that he had fled, they became even more suspicious.

Waddell was detained several days later and after questioning was charged with the murder. He was hanged by James Berry after leaving a full confession, blaming drink as the cause.

1889

Cases where no executioner is recorded are multiple executions, and readers are asked to refer to the entries before or after for details of the hangman.

1889

January 1st: Thomas CLEWES (27) Stafford

A collier convicted, at Staffordshire Assizes, of the murder of Mary Jane Bovell.

Clewes and Miss Bovell lived together at Washerwall, near Stoke, but during the summer their relationship grew strained when he became jealous of her seeing someone else.

One night in September he lay in wait, then attacked her with a hatchet.

Hanged by Berry.

January 1st: Charles BULMER (51) Leeds

Bulmer, a groom from Huddersfield, had been unhappily married to his wife for a dozen years and finally, during the autumn of 1888, they had a fight, which resulted in him being bound over to keep the peace, and following this they decided to separate.

Moving out of the house, he found lodgings but returned on 12 September 1888 to collect the remainder of his possessions. Mrs Bulmer refused entry on account of him being drunk and abusive. When a neighbour called round later, Mrs Bulmer was found stabbed to death on the kitchen floor. Bulmer gave himself up and blamed the crime on drink.

Hanged by James Billington.

January 2nd: Charles DOBELL (17) Maidstone
   William GOWER (18)

On the night of 20 July, Bensley Cyrus Lawrence, an engine driver and time keeper at a Tunbridge Wells sawmill, was called from his home with a message that someone wanted to see him. Minutes later a shot was heard and soon afterwards, his body was discovered.

A witness had seen Lawrence talking to two young men just before the shot was heard but despite an intensive investigation, the police had no clues as to the identity of the assailants.

It was almost six months later before the police had the suspects in custody, after one of them confessed to a friend. The Whitechapel murders of Jack the Ripper were filling the headlines. Discussing the atrocities with friends, Dobell confessed that he had killed the man at Tunbridge Wells. Word got back to detectives, and soon both Dobell and Gower were in custody, where they made a full confession. Police blamed the crime on the

influence of 'penny-dreadfuls' comic books, which had fired their imaginations.
Hanged by Berry.

January 8th: George NICHOLSON (52) Warwick

A journeyman baker sentenced to death at Warwick Assizes on 17 December 1888 for the murder of his wife at Aston.

During a quarrel at their home on 22 September, he struck her over the head with a hatchet, fracturing her skull.

Nicholson fled to Walsall where he was identified and arrested later that day. He confessed his guilt in the condemned cell and had to be supported on the way to the scaffold where he was hanged by Berry.

January 14th: Arthur McKEOWN (32) Belfast

Sentenced to death at Belfast Assizes before Mr Justice Holmes, for the murder of his paramour, Mary Jane Phillips.

The couple lived in a house on Robert Street, one of the roughest areas of Belfast. On Sunday morning, 26 August 1888, her body was discovered battered to death in the kitchen. Police arrested McKeown who had already served a six month sentence for assaulting her.

Hanged by James Berry.

March 6th: Ebeneezer Samuel JENKINS (20) Wandsworth

Aka Wheatcroft, convicted of the murder of his fiancee at Godalming.

Jenkins was an artist who rented a studio in the town. His fiancee had told him she wanted to end the relationship but they agreed to meet later that week on 7 January at the Three Crowns Inn, Godalming. After leaving the inn, they walked to his studio where she was found strangled the next morning after he had confessed to his crime.

He left a note for his mother saying that he would never let his fiancee leave him, and when arrested he told detectives that he wanted to be buried next to her.

Hanged by Berry, who experimented at the execution when he stood Jenkins on the drop and strapped seven pound weights to each leg to compensate for the prisoner's small & light frame. The additional poundage allowed Berry to use a drop of six feet six inches which resulted in a satisfactory execution. This was the only time the procedure was adopted.

March 11th: Jessie KING (27) Edinburgh

A Glasgow born mill worker sentenced to death by Lord Justice Clerk at Edinburgh High Court on 18 February, for the murder of two children who were in her care.

Mrs King was a baby farmer who murdered the children by first drugging them with whisky, then strangling and suffocating them. Police suspected she had also killed several other children.

She confidently predicted that she would only get a short sentence, but when the judge sentenced her to death, she began to scream hysterically and had to be escorted from the dock.

While in the death cell, she twice attempted to commit suicide before she was led to the gallows and hanged by James Berry.

March 13th: Samuel RYLANDS Shepton Mallet

A labourer convicted of the murder of Emma Jane Davies (10), at Yeobridge, Somerset.

On Wednesday 2 January, Emma went out on her daily walk to a local farm to fetch the family some milk for breakfast. The farm was only a mile away and when she failed to return after a couple of hours, the family set out in search of her. Later that afternoon Emma's younger brother stumbled across her body in a ditch. She had been battered about the head with her milk churn and then strangled with a piece of rope. Police also thought that the attacker had tried to sever her head while she lay dead.

A search was mounted for a man who had been seen in the area earlier that morning. Several days later Rylands was arrested and charged with the murder after milk and blood stains were found on his clothing.

He was convicted at Taunton Assizes on 20 February and made a full confession after being sentenced to death. In a note to his parents he claimed that he had killed Emma because he bore a grudge against her father.

Rylands was the first man to be hanged at the 200 year old Somerset gaol. James Berry carried out the sentence.

April 8th: Peter STAFFORD   Dublin

Sentenced to death at Maryboro Assizes on 9 March for the murder of Patrick Crawley in County Meath.

The two men had had a long standing quarrel stemming from a disagreement while attending Kingscourt fair. On 28 January, they were drinking in a public house when they had an altercation, during which Stafford pulled out a revolver and shot Crawley. He died later from his wounds in hospital. Stafford was arrested but claimed he was innocent and had an alibi for the time of the crime.

On conviction he declared to the court that he was as 'innocent as a priest'! He resisted violently when James Berry tried to pinion him in the condemned cell.

April 10th: Thomas ALLEN (25)   Swansea

Allen was a Zulu who had arrived in Swansea on a Cuban ship on which he served as a steward. On 10 February he called into the Gloucester Hotel, a dockside pub frequented by sailors, the landlord of which was Frederick Kent (38). At 4am the next morning, the landlord's wife heard someone strike a match in their bedroom and woke her husband. Kent climbed from his bed and began to struggle with the intruder, who attacked him with a knife. His wife reached under the pillow for their revolver but hesitated to use the gun for fear of shooting her husband. She finally got the stranger in sight and shot him in the leg. He fled from the building, leaving Kent mortally wounded on the bedroom floor.

Detectives found a sailor's cap which had been lost in the fracas. They soon traced it to Allen who was arrested when found hiding in the nearby docks. He was taken into custody after nearly being lynched by an angry public. It was alleged that he had hidden on the premises after closing time, and police suspected that he may have been guilty of other recent unsolved crimes in the area.

Hanged by Berry.

1889

April 11th: John WITHEY   **Bristol**

On Saturday 15 February, a butcher's wife Jane Withey was found stabbed to death in the St Paul's district of Bristol. Her husband was questioned and claimed that she had fallen on a knife whilst drunk.
    Withey was tried at Bristol Assizes along with an Elizabeth Knutt, who was charged with harbouring him and being an accessory to the murder. After a three day trial, Knutt was sent to prison for five years; Withey was sentenced to death.
    Hanged by Berry.

April 24th: William Henry BURY (29)   **Dundee**

On 3 February, Bury, a Wolverhampton born sawdust merchant, rushed into his local police station and cried: 'I am Jack the Ripper! If you go to my house you will find the body of my wife which I have cut up and put into a box.' After first treating the confession as a joke, the police were horrified to find that he was indeed telling the truth, certainly about his wife, if not his other astonishing claim, for when they checked at the house they found Mrs Bury's body. She had been strangled, horribly mutilated and locked in a trunk.
    He was tried at the High Court on 25 March and sentenced to death. He made a full written confession in his cell, and forwarded to the Home Secretary a document containing startling revelations on the Jack the Ripper killings. The statement was not made public at the time but it is a fact that Bury was living in the east end of London when the murders took place, and when he moved up to Scotland, the killings ceased. A former landlord in London gave him bad references and claimed that blood stains had been found in his room.
    Hanged by Berry.

August 7th: Lawrence Maurice HICKEY   **Dublin**

Convicted at Maryboro Assizes in July, for the murder of his brother-in-law, Dennis Daly (40), a wealthy farmer.
    On Thursday 22 November 1888, Daly was found shot dead on a road leading from Tralee to Castleisland. During the investigation, police

learned of a family feud that had been going on for several months, and questioned Hickey and another man.

The other man, also a relative, was acquitted. Hickey was convicted and hanged by James Berry.

August 21st: George HORTON (37) — Derby

A miner from Stanwick, convicted of the murder of his young daughter, whom he poisoned in order to obtain a small sum of insurance money. He was in a terrible state in the condemned cell and suffered continually from nervous fever.

Hanged by James Berry.

December 9th: Benjamin PURCELL (50) — Devizes

Purcell and his wife Emily (44) lived unhappily together at Bradford-upon-Avon, and as a result would quarrel over the slightest matter. On 9 November she returned home from shopping and they had an argument over a floral petticoat she had just purchased. In a rage, he picked up an axe and split her head open, then beat her about the head and body with the blunt end. When he was satisfied that she was dead, he walked to the nearest police station and confessed. Sentenced to death at Wiltshire Assizes by Baron Pollock.

Hanged by Berry.

December 24th: William DUKES — Manchester

George Gordon and his father ran a successful furniture business which had warehouses in Burnley and Bury. Dukes was the manager of the Bury branch and part of his duties was to prepare the monthly accounts for George Gordon to assess.

During August, Dukes got into trouble over his failure to produce the accounts and warned that if he slipped up again he would be dismissed. He was also cautioned for drinking at work.

On the morning of 25 September, Gordon came to the shop to see the books. Dukes, who had been drinking all morning, avoided him but when Gordon returned again that afternoon, he had to face his boss and knew he would be in trouble. Later that afternoon, Gordon's body was found in a wardrobe at the warehouse.

Police accused Dukes of beating Gordon to death with a hammer after he had been threatened with the sack. He denied the charges but later claimed it was an accident.

Sentenced to death at Manchester Assizes by Mr Justice Charles on 4 December, and hanged by Berry.

December 31st: William Thomas HOOK (40) Maidstone

Sentenced to death by Mr Justice Denman, at Kent Assizes, for the murder of his wife Julia, at Gravesend.

She had left him and taken their two sons, and in a jealous rage, he beat her head in. There was a very moving scene when he was visited in the condemned cell by his two sons.

Hanged by Berry.

December 31st: Frederick BRETT (39) Leeds

On 20 October, Brett, a Halifax railway labourer, drunkenly accused his wife of being too friendly with some of his workmates, then cut her throat with a clasp knife. When arrested he said: 'Yes, I have done it and it can't be undone. I was only playing at Jack the Ripper.'

December 31st: Robert WEST (45) Leeds

West was a travelling showman from Oxford, who came to Sheffield to take part in the annual Handsworth village fete. On 22 August, he parked his coconut van, and while his son went for a walk, he started drinking and began to curse his wife for being too friendly with another showman called 'Leicester Jack'.

Next morning, he went up to a policeman and confessed that he had killed his wife. She was later found by the police with a horrific throat wound.

Hanged by James Billington alongside **BRETT** [above].

1890

Cases where no executioner is recorded are multiple executions, and readers are asked to refer to the entries before or after for details of the hangman.

1890

January 7th: Charles Lister HIGGENBOTHAM (63)   Warwick

A former employee of Birmingham Corporation, convicted of the murder of his landlady, Winifred Whittaker Phillips (76), whom he killed by cutting her throat with a carving knife.

    He had no friends and no one took any notice of his fate after conviction. He was hanged by Berry, who gave him a drop of four feet six inches, but the force of the drop re-opened an old neck wound and blood gushed all over the walls of the pit. Death was seen to be instantaneous but the blood continued to spurt for several minutes.

March 11th: Joseph BOSWELL (29)   Worcester
Samuel BOSWELL (39)

The Boswell brothers, and Alfred Hill, were three gardeners who often turned their hand to poaching. One night they were in the grounds of the Duc D'Aumale at Evesham when they were surprised by Frank Stephens, the gamekeeper, whom they shot dead.

    All three were convicted at Worcester Assizes, and sentenced to death. Their appeal against the sentence, on the grounds that although they were guilty of poaching, they hadn't set out to commit murder, was rejected. The Government later announced that a reprieve had been granted in the case of Hill, who would now serve a life sentence. The news was kept from the brothers although it caused outrage in the city as many believed, including the jury, that Hill was by far the more guilty.

    The Boswells were hanged by Berry and an unnamed assistant. As they were pinioned, they turned to Berry and asked: 'Where's Hill?' On being told he had been reprieved, they broke down and had to be supported on the short steps to the drop.

March 12th: William ROW (40)   Newcastle

In October 1889, Row, a Manchester shoemaker, left his wife and fled to Newcastle with Lily McClaren Wilson, a woman of disreputable means, with whom he had been having an affair. An uncle had recently left him a large legacy but he soon frittered it away and had to look for a job.

    On 3 January, he returned home from work and argued with Lily after accusing her of having more money than she could have earned legitimately. In a fit of passion he cut her throat with his shoemaker's knife. He confessed to the crime and was sentenced to death by Mr Justice Grantham on 21 February.

The jury strongly recommended him to mercy but he was hanged by Berry.

March 26th: John NEAL (64) Newgate

On 24 January, Neal, a bricklayer, and his much younger wife, Theresa, moved into new lodgings at Islington. Four days later he stabbed her to death in a fit of jealousy and was arrested.

On the gallows, he claimed: 'I'm sorry I committed the murder but she was a bad wife to me.'

Hanged by Berry.

April 8th: Richard DAVIES (18) Knutsford

On Saturday 25 January, George Davies (16), rushed into the family home and claimed that their father had been attacked by two men on a Crewe road. He took police to the scene where they found the body of Richard Davies senior (50), a tailor. He had been battered about the head with a large tree branch that lay close by, covered in blood.

Detectives from Cheshire Constabulary questioned the family and learned that the father frequently bullied his children. A search for the two assailants had yielded no clues so they set about re-checking the statements made by his two sons. Richard Davies junior trapped himself when he revealed more about the murder than he should have and soon both he and George were charged.

They were tried before Mr Justice Wills at Chester on 20 March and after a fair trial, both were convicted. George was reprieved a few days before the scheduled execution on account of his age, although he was just as guilty, if not more so, than his brother.

Richard Davies was hanged by James Berry, who later wrote that the spectre of the young man frequently came back to haunt him.

1890

April 15th: William Matthew CHADWICK (23)   Liverpool

On the morning of Monday 22 July 1889, Walter Davies, a pawnbroker's assistant at Atherton, near Bolton, was cleaning out the cellar when he heard the shop door open. He came upstairs and saw a man stealing watches from behind the counter.

The two men began to fight and Davies received a fatal knife wound in the neck and fell down the cellar stairs. The assailant then emptied the victim's pockets, stole his watch and chain, and after taking the contents of a display cabinet, he disappeared.

An intensive enquiry eventually produced some of the missing watches, and in October police arrested Chadwick for another offence. Witnesses identified him as the man who was selling the stolen goods. A search of Chadwick's house resulted in further evidence linking him with the murder and he was charged.

He was tried before Mr Justice Matthews at Liverpool Assizes on 22 March 1890, and after a short trial was sentenced to death.

Hanged by James Berry, on a new type of scaffold which was built on a level floor without steps leading up to it. This design became the blueprint for all future scaffolds.

June 10th: Daniel Stewart GORRIE (30)   Wandsworth

On 12 April, Thomas Furlonger, a baker at Neville's Bakery, Brixton, picked up his week's wages. Later that night, he was found beaten to death and robbed of his money. The attacker had used an iron bar which was found lying nearby.

Gorrie was picked up after he was identified as being seen in the vicinity of the murder. When his pockets were emptied he was found to be in possession of more money than he could possibly have earned.

Hanged by Berry.

July 29th: George BOWLING (57)   Wandsworth

A labourer convicted of the murder of his paramour, Elizabeth Nightingale at Mitcham, Surrey. They were both addicted to drink, and it was during a drunken quarrel that he beat her to death with a hammer. He admitted his guilt after the death sentence was passed.

Hanged by Berry.

1890

August 22nd: Felix SPICER (60)   **Knutsford**

Mary Spicer managed a seaside cafe at New Brighton. Her husband, a former sailor and the father of their five children, ran a small guest house they owned. They lived apart at her request but Spicer was continually trying to get his wife to move back in with him. She stubbornly refused because he had made public that they weren't officially married. Finally, on 24 April, he lost patience and decided to kill her.

    He first put the children to bed but returned later and cut the throats of the two youngest. Spicer then went to the cafe where he attempted to do the same to his wife. A fierce struggle ensued and in a desperate attempt to flee, Mary Spicer jumped through the front window and ran off down the street. Spicer did likewise but the sound of breaking glass attracted the attention of a passing policeman.

    Spicer was arrested and charged with the murder of his two children, and the attempted murder of his wife.

    He was convicted at Chester Assizes and sent to Knutsford gaol to await execution. Up to this time it had always been the practice to guard the condemned man with only one prison officer, but as the execution neared Spicer made an attempt to kill his guard and then himself. He was thwarted by the warder who managed to summon help, and henceforth all condemned prisoners had two guards watching over them.

    Hanged by Berry who gave him a drop of five feet two inches.

August 26th: Frederick DAVIES (40)   **Birmingham**

Davies was a gunsmith who lived with his wife at Birmingham. They had an unhappy marriage due in most part to his intemperate habits, and as a result she left him and went to stay with her sister. On 16 May, he called at the house and asked her to come back, and she decided to give him another chance.

    Wary of threats Davies had made to kill his wife, Mrs Davies's sister and husband accompanied them back home. They had only been there a short while when Davies and his wife began to quarrel about his drinking. Without a word, he left the room, returned with a pistol and shot his wife. Mrs Davies rushed into the yard where she collapsed and died. Davies was attempting to reload when he was overpowered by his brother-in-law, who managed to hold him until police arrived.

    Sentenced to death by Mr Justice Hawkins and hanged by James Berry.

August 26th: James HARRISON (30)   Leeds

A labourer from Bowling, near Bradford, convicted of the murder of his wife Hannah, whom he battered to death in May.

    Harrison lived with his wife and the woman who had adopted him as a child. He was an easy going hard working man who was kind to his wife and mother, always giving them money when he received his wages. His wife was quick tempered and would often provoke her husband into violence.

    At 5am on the morning of 12 May, Harrison left his bed and went downstairs to light the fire. He was still enraged by something his wife had done on the previous evening, and after starting the fire he picked up the poker, went back to the bedroom, and battered her to death.

    He immediately confessed and at his trial at West Riding Assizes before Mr Justice Charles on 6 August, he pleaded guilty through extreme provocation. The jury recommended him to mercy but it was ignored and he was hanged by James Billington.

August 27th: Francois MONTEAU (51)   Newgate

Monteau was a Belgian immigrant who worked as a cabinet maker in Marylebone. He was friendly with several Belgians in the area, one of whom was a Francois de Grave. Monteau had been living with his Belgian girlfriend, Marion Du Pond, since her arrival in 1887. They had a happy relationship until the end of May 1890, when she left him and went to stay at the same house as De Grave.

    Monteau became very angry and decided to kill her if she wouldn't return to him. On 28 May, he bought a gun and arranged to meet her in Leicester Square. They talked for a while and then she returned home. Later that day, Monteau called at the house to see her and was told by De Grave that she wasn't home. He asked De Grave to come outside, and when he did so, Monteau shot him dead.

    He was tried before Mr Justice Grantham at the Old Bailey and pleaded that the gun had gone off accidentally after someone had caught his arm. The judge said that an example must be made of people firing guns in public and sentenced him to death.

Hanged by Berry.

September 23rd: Henry DELVIN (45) — Glasgow

A father of seven sentenced to death by Lord Adam at Glasgow Circuit Court on 2 September, for the murder of his wife. In June, he beat her to death with a poker at Benhar near Shotts, while their children looked on.

On the morning of the execution the hangman entered the cell and pinioned the condemned man, then had to wait until the bailie had signed a warrant before the procession formed that led to the scaffold. It was reported that Delvin behaved like an utter coward on the walk to the gallows, and had to be held erect by the warders.

After Berry pulled the lever and the trap fell, the officials were horrified to hear a snorting from the pit; it was obvious that the drop of four feet had failed to break his neck and that he had died from strangulation. This was not made public at the time as it had become standard practice to record that all executions passed off without incident.

December 23rd: Mary Eleanor WHEELER (24) — Newgate

Mary Wheeler had never married but called herself Mrs Pearcey when she had moved in with a man of that name. By 1890, she was living alone at Kentish Town in a furnished flat paid for by one of her admirers. She was, however, in love with another man called Frank Hogg. Mary became full of jealous hatred for Hogg's wife, and decided to kill her.

On 24 October she invited Phoebe Hogg to tea and then attacked her with a poker and knife. When she was dead, Mary turned her attention to Mrs Hogg's baby and strangled it. She put both victims in the pram and covered them with a blanket; then she calmly walked through the busy afternoon traffic before dumping the bodies on nearby wasteland.

After the bodies were discovered, she was soon investigated by the police because Mrs Hogg's sister had mentioned to them that she knew Phoebe had visited her for tea on the previous day. When they visited Wheeler, she played the piano while they unearthed a wealth of clues.

She was tried at the Old Bailey before Mr Justice Denman on 1 December. She would have stood a good chance of being declared insane if she had pleaded guilty, but chose to protest her innocence. The trial was straightforward, and concluded with the judge passing the death sentence.

She was hanged by Berry who recalled that she met her end very bravely. Shortly afterwards Frank Hogg sold some furniture and other objects to Madame Tussauds to accompany the new model of Wheeler, which proved a popular attraction for many years.

She was not the first in her family to wear the rope - her father Thomas had been executed ten years earlier, see **1880, November 29th**

December 30th: Thomas McDONALD (32)   Liverpool

On the morning of Saturday 15 November, a young schoolboy discovered the body of his teacher Miss Elizabeth Ann Holt, lying in a field at Belmont, near Bolton. The police ascertained that she had been kicked and stabbed to death, and although her clothes had been ripped there was no sign of rape.

Police learned that she had been missing for a week. As she spent weekends with her family at home, and weekdays staying with the headmaster at the school, both thought she was with the other. The head assumed she was off sick and the family had no idea she had failed to reach her destination.

Witnesses revealed that shortly before she had vanished, she was seen walking along a path a few hundred yards ahead of Thomas McDonald, a man well known to the police as a local villain, and until recently a suspect in a mysterious death. He had a long criminal record, which included rape and police called on him to ask for a statement. He admitted being in the area but claimed that he had passed the spot where the body was found and gone to work at a nearby pit. A quick check with the mine owner proved he was lying and he was taken into custody.

McDonald was tried at Liverpool Assizes by Mr Justice Cave on 13

December, and convicted after the prosecution put forward a strong case. Shortly before he was hanged by Berry, he was reported to have confessed to a relative that he had killed the girl.

December 30th: Robert KITCHING (34) — York

On 19 September, Kitching, a gardener from Bedale, near York, was reprimanded by a PC Weedey for leaving his conveyance parked outside the Leeming Bar Hotel. Kitching told the officer to mind his own business and threatened to blow his brains out. Next morning, the officer was found shot dead and evidence led police to Kitching. In his defence, he claimed that the gun had gone off accidentally but he was convicted of murder.
Hanged by Billington.

1891

Cases where no executioner is recorded are multiple executions, and readers are asked to refer to the entries before or after for details of the hangman.

January 11th: Frederick Thomas STOREY (54)   Greenock

A circus manager found guilty at Glasgow for the murder of Lizzie Pastor, a fellow worker at Cooke's Circus in Greenock, whom he stabbed to death in Argyle Street, Greenock, on 14 November 1890. He killed her through jealousy when she refused his offers of romance.
       Hanged by Berry. It was the last execution at Nelson Street Prison before it was demolished.

February 2nd: Bartholomew SULLIVAN (35)   Tralee

Convicted at Munster Assizes before Mr Justice O'Brien, of the murder of Patrick Fishive, a farmer from Ballyheige, Co Kerry. He was found dead in a field on 30 August 1886.
       It was alleged that the farmer was attempting to harvest some crops in a field he had been evicted from, despite threats that he would regret it if he did.
       Eventually, investigations led police to charge Sullivan, who strongly protested his innocence.
       Hanged by Berry.

March 13th: John PURCELL (40)   Dublin

A blacksmith convicted of the murder of Bridget Smith (60), who was found battered to death in her home at Naul, Co Dublin, on 21 November 1890.
       Hanged by Berry.

May 19th: Alfred William TURNER (20)   Manchester

On Sunday 29 March, Turner, an Oldham labourer, called at the lodgings of his sweetheart, Mary Ellen Moran (18), and suggested that they go for a walk. When they reached a secluded woodland, he accused her of going out with another man. She vigorously denied the accusation but Turner withdrew a knife and stabbed her in the throat.
       He later went to the local police and reported how he and the girl had been attacked by two men and after knocking him unconscious, they had murdered her. Detectives asked him to show them where the incident had occurred and together they rushed to the spot.

Arriving at the scene, Turner was horrified to find that Mary was still alive. When an officer asked who had attacked her, she weakly pointed at Turner, who then fled. He was quickly detained and charged with murder after she died the following day.

Hanged by Berry.

July 21st: Franz Joseph MUNCH (31)   **Wandsworth**

Munch was born in Germany but when he was ordered to sign on as a conscript in the army, he emigrated and settled in London. He found work as a foreman baker for a Mrs Bridget Kenrath at Bermondsey, and was much enamoured with his employer, although a rival for her affections existed in the shape of one James Hickey, an Irishman who had come to the bakery from Manchester.

On 22 April, Munch went out for the evening and after becoming rather drunk, he lay in wait for Hickey, eventually shooting him dead in a dark alley.

After he was sentenced to death, Munch appealed for a reprieve on account of extreme provocation. He also contacted the German Embassy to act on his behalf but when they learned why he had left his native country, they refused to have anything to do with him.

Hanged by Berry.

July 28th: Arthur SPENCER (22)   **Lincoln**

Spencer was a native of Retford, Nottinghamshire, who came to Lincoln to apprentice as a pork butcher. He fell in love with Mary Ann Gardner (32), a widow to whom he proposed marriage. For some reason she refused and when he threatened to shoot her if she didn't change her mind, she just laughed.

On 31 March, he called at her house and after she told him she hadn't changed her mind and still had no intention of marrying him, he shot her twice in the chest. He then turned the gun on himself and fired two shots. The first, at his chest, caused nothing more harmful than a flesh wound so he put the gun into his mouth and fired again. Amazingly, the bullet passed straight through his head, exiting at the back of his neck without causing any serious damage!

He pleaded guilty at Lincoln Assizes before Mr Justice Vaughan

Williams, and while in the condemned cell, he put on over two stones in 'grief fat'.

Hanged by Berry.

August 18th: Walter Lewis TURNER (32)   Leeds

On 6 June, Barbara Waterhouse (6) disappeared while playing outside her house at Horsforth, Leeds. Despite a frantic search of the area, police could find no sign of her. Four days later her mutilated body was discovered in a tin trunk left outside Horsforth Town Hall. The body had been wrapped in a shawl and had its throat cut.

On 12 June, a Mrs Turner was questioned after the shawl had been traced to her and she confessed to helping her son dispose of the body. He denied murdering the child and claimed that a quarryman called Jack had asked him to dispose of the trunk. He wasn't believed, and both he and his mother were charged with murder.

They were tried at Leeds Assizes with the conclusion that Turner was sentenced to death, his mother to life imprisonment.

Hanged by James Billington.

August 18th: Thomas SADLER   Chelmsford

A labourer convicted at Essex Summer Assizes for the murder of William Wass at Colchester.

Sadler persuaded Mrs Wass to leave her husband and move in with him. During a dispute over the custody of her children, Sadler stabbed Wass behind the ear with a penknife, killing him instantly.

He remained very calm after sentencing until his last interview with his father and sister, after which he became exceedingly distressed. He was hanged by James Berry on a permanent gallows erected inside Springfield Gaol.

1891

August 19th: Robert BRADSHAW (56)   Wandsworth

In the spring of 1891, Bradshaw's wife took out a summons against her husband after he repeatedly threatened her. Bradshaw, a man of intemperate habits, told her that he would kill her if she didn't withdraw the summons. When she told him she had no intention of doing so, Bradshaw enticed her into his room and cut her throat so severely that he almost cut her head off.

Hanged by Berry.

August 20th: John CONWAY (62)   Liverpool

Aka Owen Gilbin, a marine fireman convicted of the murder of Nicholas Martin (9). On 16 May, the boy's mutilated body was found floating inside a sailor's kitbag in Liverpool docks. The bag also contained a knife and a saw which police proved to be the murder weapons. The bag was traced to Conway, and witnesses came forward to say they had seen him and the boy together shortly before the body was found. Conway later confessed to the crime which he blamed on drink.

He was hanged by Berry, who had a disagreement with the prison doctor over the proposed length of the drop. Berry had his way, and gave Conway a fairly long drop, only to be horrified when the head was almost torn off by the force.

August 25th: Edward Henry FAWCETT   Winchester

Aka Watts. Fawcett and his wife lived at Greenwich with their only child. They had been married sixteen years but had lately become unhappy. After a quarrel, she left home and took the child to live at Portsea.

On 4 April, he also went to Portsea. After failing to persuade to return, he shot her four times with a revolver.

Sentenced to death at Winchester Assizes, he was the last man hanged by James Berry, who resigned following the upsetting experience at Liverpool the previous week involving **CONWAY** [above].

1891

December 15th: Henry DAINTON (34)   Shepton Mallet

A stonemason from Bath convicted of the murder of his wife, who was found drowned in the River Avon on 8 September.

Witnesses claimed they had heard a woman screaming 'Don't Harry!' shortly before the body was found. When she was identified, the police visited Henry Dainton at his home and found a bundle of saturated clothes and a pair of muddy boots. He was arrested immediately, and the police were lucky to get him to the station alive as he was almost lynched by an angry mob that had formed outside the front door. He claimed he was innocent and that his wife had frequently told him she intended to drown herself in the river.

Hanged by James Billington, now promoted to the number one hangman following Berry's resignation.

December 22nd: John William JOHNSON (49)   Durham

A farm labourer from Hetton-le-Hole, Durham who had been living with a Mary Addison for sometime. In September she told him of her intention to marry someone else. After she left, he followed her and shot her dead.

He refused any form of legal aid and insisted on pleading guilty.

Hanged by James Billington.

December 23rd: Charles SAUNDERS (31)   Hereford

A blacksmith sentenced to death at Hereford Assizes for the murder of a young child.

Saunders persuaded the parents of Walter Charles Steers (2), to let him look after the boy while they stayed in London. During May, Saunders and his girlfriend 'tramped' to Leominster, using the child to help them beg for food and money but Walter soon became a burden.

They took shelter in a disused cottage, and one night Walter's crying kept Saunders awake so he picked the child up and bashed its head on the floor. He buried the body under a pile of straw where it lay undiscovered for sixteen weeks.

He was convicted on the testimony of his girlfriend and hanged by James Billington. The execution had to be put back a while as the hangman's journey from Durham was delayed by thick fog.

Billington didn't arrive until after 9am and after a quick check of the equipment, he started the execution. It was noted that after the drop fell the body swung from side to side and the arms seemed to twitch for several seconds.

1892

Cases where no executioner is recorded are multiple executions, and readers are asked to refer to the entries before or after for details of the hangman.

1892

January 5th: James STOCKWELL (26) — Leeds

On the afternoon of 21 August, Mrs Brooke, the landlady of the 'Ivy Bridge' public house at Milne Bridge, near Huddersfield, went into town. She left the bar in the hands of her waitress, Catherine 'Kate' Dennis, a sixteen year old Irish girl.

The only customer at the time was Stockwell who was sitting in the kitchen eating a pie with a sharp knife. At 3pm, another customer, John Iredale, entered and stayed for fifteen minutes, thinking he was the only person apart from the girl in the building. As he left, he passed two men and saw them enter the pub.

An hour later, a butcher's boy called on an errand but was unable to gain entry. Alarmed at this, he called on a neighbour and between them they forced entry and found Kate dead on the floor. She had been stabbed in the neck.

On hearing about the murder, John Iredale quickly contacted the police and told them about the two men he had seen enter the pub. They were soon picked up and although one of them was carrying a knife, they were able to satisfy detectives of their innocence. When Mrs Brooks returned she told the police about James Stockwell being in the kitchen; when police went to interview him, he had vanished.

Stockwell was at liberty for several days, hiding on the moors until he eventually tired of running and surrendered. At his trial at Leeds Assizes he claimed that the girl had pulled his hair as he lay asleep on a bench and in a rage he had picked up the knife and stabbed her.

Hanged by James Billington.

January 12th: James HEANEY — Mullingar

Convicted of the brutal murder of his wife at Longford. Heaney cut her to pieces with a scythe while in a rage. He claimed that he had been provoked into the assault after she struck him with a spade.

Hanged by Thomas Scott, who was officiating at his first execution.

March 1st: James MUIR   Newgate

A shoemaker from Whitechapel, Muir had split up from his paramour, Abigail Sullivan after a drunken row. He went to live with another woman but Sullivan still pestered him for money and took to calling on him at work. Muir told her that if she came to the works again, he would stab her, and later told a friend: 'Something will happen tonight and if anyone tries to interfere they will be served the same.'

After work, he called at her house and was told to leave. He refused and stabbed her fatally in the breast.

Hanged by James Billington.

March 17th: Charles RAYNOR   Oxford
Frederick EGGLESTON

On 12 December 1891, the two men, together with a third man, Charles Smith, were poaching in a wood at Bilstone, near Aylesbury. The three were set upon by gamekeeper Joseph Crawley and watchman William Puddipant, and in the ensuing brawl, both men were beaten to death.

Blood was found on their clothing and their guns were found in the wood. They were tried at Buckinghamshire Assizes before Mr Justice Lawrence. Smith received twenty years for manslaughter, and the other two were sentenced to death.

James Billington gave Eggleston a drop of six feet nine inches, and Raynor seven feet.

March 22nd: Joseph WILSON (24)   Carlisle

Wilson was a quarryman who lodged with Mrs Maria Crossman at Millom, near Barrow. On New Year's Day, they had a quarrel after he complained about his breakfast, and in a rage he took down her husband's gun and shot her dead.

Hanged by James Billington.

March 29th: John NOBLE (46) — Newgate

A chimney sweep convicted of the murder of Mrs Mary Elizabeth Swift at Chelsea on 4 February. They had lived together for four years after she had split up from her husband. When she announced to a drunken Noble that she was leaving him as well, he cut her throat in a jealous rage. She ran from their house and made it as far as the local pub where she collapsed and died.
    Hanged by James Billington.

April 4th: James CAMPBELL — Tullamore

Convicted after a second trial of the murder of Mary Kate Keenan (6), who was assaulted and strangled in Co Clare on 19 December 1891.
    Hanged by Thomas Scott.

April 19th: Daniel HANDLEY — Wexford

Convicted, along with his younger brother James (15), of the murder of an aged widow, Mary Ann Lyons, who was found battered to death at home in Bandarren, County Wicklow in 1890.
    James Handley was reprieved because of his age and was sent to Mountjoy Prison.
    Daniel Handley was hanged by Thomas Scott.

April 26th: George Henry WOOD (29) — Lewes

One morning in December 1891, the body of a young girl, Edith Jeal (5), was found partially naked in a shed at Brighton. She had been raped and strangled. Suspicion fell on Wood, a railway porter who was known to have been drunk on the night before the murder, and had a record for accosting young children in the street.
    He was convicted on strong circumstantial evidence and sentenced to death. A petition for a reprieve on the grounds of insanity was refused and he was hanged by Billington.

1892

June 14th: Henry PICKERING (29)   Leeds

Pickering was a mechanic by trade but after getting married in January, he had been unable to find work. As a result, he and his wife had to live with his parents at Holbeck, near Leeds.

On 23 April, the younger Pickering and his wife had a quarrel, and she retired upstairs to their room. He followed, then cut her head off with a carving knife.

He gave himself up and said he wanted to be hanged. James Billington saw that he got his wish.

July 26th: John GURD (29)   Devizes

Gurd was engaged to Miss Florence Adams and was looking forward to getting married. They had sorted out most of the arrangements and had the banns read out in the local church. On 19 April, Florence told him she wanted to call the wedding off but could give him no satisfactory explanation. Gurd suspected that her uncle Henry Richards was behind the break up and decided to confront him. During the ensuing argument he shot Richards then fled.

The local police started a manhunt for the missing gunman, and on 2 June he was accosted by two officers, Superintendent Perret and Sergeant Moulden. In a desperate attempt to avoid capture, he fired two shots at the pursuing officers, hitting Sergeant Moulden, who later died from his injuries in hospital.

Gurd was finally arrested, and after his trial at Wiltshire Assizes, he was sentenced to death. He was hanged by Billington.

At the inquest held after the execution, it was claimed that the drop had failed to break his neck which had very strong muscles.

August 16th: John George WENZEL (25)   Newgate

A German butcher convicted at the Old Bailey for the murder of a Detective Joyce on 27 July, and also of the attempted murder of two gentlemen, Henry Selzer and Frederick Reuman.

Wenzel was involved in a robbery at Dalston; when Joyce, Selzer and Reuman tried to arrest him, he opened fire and the police officer was killed.

He pleaded that the charge should be manslaughter as he hadn't intended to kill Joyce, and also that the gun had gone off accidentally.

1892

August 16th: James TAYLOR (60) Newgate

An army pensioner convicted of the murder of his wife at Westminster on 14 June. Both were addicted to drink, and he beat her to death with a mangle roller while drunk.

Sentenced to death by Baron Pollock at the Old Bailey on 28 July, and hanged alongside **WENZEL** [above] by Billington & Scott.

August 17th: Patrick GIBBONS (33) Liverpool

Sentenced to death by Mr Justice Denman at Liverpool Assizes for the murder of his mother.

Gibbons lived with his parents at Royton, near Oldham. On Saturday 9 July, he returned home drunk, entered her bedroom and cut her throat as she slept. It was alleged that they had had a quarrel earlier but Gibbons denied this and said he couldn't recall anything about the day of the crime.

He was hanged by James Billington at Walton Prison which had recently taken over as the sole execution prison in Liverpool.

August 18th: Moses CUDWORTH (40) Leeds

On 4 June, Cudworth, a weaver from Earby, took his wife and child for a walk up a quiet country lane near his home at Skipton. He later returned with the child and when friends asked the whereabouts of his wife, he confessed that he had battered her to death with a large stone. Cudworth said he was drunk at the time and that he didn't regret his actions.

Hanged by James Billington.

October 11th: John James BANBURY (22) Wandsworth

Convicted of the murder of Annie Emma Oakley at Walworth in June. He frequently called on her, and during one such visit he shot her dead in a jealous rage.

At his trial, the jury was out for four hours before returning with a guilty verdict. They added a strong recommendation for mercy on account of his age, but later it became known that two members of the jury were hard of hearing and had to have some of the evidence repeated to them while the verdict was discussed. The judge ordered a retrial, but the new jury came to the same conclusion as the first, and Banbury was hanged by James Billington.

November 15th: Thomas CREAM (42)   Newgate

In 1881, Cream, a Glasgow born medicine graduate, was sentenced to life imprisonment in Chicago for murder. He had poisoned his mistress' husband with strychnine. Dr Cream had convicted himself when he contacted the District Attorney's office and advised them to have the body exhumed.

After serving ten years, he was released and returned to Britain where he settled in Lambeth, south London. During the winter of 1891 four prostitutes - Ellen Donworth, Matilda Clover, Emma Shrivell and Alice Marsh, died as a result of strychnine poisoning. Dr Cream had persuaded the women to take his 'tonics' with promises that they would cure a variety of ailments from acne to migraine.

As he had done in Chicago, Cream incriminated himself by contacting the police. He offered to reveal the identity of the Lambeth Poisoner in exchange for a large sum of money. In June he was arrested and charged.

A prostitute came forward to say how he had tried to get her to swallow a tablet but she managed to spit it out without him noticing, and a chemist testified that he had sold him the poison.

Cream was hanged by Billington and claimed on the scaffold: 'I am Jack the ...' He died before he could finish the sentence. Although the hangman was convinced he was telling the truth, the fact that he was safely locked away in Chicago's Joliet State Penitentiary while the Ripper was at large, dismisses him from the list of suspects.

December 20th: James MELLOR (33)   Manchester

On 17 October, the body of Mary Jane Mellor was discovered buried beneath the staircase at her home in Oldham. She had last been seen alive on 3 September and since that time her husband had behaved as normal.

A search had failed to reveal her whereabouts and she was treated as a missing person until the police were told that Mellor may be hiding something. Detectives ordered a thorough search of his house and found her body: she had been stabbed to death and her throat had been ripped from ear to ear.

Mellor, a factory worker, was tried at Manchester Assizes and convicted of her murder.

Hanged by James Billington.

December 22nd: Thomas EDWARDS (30)   Usk

Convicted of the murder of Mary Connely, a down and out, at Abergavenny on 16 September. He cut her throat with a razor after accusing her of stealing from him, and then confessed to the police.

He was sentenced to death by Mr Justice Day at Monmouth Assizes. It was revealed at his trial that he had a pathological hatred of tramps ever since one of them murdered an old army colleague at Birmingham, and he had sworn to avenge the death.

Hanged by James Billington.

1893

Cases where no executioner is recorded are multiple executions, and readers are asked to refer to the entries before or after for details of the hangman.

1893

January 3rd: Cross DUCKWORTH (32)   Liverpool

On 8 November 1892, the body of Alice Barnes was found suffocated at Witton Park, Blackburn. From the position of her clothing, it looked as if she had been the victim of a sexual attack, although police could not be certain whether any assault had taken place.

They had an immediate suspect in Cross Duckworth and he reinforced their suspicions by greeting them with the question 'Have you come to see me about the murder?' A search of his house uncovered a pair of muddy boots that matched prints found at the scene and also a handkerchief similar to the one used to gag the victim. His alibi for the time of the murder was weak and he was charged.

Duckworth was convicted at Liverpool Assizes on 12 December and the jury took less than an hour to find him guilty.

Hanged by James Billington.

January 6th: John BOYLE   Londonderry

On 2 November 1892, Boyle killed his wife by beating her about the head until she fell unconscious. He then broke her spine by repeatedly bashing her against the walls of their cabin at Aughnacloy, Co Tyrone. Boyle then danced on her body as she lay dead on the floor.

Hanged by Scott, who was pelted with rotting vegetables as he was driven to the gaol in a cab.

January 10th: Andrew George McCRAE (36)   Northampton

On 6 August 1892, the dismembered body of a woman was discovered inside a sack beside the Northampton to Rugby road. The sack was traced to a Northampton butcher, Edward McCrae, who told police that he and his brother often sold bags to the public. The police requested that McCrae tell his brother to call at the station to clear himself.

The police had no further leads and on 29 August the coroner recorded an open verdict. Police received information that a man named McCrae had sold a bundle of women's clothing. When they learned that Edward McCrae's brother Andrew had failed to report to the station as requested, they decided to track him down.

It was learned that Andrew McCrae had a wife and family in Birmingham but had moved to Northampton to work with his brother.

Police also discovered that he had had an affair with a young woman called Annie Pritchard. It was thought that she had sailed to New York with a man named Anderson after she had become pregnant. Police decided that Anderson and McCrae were the same person, and concluded that he had killed his lover when she became pregnant, probably to rid himself of the financial burden. A search of McCrae's property produced the calcined remains of human bone and other parts of the body.

McCrae was tried at Northampton Assizes on 20 December. He strongly protested his innocence but the case against him was strong and the jury took only a short time to return a guilty verdict.

Hanged by James Billington.

January 18th: William McKEOWN   **Glasgow**

In October 1892, McKeown, a gardener, had been left in charge of his employer's house on Maxwell Drive, Pollokshields, Glasgow. He was joined by a sailor, Thomas McNeilly, and during the afternoon they were visited by Elizabeth Connor.

When Connor was later reported missing, enquiries were made and it was discovered that she had been seen in the vicinity of the house. The police searched the garden where they found the stabbed and mutilated body buried.

McKeown had fled the scene and when he was later arrested at Cardonald, he had made an attempt to cut his own throat. McNeilly was also found but he had an alibi for the time of the crime and was discharged.

McKeown was tried at Glasgow Circuit Court on 28 December before Lord Adam. He pleaded guilty to culpable homicide in an attempt to escape the gallows but the jury convicted him of murder.

He was hanged by James Billington.

March 16th: Albert MANNING (37)   **Gloucester**

In 1873, Manning took up lodgings with a Mrs and Mrs Flew at Kingswood, near Bristol. He became very friendly with his landlady, so much so that her husband left home and emigrated, leaving them to carry on with their relationship.

Ten years later, Manning returned to his native south Wales and married his long time sweetheart but he soon left his wife at home and returned to Mrs Flew. By 1890, he was very jealous of another man who vied with him for her attention.

On 28 September he left work and called at her shop, which he had helped her to purchase. Soon after he entered, a passer-by heard a shot, and moments later Manning ran from the shop as Mrs Flew staggered outside and collapsed. Manning returned to the shop and hid upstairs but was discovered, arrested and charged with murder.

He refused to plead at his trial at Gloucester; he was found guilty, and hanged by Billington and Thomas Scott.

March 28th: William WILLIAMS (19) — Exeter

Williams had been regularly courting Emma Holmes Dodge (17), until she suddenly called off their relationship after finding someone else.

On 13 November 1892, Emma attended church at Tavistock and witnesses overheard Williams threaten her as she walked home with her new boyfriend, William Rowe (21). He followed them along the road and shot both dead, but as he reloaded with the intention of shooting himself, he was disarmed.

Sentenced to death at Devon Assizes by Mr Justice Denman and hanged by James Billington and Thomas Scott.

April 4th: Edward HEMMINGS (26) — Leeds

A collier from Normanton, convicted of the murder of his wife at Handsworth, near Sheffield, on 16 February. They had married in September but he soon became very jealous of her talking to any other men.

They moved to new lodgings and immediately he was jealous when she became very friendly with several of the lodgers at the house. In a rage, he killed her as she slept, attacking her with an axe and then cutting her throat. He fled from the house and discarded the axe which police later found under a railway arch.

He was arrested at Normanton, and after conviction he left a full confession. Hanged by James Billington.

1893

July 10th: Edward LEIGH — Dublin

A young man sentenced to death on 9 June, for the murder of an old woman, Bridget Knight, on 28 February. The victim was found stabbed to death at her home on the outskirts of Dublin.

Hanged by Thomas Scott despite the jury's recommendation for mercy on account of Leigh's youth.

July 18th: Richard SABEY (45) — Northampton

Sabey, an ex-sailor, lived happily with Louisa Johnson at Burton Latimer, near Northampton. His wife, a half-caste, whom he had met and married in India suddenly made an appearance. This upset Louisa and she put an affiliation order out on Sabey before moving with their offspring to Liverpool. Sabey followed, enticed her from her home, then cut her throat in the street.

He was indicted at Nottingham Assizes on 29 June and admitted that he had killed her because of the affiliation order she took out on him.

Sabey was sentenced to death. There was a petition for a reprieve on account of his epilepsy, but he was hanged by James Billington.

July 19th: Amie Holman MEUNIER (25) — Worcester

A German immigrant sentenced to death by Baron Pollock at Worcester Assizes on 28 June, for the murder of Charlotte Pearcey (71).

Mrs Pearcey and her husband lived in a cottage near Bromsgrove and kept a shop. Meunier had fallen on hard times and on 13 January entered the shop with the intention of stealing something. It would seem that the old lady caught him and as a result Meunier pulled out an axe and hacked her to death.

He was identified by a witness as the murderer but when police went to arrest him he had fled the country. He was traced to Belgium where he was detained and extradited to face a murder charge.

He attempted suicide in the condemned cell before he was hanged by James Billington.

1893

July 25th: George Samuel COOK (27)   Newgate

On 7 June, a warder at Wormwood Scrubs gaol saw a policeman and a young girl walking together across the common adjacent to the prison. Early next morning a shepherd crossing the common stumbled across a female body. She had been battered to death and was covered in blood, though there was no sign of any sexual assault.

Police identified the victim as Maud Smith, and when the gaol warder offered his information, detectives interviewed a PC Cook whose beat took him past the prison. He denied knowing Smith but they soon discovered he had been having an affair with her. A search of his lodgings unearthed a bloody uniform, and in the garden a bloodstained truncheon.

Despite his infidelity his fiancee made strenuous efforts for a reprieve but it was to no avail and he was hanged by James Billington.

August 10th: Charles SQUIRES (28)   Shepton Mallet

Sentenced to death at Wells Assizes for the murder of his wife's two year old illegitimate child. The child had woken him up by crying during the night and in a temper he suffocated it.

Squires asked his wife if she would say that the death had been an accident but she refused. He was hanged by James Billington.

August 15th: John Thomas HEWITT (19)   Stafford

Convicted of the murder of William Masfen, a gentleman farmer from Cannock, who was shot dead after catching Hewitt poaching on his land. Hewitt pleaded that the shooting was an accident, and that the gun had gone off during a struggle. Evidence was shown in court that the shot had been fired from a distance and there was no way that the wound could have been inflicted at close range.

Hanged by Thomas Scott, of Huddersfield, who was officiating as number one at his first execution in England.

1893

August 16th: John DAVIS (34) **Chelmsford**

On the afternoon of Sunday 15 April, a courting couple came across the body of Police Sergeant Adam John Eves lying in a ditch at Purleigh, Essex. He had been battered about the head and his throat had been cut from ear to ear. It appeared he had been taken unawares as his truncheon hadn't been drawn and his lamp was switched off. Beside the body was a number of broken sticks and several sacks of corn.

Next day, four poachers were arrested on suspicion. They had been under investigation after some corn had been stolen. When the men were examined, two of them had bloodstains on their clothes which they claimed were from an animal.

All four stood trial at Essex Assizes at the beginning of August before Mr Justice Matthew. The jury took less than half an hour to find Davis and his younger brother Richard guilty; the other two not guilty. John Davis made a full confession while awaiting execution which partially exonerated his brother who was granted an eleventh hour reprieve.

Hanged by James Billington and William Warbrick.

September 2nd: James REILLY **Dublin**

A labourer convicted of the murder of Bernard Cox, an insurance agent, who was waylaid on a quiet road in May. Reilly robbed and beat him to death with an iron bar.

Hanged by Thomas Scott.

November 28th: Emanuel HAMER (33) **Manchester**

Hamer was one of a gang of painters working on a small row of terrace houses in Salford, one of which was occupied by a Mrs Tyrer (74). For several days she had supplied the men with hot water for their tea break but had made it clear she didn't like Hamer because she thought he was crude and rough spoken.

At 6pm on 28 October, Mrs Tyrer's next door neighbour, a Mr Denson, heard a bang which he thought may have been a fall, and rushed to her front door to see if he could be of any help. Unable to open the door, he hurried around the back and found Hamer in the yard, who attempted to run away. Denson managed to detain him while another neighbour contacted the police. Mrs Tyrer was found lying in a pool of blood inside the house, and later died in hospital from massive head injuries.

Hamer was convicted at Manchester Assizes on 10 December before Mr Justice Grantham. No motive was ever clearly established although police suspected that he had gone to the house to commit robbery and was surprised by the victim, whom he then pushed down the stairs.

Hanged by James Billington.

December 5th: John CARTER (43) Reading

An agricultural labourer convicted at Berkshire Assizes for the murder of his third wife.

On 20 June, their son heard banging coming from his parents' bedroom at Bronledge Farm, Watchfield, near Faringdon. The next morning, Carter forbade his son to enter the bedroom, and the boy later noticed that something had been burnt in the grate.

Carter told his son and neighbours that his wife had gone to stay with relatives but eventually suspicions were aroused and the house was visited by detectives. A thorough search unearthed the body of Mrs Carter beneath the washroom floor. She had been beaten to death, burned and then buried.

He left a note confessing to the murder of his second wife whose body was also buried at the house. He also wrote that he wanted her remains to be given a decent burial and described where she could be found. A female skeleton was later unearthed.

He was hanged by James Billington.

December 6th: George MASON (19) Winchester

Aka George Beckworth. Mason was a former costermonger who had enlisted in the 3rd Battalion of the East Surrey Regiment, stationed at Portsdown Hill.

On 26 June, he was confined to barracks after being reported by Sergeant James Robinson. The next day while taking part in rifle practise, Mason pointed the gun at Robinson and shouted: 'Now I am level with you,' and shot him in the chest.

His defence at Winchester Assizes was based on hereditary insanity but he was convicted of murder and hanged by James Billington.

December 19th: Henry RUMBOLD   Lincoln

A skipper convicted of the murder of his sweetheart, a Miss Rushby. Rumbold returned home from sea unexpected and found she had been unfaithful. On 7 November, he met her in the street and together they walked back to her lodgings, where after a row he shot her three times.
    Hanged by James Billington & William Warbrick.

December 21st: Frederick WYNDHAM (45)   Gloucester

A butcher sentenced to death by Mr Justice Cave for the murder of his father, James (72), at Oakridge on 19 October.
    They were taking part in some shooting on his father's farmland. During a quarrel he accused his father of ill treating his sister and shot him dead.
    Hanged by James Billington and Thomas Scott.

1894

Cases where no executioner is recorded are multiple executions, and readers are asked to refer to the entries before or after for details of the hangman.

1894

January 2nd: William HARRIS   **Warwick**

Aka William Haynes. Florence Clifford (17), Harris's girlfriend, lodged with him and his mother at Ashtown. She became upset at his ill treatment and told her mother, who advised her to come home.

On 20 September, Florence and her mother went to the lodgings to collect her things. Mrs Clifford waited outside as her daughter entered, and soon after she saw the shadow of a man swinging an axe. She rushed inside and saw Harris leaning over her daughter, and as she entered the room Harris stood up and chased her out into the street. He then disappeared, but later gave himself up.

After he had been sentenced to death on 13 December, he turned to the packed courtroom and declared: 'I wish I could have got her mother as well. I would have chopped her into mincemeat and made sausages of her, and then I should have been satisfied.'

Hanged by James Billington.

February 13th: George THOMAS (25)   **Carmarthen**

Thomas, a young army reservist, had been courting Mary Jane Jones (15) for several weeks. In the autumn she tired of his affections and began to avoid him.

On Sunday 19 November, while out walking, he tried to force his advances on her but she pushed him away, and in a rage he cut her throat. He confessed to police immediately and took them to the body, claiming he had planned the crime.

Hanged by James Billington.

March 27th: Walter SMITH (32)   **Nottingham**

Convicted at Notts Assizes for the murder of Catherine Cross (25), a nurse from Liverpool. Cross had recently become engaged in her native Liverpool and had come to Nottingham to visit her mother. While she was in the city, she became friendly with Smith who invited her to his lace factory after they discussed a new machine he had invented.

While they were at the deserted factory, Smith pulled out a gun and shot her in the chest. In a panic, he fired two more shots into her and then left her for dead. When the crime was discovered, Cross was still alive and before she passed away she managed to tell the police that she thought the first shot was an accident but the other two deliberate.

Smith maintained that he had panicked after the first shot, but the fact that he had fired again destroyed his defence that her death was accidental. After a three day trial, he was sentenced to death by Mr Justice Hawkins.

Hanged by James Billington.

April 2nd: Margaret WALBER (53)   **Liverpool**

Mrs Walber and her second husband had been married for five years and ran a small shop together, but had lately become unhappy because of his drinking.

In May 1893, she found that he had been seeing an old girlfriend and in a rage, she locked him in their flat and threatened to poison him if he tried to escape.

On 16 November, a great disturbance was heard in the flat, and later James Walber was found beaten to death. Mrs Walber blamed her son for the crime, claiming that he had beaten him with a heavy chain.

She was convicted by Mr Justice Day at Liverpool Assizes and hanged by Billington and his assistant Thompson.

April 3rd: Philip GARNER (49)   **Leeds**

Garner was a former army officer who had met and married his wife while serving in Belfast. They had returned to England and settled in his native Doncaster, and for a while they got on well.

They went for a walk together but he returned alone. She was later found battered to death and he was charged with murder.

Hanged by James Billington.

April 4th: Frederick William FENTON (32)   **Birmingham**

Fenton was a silversmith at Birmingham, and had become engaged to Florence Elbrough, a barmaid. To impress her, he exaggerated about his financial status, and as a result she kept on at him to buy some new furniture for their house.

She eventually challenged him as to why he was so reluctant to spend any money and during a quarrel, he shot her dead and then turned the gun on himself, but failed in his suicide attempt.

Hanged by James Billington.

May 22nd: John LANGFORD   Liverpool

Langford was a foreman baker who co-habited with Elizabeth Stevens, a woman with a young family who had separated from her husband. They had been together for three years but he was very jealous of her and suspected she was having an affair.

One day in September he found her drinking in public with another man and confronted her. They had a quarrel and she slapped him across the face before storming off. He followed her and, during a struggle, stabbed her to death with a clasp knife.

Hanged by James Billington.

July 18th: Samuel ELKINS   Winchester

Pleaded guilty at Hampshire Assizes for the murder of William Mitchel, a tramyard manager at Bournemouth. Mitchell had reported Elkins for a breach of duty, and in a rage Elkins had bought a gun and shot him dead.

Hanged by James Billington on a scaffold constructed in a shed that normally housed the prison van.

July 31st: William CROSSLEY (42)   Manchester

Aka William Sellers. Crossley was a labourer in an iron foundry and lived in a large cottage at Burnley with Mary Ann Allen (56), and five other people. In September 1893, Mrs Allen's daughter came to live with them, and from then on Crossley became irritated.

On 11 June, he and Mrs Allen had a disagreement and he was told to find fresh lodgings and that his dinner that night would be his last in the house. Later that afternoon, he was seen going down into the cellar and returning with something hidden inside his coat. He sat down for dinner in the evening, and when Mrs Allen went into the kitchen he followed and struck her with an axe. One tenant tried to disarm him while another called for the police.

He was condemned to death by Mr Justice Bruce at Manchester Assizes on 12 June, and after leaving a full confession he was hanged by Billington.

August 14th: Paul KOEZULA (24) — Newgate

A German immigrant convicted, along with another German called Schmerfedlt, of strangling a lodging house keeper, Mrs Rasch, in Shaftesbury Avenue.

Schmerfedlt was sentenced to death but reprieved; Koezula pleaded his innocence as he was led to the gallows. Hanged by Billington and Thompson.

August 17th: John GILMOUR (22) — Belfast

Convicted of the murder of Lyle Gardner (73), a farmer at Ballyhavistock, in April.

Gilmour had seduced the old man's daughter, and fearing legal proceedings he deliberately went out one night and shot Gardner through a window.

Hanged by Scott.

August 21st: Alfred DEWS (28) — Leeds

An iron moulder from Wakefield, sentenced to death at Leeds Assizes for the murder of his infant son. Dews poisoned the child after a jealous quarrel with his wife when he became convinced he wasn't the child's father.

He claimed he was innocent to the last and left a will telling his wife how to dispose of his property.

Hanged by James Billington.

November 27th: James Wilshaw WHITEHEAD — Manchester

Whitehead was a young married man from Oldham, employed in the cotton industry.

During the summer of 1894, his marriage collapsed, and in spite of his repeated pleas to her to try and save it, his wife left him.

On 20 August, they met up in the street and he made another desperate plea for her to come home. When she refused, he withdrew a razor and cut her throat, then turned the weapon on himself.

He was hanged by Billington, who gave him a long drop, the force of which re-opened the neck wound and sprayed the walls of the pit with blood.

November 29th: Thomas RICHARDS   **Carmarthen**

On 21 September, Richards broke into the house of his sister-in-law, Mary Davis, at Borth. After smothering her with a pillow he stole a pony, some money, and her wedding ring.

He was suspected at once but despite an extensive search, he was at liberty for several days until he was detained at Neath and charged with murder.

Hanged by James Billington.

December 4th: James Canham READ   **Chelmsford**

Read was a middle-aged book-keeper at London docks earning a respectable income for his wife and eight children. He was, however, not content with his large family and had taken a number of mistresses, one of whom was a Mrs Ayriss.

He further complicated his love life by becoming involved with Mrs Ayriss' sister, Florence Dennis (18). They soon became lovers and in the spring she became pregnant. She named him as the father and wrote asking what he intended to do about it.

Read arranged to meet her at Southend, and she was never seen alive again. Florence had been seen in his company, and when Mrs Ayriss wrote to Read asking what had happened to her sister, he panicked. He stole some money from his office and fled to another of his mistresses at Mitcham, Surrey.

Florence's body was later found shot dead in a field. Read was arrested after police traced a letter he had sent to a relative. He was convicted at Chelmsford Assizes in November.

Hanged by Billington.

1894

December 10th: John William NEWELL (42) — Leicester

A former Royal Marine sentenced to death on 21 November for the murder of his wife, Isabella, at Loughborough. On 21 August, they had a quarrel during which he accused her of being unfaithful and in a rage he beat her to death with a coal hammer.

After he was arrested, he declared: 'I'll go to the gallows in good heart if I know she is dead.'

Hanged by James Billington.

December 11th: Samuel George EMERY (20) — Newcastle

A private in the South Staffordshire Regiment, convicted of the murder of Mary Ann Marshall, whom he stabbed to death on a road at Tynemouth on 23 July.

Billington recalled after the execution that he was the gamest man he had ever hanged because of the cool and totally unafraid manner in which he went to the scaffold.

December 12th: Cyrus KNIGHT (45) — Winchester

A carter convicted at Winchester Assizes of the murder of his wife at Binstead, near Alton. He cut her throat during a quarrel.

Knight had attempted suicide after the crime and as a result of the six feet four inches drop James Billington gave him, the wound opened up after execution.

December 12th: William ROGERS — Winchester

Rogers was a sailor who lived with Sarah Jupe. He was convicted of murder after shooting her dead. As he walked in the procession towards the gallows, he kicked off his shoes and declared: 'That's better. I'll not die in those. It was them that brought me here.'

Hanged by James Billington with **KNIGHT** [above].

1895

Cases where no executioner is recorded are multiple executions, and readers are asked to refer to the entries before or after for details of the hangman.

February 9th: John TWISS — Cork

A native of Cordal, Castleisland, Co Kerry. On 21 April 1894 he was convicted of the murder of James Donovan, the caretaker of an evicted holding on Lord Cork's estate at Glenlara, Haymarket. Another man named Keefe was acquitted at the trial.

Donovan had been dragged from his bed and beaten to death by Twiss, who was identified by the victim's son.

He put on over two stone while in the condemned cell, and broke down saying: 'Oh my poor sister, she will be so lonely.' He regained his composure and walked firmly to the scaffold where he was hanged by James Billington.

March 26th: Edmund KESTEVEN — Nottingham

Kesteven was a well known former county cricket player who had lived with Sarah Ann Oldham at Sutton-in-Ashfield for several years. Both were addicted to drink and frequently quarrelled. On New Year's Day 1895, she staggered to her sister's house with her throat cut. She managed to say what had happened just before dying.

Kesteven admitted the crime and claimed he had killed her because she had deceived him. He pleaded insanity at his trial.

Hanged by James Billington.

June 4th: William MILLER — Liverpool

Convicted of the murder of Edward Moyse, who kept a bookstall at the Liverpool ferry landing stage. The two men were homosexuals, and Miller stabbed Moyse to death during a jealous quarrel after he had seen him with another man. Moyse was found dead in his bed, and Miller was identified as being seen to leave the house on the morning of the crime.

Hanged by James Billington who gave him a drop of seven feet five inches, assisted by William Warbrick.

1895

June 18th: James CANNING (32)   **Wandsworth**

A Jersey born army pensioner sentenced to death by Baron Pollock on 27 May at the Old Bailey, for the murder of his sweetheart Jane Youell.

Canning worked as a male nurse and lodged with Youell's parents at Bermondsey. They had a jealous quarrel one night around Easter and he cut her throat.

Hanged by James Billington and Thomas Scott.

July 2nd: Henry TICKNER (42)   **Wandsworth**

A former soldier sentenced to death at Guildford Assizes on 12 June for the murder of his wife.

They lived apart but on 11 February he called on her, then attacked her with a billhook, inflicting fatal injuries. At his trial he admitted that he had become jealous of her affection for another man, and pleaded guilty through insanity.

Hanged by James Billington and Thomas Scott.

August 13th: Robert Heseltine HUDSON   **York**

Convicted of the murder of his wife Kate, and son Heseltine, whom he stabbed to death between 21 May and 8 June, and then buried their bodies on the Yorkshire Moors.

He never attempted to cover his tracks and confessed when arrested at Birmingham on 22 June.

Hanged by James Billington.

August 20th: Thomas BOND (29)   **Stafford**

Bond was a Staffordshire labourer and on 31 May, he called at the Orgreave home of Fred Bakewell, a farmer. After knocking on the door, he was greeted by George Hackett, Bakewell's son-in-law. Bond pulled out his gun and shot Hackett dead, then entered the house and shot Bakewell dead as he sat in his chair. Bond then fired at Mrs Bakewell but she received only a minor wound and managed to escape through the back door.

Bond was convicted on the testimony of Mrs Bakewell, and hanged by Scott.

1895

November 13th: Richard WINGROVE (37)   Newgate

On Saturday 7 September, the body of a woman was found close to a railway line at Kensal Rise, near Willesden. She had been battered to death with a sharp piece of paving stone and then her throat had been cut.

The area was a popular resting place for vagrants and she was soon identified as Jane Eagle (35), a single woman with two children. No sooner had police identified the victim than they had a man in custody. Wingrove, an army reservist, walked into a police station and confessed that he had killed her but never offered a motive although she was his former paramour.

Hanged by James Billington.

December 3rd: Arthur COVINGTON (27)   Bedford

Convicted of the murder of his cousin, Effie Burgen (20), in June. He had been paying her some attention while she was visiting his parents, and while they were left alone he shot her three times with his revolver. His defence of insanity was rejected and he was hanged by Billington.

One of the last acts that the condemned man did was to fill in the census form. He gave his address as 'The Condemned Cell, Bedford Gaol.'

December 17th: Elijah WINSTANLEY (28)   Liverpool

Convicted of the murder of a railway policeman at Ince, near Wigan.

To combat the increasing number of thefts from railway wagons parked at Kay's House Sidings, the LNW Railway had employed extra police to patrol the area.

On the evening of Sunday 3 September, Detective Sergeant Robert Kidd, a Salford born father of seven, and his colleague DS Osborne, spotted a gang climbing aboard one of the wagons. As the thieves pulled back the tarpaulin, the two policemen shouted at them and ran to make the arrests.

Instead of running, the gang stood their ground, and when DS Kidd tried to arrest one of them, he was stabbed several times in the chest and head. Osborne went to his aid and he too was attacked, and although he was only kicked and punched, he still received severe injuries.

The police soon had a group of suspects in custody and when they were taken to DS Osborne's bedside he was able to identify Winstanley as the attacker, who was then charged with Kidd's murder.

Winstanley was sentenced to death, while another man, William

Kearsley received life imprisonment for his part in the attack. In the death cell, Winstanley pleaded unsuccessfuly for the release of his friend, whom he claimed was innocent. Kearsley remained in gaol until he died in 1918.

Winstanley was hanged by James Billington and Thomas Scott.

December 24th: Henry WRIGHT (35) — Nottingham

Wright lived in lodgings at Mansfield with a Mrs Reynolds and her family. He repeatedly made advances towards her which she rebuffed, and after one such rejection he cut her throat and then killed her two sons and grandson. Wright then set the house alight and rushed naked to the police station where he gave a detailed confession. At his trial, he pleaded insanity.

Wright was convicted, and hanged by Billington and his assistant, William Warbrick.

December 31st: Patrick MORLEY (38) — Leeds

An Irish labourer convicted of the murder of his wife, Elizabeth, at Batley, after she had left him and refused to return. She had walked out on him because of his constant violence towards her. On 21 September, while drunk, he called on her and asked her to lend him a shilling. When she refused, he shot her.

He was tried before Mr Justice Grantham and pleaded insanity, also claiming that the gun had gone off accidentally. Unfortunately for Morley, Grantham's summing up was heavily in favour of the prosecution and he was found guilty.

Hanged by Billington.

1896

Cases where no executioner is recorded are multiple executions, and readers are asked to refer to the entries before or after for details of the hangman.

1896

February 4th: William James MORGAN (56) — Wandsworth

A hawker convicted of the murder of his wife at Lewisham in September, 1895. They had been living apart and met up one night in the street. A quarrel ensued and Mrs Morgan threatened to set her son on her husband if he didn't leave her alone. In anger, Morgan pulled out his knife and stabbed her to death.

After his conviction, Morgan, a former champion sculler who had been presented with cups by Gladstone, bequeathed his trophies to his former colleagues.

Hanged by James Billington and William Warbrick.

February 25th: Alfred CHIPPERFIELD — Newgate

Chipperfield was a young clerk who met up with a barmaid at Islington and persuaded her to elope with him. They went to Cork, and within a fortnight they had married. They returned to Islington, and while travelling together in a taxi, he cut her throat and then his own.

He was tried at the Old Bailey and his defence claimed that she had committed suicide while of unsound mind. Evidence suggested otherwise and he was convicted.

Hanged by James Billington & William Warbrick.

June 9th: Henry FOWLER (31) — Newgate
Albert MILSOM (33)

On 14 February, the body of Henry Smith (79), a wealthy retired engineer, was discovered battered to death in the kitchen of his home at Muswell Hill. He had been bound and gagged. Evidence suggested he had been tortured, probably to reveal the combination of his safe which stood empty.

Fowler and Milsom, two well known thugs had been seen in the area on the day before the crime, but the only clue the police had was a child's toy lantern found in the grounds outside the house. When detectives learned that the toy had once belonged to a relative of Milsom, a manhunt was started.

The two were eventually located in Bath, and although Fowler strenuously denied any involvement with the crime, Milsom cracked under interrogation and made a full confession.

They were convicted on overwhelming evidence at the Old Bailey and as they were sentenced to death, Fowler made a desperate attempt to strangle his former associate who had landed him in the dock.

June 9th: William SEAMAN (46) Newgate

A sailor, with a long criminal record, convicted of a double murder in Whitechapel.

On 4 April, he called at the house of Jonathon Goodman Levy (75), a retired umbrella maker, who lived in a predominantly Jewish area of Whitechapel. He chose a time when most of the locals were at the Synagogue, and he was received at the door by Levy's housekeeper, Mrs Annie Sarah Gale (31). Seaman told the woman that he was begging alms but when she refused to help him he attacked her.

Mrs Gale fled up the stairs but Seaman caught up with her and battered her about the head with a poker which he had picked up from the grate. Seaman then set about ransacking the house in search of money and when he was surprised by Levy, who had been in the workshop at the back of the house, he killed him in a similar fashion.

A neighbour called round and discovered the body of Levy and heard a sound coming from upstairs which she took to be the intruder. Police rushed to the house and chased Seaman onto the roof from where he attempted to escape by jumping into the crowd that had gathered some thirty feet below to watch the drama unfold above them. Faced with no alternative, Seaman jumped, seriously injuring one of the onlookers. He was taken to the hospital unconscious but made a full recovery before his trial.

He was hanged between the two Muswell Hill killers **FOWLER and MILSOM** [above], and as he took his position on the drop, he remarked that it was the first time he had been a peacemaker.

Fearing that there would be a fight on the scaffold, the prison authorities posted an extra number of warders on condemned duty. When Billington and his assistants, Robert Wade and William Warbrick began, the warders closed in on the prisoners.

According to the execution report, Warbrick was still strapping Milsom's ankles when Billington pulled the lever, and he grabbed Milsom's legs to stop himself from falling into the pit. This would seem unlikely however as the combined weight of Milsom and Warbrick would have been enough to decapitate the prisoner. Billington always denied that anything untoward had happened, as did the priest in attendance.

June 10th: Amelia Elizabeth DYER (57)　　　　　　　　　　Newgate

'The Reading Baby Farmer'. A former member of the Salvation Army, Mrs Dyer had been convicted of cruelty to children while living in Bristol in the 1880s.

In 1895, she moved to London and began to advertise that she would take in children for board and adoption. On 31 March, she took care of a young girl, Doris Marmon, and two days later police found the bodies of two young children floating in the River Thames, one of whom was identified as Doris. Mrs Dyer was questioned and as more bodies of young children were pulled from the river she was charged with multiple murder.

Mrs Dyer was tried before Mr Justice Hawkins at the Old Bailey, on the same day as Milsom and Fowler [see above], and her defence was guilty but insane. The prosecution, however, alleged that the motive for the mass killings was gain, and the jury took just five minutes to find her guilty of murder.

She was hanged by Billington and two assistants.

July 7th: Charles Thomas WOOLDRIDGE (30)　　　　　　　　Reading

Woolridge had met his wife Laura while he was serving in the Royal Horse Guards at Windsor. His commanding officer had refused him permission to marry and so they had wed in secret. The marriage wasn't a happy one due to his drunken violent outbursts.

During the spring he was posted to London, and because the army didn't recognise Laura as his wife she was unable to go with him. They parted on bad terms and the relationship seemed to be over. Soon after his departure she began an affair with another soldier.

On 29 March, she agreed to meet Wooldridge in London but failed to turn up. He learned from a friend of her affair with the other soldier, and after borrowing a razor, travelled to her house at Windsor. Once there, he managed to gain entry by asking her to sign some papers, but then pulled out the razor and slit her throat. He gave himself up immediately and was charged with murder.

He was convicted at Berkshire Assizes and returned to Reading to await execution. The playwright Oscar Wilde was at the prison, serving two years for homosexuality, and after seeing the prisoner at exercise, he was inspired to pen his classic work 'The Ballad of Reading Gaol', which he dedicated to the soldier's memory.

Hanged by James Billington.

July 21st: Philip MATTHEWS (32)　　　　　　　　　　**Winchester**

A coachman employed by Teignmouth Council and convicted of the murder of his daughter.

Matthews had married his second wife in 1892 and she cared for his daughter from his first marriage as if she were her own. In the autumn of 1895 he met Charlotte Mahoney and concealed from her the details of his family circumstances, leading her to believe he was a wealthy single man. He was so infatuated with her that he proposed marriage and when she accepted he had invitations printed.

He was then faced with the difficulty of telling his wife, and when he did, she threw him out and refused to accept any further responsibility for his child. Matthews looked after the child but kept it secret from his intended bride and eventually it became a serious problem for him.

On 7 April, a child's body was found strangled in a wood at Teignmouth. Enquiries soon led officers to Matthews who was arrested and charged with murder.

July 21st: Frederick BURDEN (24)　　　　　　　　　　**Winchester**

A Southampton labourer sentenced to death by Mr Justice Day at Winchester Assizes on 1 July for the murder of Mrs Angeline Faithfull.

Mrs Faithfull had walked out on her husband in 1893 and gone to live with Burden. They had a tempestuous relationship and neighbours could often hear them quarrelling. On 18 February 1896, they had a fierce row and he was heard to threaten her.

The next morning, she was found dead in bed with her throat cut and holding a bloodstained razor in her hand. Police soon dismissed any theory of suicide and began searching for Burden. He had disappeared from his workplace but was traced to Salisbury, where they found blood stains on his clothing and he was arrested.

Burden claimed he was innocent and that the real killer was one of the numerous men friends who called on Mrs Faithfull while he was at work.

At his trial, the first jury could not reach a verdict, so they were dismissed and a new jury sworn in. This time he was convicted, and hanged in the last triple execution.

July 21st: Samuel Edward SMITH (18)   **Winchester**

A soldier in the 4th King's Royal Rifles convicted of the deliberate, premeditated murder of a Corporal Payne, at Aldershot. Smith had been reported by Payne and he shot him dead in a revenge attack.

Hanged alongside **BURDEN** and **MATTHEWS** [above] by Billington and Warbrick. It was the last triple execution in Britain.

August 4th: Joseph HIRST (26)   **Manchester**

Hirst, a bricklayer, and his sweetheart Martha Ann Goddard (20), a laundress, had lived in various parts of the country before they settled in Chorlton-on-Medlock, Manchester. Soon after, Martha gave birth to a baby girl. In March they moved again to new lodgings but still in the same district.

On 2 April, they left the house carrying the child, after telling their landlady they were taking her to Stockport to be cared for by Hirst's mother. Hirst and Goddard returned later without the child; soon afterwards a body was found floating in a nearby canal. Acting on information received, the police called on the couple, and after satisfying themselves that it was their child in the canal, they charged them with murder.

They stood trial at Manchester Assizes on 14 July. Although Goddard was to be charged as an accessory, the prosecution offered no evidence against her and she was discharged. Hirst confessed that he had strangled the child after he had become tired of it.

Hanged by James Billington.

1896

August 5th: William PUGH (21)   Derby

Pugh, a collier, called at a farm at Brackenfield, Derbyshire, where Miss Elizabeth Boot (19), was a housekeeper. A young girl at the farm told how she saw Pugh persuade Elizabeth to accompany him to a barn, where she was later found beaten to death.

Pugh was arrested and denied the murder, claiming: 'Why should it be me, what motive could I have?' He did confess to helping a friend move the body, hence the bloodstains found on his clothing, but the jury wasn't convinced by his story and he was convicted.

Hanged by James Billington and William Warbrick.

August 11th: John ROSE   Nottingham

A baker sentenced to death at Nottingham Assizes on 22 July for the murder of his wife Mary.

On 12 February, he cut her throat at their home on Lincoln Street, Nottingham, and then tried to take his own life in the same way.

August 11th: Samuel WILKINSON   Nottingham

On 14 February, Wilkinson, a gardener, called at the house of a family called Powley, at Arnold, Nottingham. He claimed that Mr Powley had been taken ill at a local inn. Mrs Powley rushed there leaving her friend, an elderly widow called Mary Kay, in charge of the house.

After discovering that the call was a false alarm, she returned home and found Mrs Kay dead on the floor with her skull caved in. She had been battered about the head before the house was ransacked.

A description of the mystery caller was circulated which led the police to Wilkinson. He was being held at Manchester's Strangeways Prison after breaking into a golf pavilion. A search of his belongings revealed articles stolen from the Powley house and he was charged with the murder.

He was convicted at the same Assizes as **ROSE** [above], and hanged alongside him by James Billington and William Warbrick.

1896

August 18th: Frank TAYLOR (23)   Birmingham

On 10 March, May Lewis (10) did not return home after school and all enquiries failed to trace her whereabouts. Early next morning, some workmen passing by land adjacent to the Taylor house found a child's body with its skull battered in.

Police searched the house and after finding evidence that the crime had taken place in an upstairs bedroom, arrested Mr and Mrs Taylor but later released them after their son, Frank, confessed.

Witnesses came forward to say they had seen Taylor decoy May Lewis into the house while his parents were out for the night. It was later discovered that Taylor had tried to drown himself on the night of the crime by throwing himself into a canal, only to be pulled out by a passer-by.

Hanged by James Billington.

August 25th: Joseph Robert ELLIS (22)   Leeds

A seaman convicted of the murder of his wife at Goole. They had been married for only fifteen months before they separated and she went back to live with her mother. Ellis called at the house and chased his wife and her mother out into the street where he stabbed them both, fatally wounding his wife.

Hanged by James Billington.

October 6th: James JONES (26)   Newgate

A ship's fireman sentenced to death at the Old Bailey for the murder of Edward White at Wapping. He stabbed him to death when ill feeling evolved after a family quarrel. No effort was made to secure a reprieve and Jones claimed he didn't want or expect one.

Hanged by James Billington.

1896

December 22nd: August CARLSEN (43)   York

A Swedish sailor convicted of the murder of Juliet Wood, with whom he lived at York. At 8pm on 23 July, Carlsen went to their landlord and confessed that he had killed his sweetheart. She was found dead in bed with her throat cut. Carlsen was drunk when arrested.
        Hanged by James Billington.

December 23rd: Joseph ALLCOCK (26)   Nottingham

In September, Allcock, a collier's agent, was drinking in a Nottingham pub, when he told a friend that he was heartbroken and that his wife had wronged him. He returned home, and after a quarrel he cut his wife's throat then gave himself up to the police.
        There was no evidence that his wife had ever been unfaithful, and it seemed that he had wrongly imagined her adultery. He was hanged by Billington and Warbrick.

1897

Cases where no executioner is recorded are multiple executions, and readers are asked to refer to the entries before or after for details of the hangman.

1897

January 5th: Henry BROWN (32)　　　　　　　　　　　　**Wandsworth**

After serving a term of imprisonment, Brown came out and went to live with his wife and mother-in-law at Clapham. After a quarrel broke out in November 1896, he attacked both women with a coal hammer. As a result, his wife died.
    Sentenced to death at the Old Bailey and hanged by Billington.

February 9th: Robert HAYMAN　　　　　　　　　　　　**Maidstone**

Convicted of the murder of Esther Allchin (51), a widow with whom he lived. The couple quarrelled in a public house at Plaxtol, near Sevenoaks, Kent, because she had been drinking with another man. On leaving the premises, he knocked her down and kicked her about the head and body while wearing a pair of heavy boots. The body was found hidden in a shed the following day.
    Hanged by James Billington.

June 7th: George PATERSON　　　　　　　　　　　　**Glasgow**

An aged soldier sentenced to death by Lord Young at Edinburgh High Court for the horrific murder of his paramour, Mary McGuire, whom he beat to death with a red hot poker in their home at Milton Lane, Glasgow, in February. When the body was discovered police counted forty burns on the upper body.
    His defence attributed the murder to the fact that Paterson was insane as a result of sun-stroke he had suffered while serving in India. The jury found him guilty by a majority of 8-7 and on 17 May he was sentenced to death; they also added a unanimous recommendation for mercy on account of provocation.
    It was expected that Paterson would be reprieved as the execution was due to take place amidst the celebration of Queen Victoria's Diamond Jubilee, but on Whit Monday he was hanged by James Billington on a scaffold specially constructed in a part of the gaol known as the joiner's shop.

1897

July 27th: Joseph BOWSER   **Lincoln**

A wealthy farmer, with over 800 acres of land, who murdered his wife, Susan, on 25 May at Donnington, by kicking her unconscious while she was feeding chickens. He then returned to the house, took out his shotgun, and blew her brains out.

He pleaded manslaughter through insanity but was convicted of murder and sentenced to death. He was hanged by James Billington, with his eldest son Thomas assisting for the first time. As Bowser was over seventeen stone he was given a short drop of only four feet six inches.

August 17th: Joseph ROBINSON (33)   **Leeds**

Convicted at Leeds Assizes of the murder of his wife at Monk Bretton, Barnsley, after she walked out on him. They met up one day in the street and after a quarrel, he shot her dead.

He made an unsuccessful attempt to poison himself before he was arrested. On the gallows he was very firm, and said he was sorry for the pain he had caused his little daughter.

August 17th: Walter ROBINSON (33)   **Leeds**

A former soldier who quarrelled with his cousin, Sarah Pickles, and after making threats to her, was bound over to keep the peace. This infuriated him to such an extent that when he met her later, he attacked her with a razor, and while she lay dead he said: 'I am satisfied, I have got my revenge.'

As he awaited execution, the authorities laid on extra warders as they feared he would try to pre-empt the sentence. He blamed drink for the crime.

Hanged by James and Thomas Billington alongside **ROBINSON** [above]; the two condemned men were not related.

August 18th: Thomas LLOYD   **Liverpool**

Convicted of the murder of his wife, with whom he had a stormy, unhappy marriage.

On 25 June he was arrested for attempted murder after he struck her with an axe several times following a drunken quarrel. He confessed that he had tried to kill her and declared that if she died he would 'Swing for her like a man.'

Mrs Lloyd later died from her injuries. At his trial at Liverpool Assizes in July, Lloyd claimed that her bad temper had provoked him into committing the crime while in a drunken rage.

Hanged by James and Thomas Billington.

December 16th: William BETTS (47)   **Maidstone**

A labourer sentenced to death at Maidstone Assizes for the murder of his father near Teston.

On 22 July, William Betts senior received eight pence off a friend as payment for a debt and later his son claimed that some of the money should be given to him. When the old man refused to hand any over, his son attacked him with an axe.

Betts immediately surrendered to the police and told them: 'I have knocked my old man down.' Police went to the house and found the victim with terrible head injuries.

Despite the jury recommending him to mercy, he was hanged by James Billington.

1898

Cases where no executioner is recorded are multiple executions, and readers are asked to refer to the entries before or after for details of the hangman.

1898

January 14th: Patrick HESTOR   Tullamore

Convicted of the murder of Bernard Keegan, his father in law, the previous October.
Hanged by Scott.

February 22nd: George William HOWE (34)   Manchester

John Kirby Pickup was the manager of a Burnley brickworks where George Howe was employed until he was sacked shortly before Christmas 1897. Howe blamed the manager for his dismissal and began to harbour a grudge against him.
    On New Year's Eve, Pickup was found beside a level crossing. He had been beaten about the head with a stick and died later in hospital. Howe was an immediate suspect and when questioned he confessed.
    Sentenced to death at Manchester Assizes and hanged by James and Thomas Billington.

March 12th: John HERDMAN (52)   Edinburgh

A printer convicted of the murder of Jane Calder, his paramour, whom he killed during a drunken quarrel at Hogmanay. The police surgeon stated that death was caused by a severe kicking and several stab wounds. The doctor claimed that the bruises were the worst he had ever seen.
    Herdman was sentenced to death at Edinburgh High Court and a petition of 11,000 signatures failed to stop the sentence being carried out by James Billington.

March 22nd: Charles SMITH (33)   Durham

On 27 December 1897, Smith, an Aberdeen born plasterer living in Gateshead, and his wife, retired to bed on good terms, although he was the worse for drink. Next morning, she was found dead on the bedroom floor; her head battered with a brush handle.
    Smith was convicted at Durham Assizes and hanged by Billington. He left a young son who was found a place in a local Dr Barnardo's home.

1898

April 5th: Wilfrid F KENNY (27)   **Clonmel**

Kenny was a German immigrant also known as Kruetze. After leaving his native country, he settled in England and enlisted in the 3rd Hussars under the name of Williams.

In 1894, he was sentenced to three years imprisonment for stealing valuable bonds from a Liverpool hotel. On his release, he joined the Hampshire Regiment but soon deserted and enlisted in the Dublin Fusiliers. Later that year, he transferred to the 8th Hussars and it was while serving in this regiment that he committed the crime that took him to the gallows.

One evening at the company's Cahir barracks, Kenny shot dead a Private Goodwin in an underground kitchen. He then dragged the body outside to an exercise ground where it was discovered the next day.

Kenny showed no emotion while he was led the two hundred yards across a courtyard and up a flight of stairs to the scaffold. He was hanged by Scott.

June 28th: William HORSFORD (26)   **Cambridge**

A farmer sentenced to death by Mr Justice Hawkins at Huntingdon Assizes for the murder of his cousin.

On 7 January, Mrs Annie Holmes (38), a widow, died suddenly after a short illness at her home in St Neots, Huntingdonshire. She had been sent a tonic through the post only a day before her death.

Suspicion grew that the death might not have been through natural causes, and on 24 January the Home Secretary agreed that the body should be exhumed. The post mortem revealed traces of strychnine, which was suspected to have been concealed in the tonic.

Horsford was eventually arrested and charged with the murder, and although he strongly denied posting the tonic he was identified as the sender. At his trial, the prosecution alleged that he had killed his cousin after she threatened to disclose to relatives that he was in some kind of trouble.

Hanged by James Billington.

1898

July 12th: James WATT   **Norwich**

A labourer from Sprowston, sentenced to death by Mr Justice Hawkins for the murder of his wife, whom he killed on 14 April. She had left him because of his brutal behaviour. However, he happened to see her on a road later and shot her. He claimed that the motive was sudden passion.

Hanged in the prison coach house after he confessed his guilt to the chaplain, by James Billington and his son William, who was assisting at his first execution.

July 19th: William WILKES   **Chelmsford**

A shepherd from Canewdon, Essex, who murdered his wife by kicking her to death after they had quarrelled over some tobacco.

At the trial he acted with total indifference to his fate but as the execution drew nearer, he broke down completely and had to be fed. As Billington placed the noose around his neck, he turned to the warder in tears and asked 'Will it hurt me?' Before the warder could reply he was dropped seven feet two inches to his death.

August 3rd: Thomas JONES (35)   **Carnavon**

A hawker, sentenced to death by Mr Justice Wills, for the murder of Mary Burton, with whom he lived. He had deserted his wife and was residing with Burton in a common lodging house at Ffestiniog. After a quarrel on 1 March, her body was found on a secluded hill, covered in bruises and wounds.

He denied the crime but was convicted, and hanged by James and Thomas Billington.

August 30th: Joseph LEWIS   **Swansea**

Robert Scott was the gamekeeper on an estate at Margam, Glamorgan. He was on the lookout for poachers who had been plaguing the estate for weeks, and despite the dangers of tackling potentially armed men, he never carried a weapon.

In spring, he surprised Lewis, who was trespassing on the estate; when challenged, Lewis shot him in cold blood, then beat him about the

head. Several other people were arrested before the police got their man. He confessed to the crime in a letter to Scott's widow, and implored her forgiveness.
Hanged by James and Thomas Billington.

November 15th: John RYAN (30)   **Newgate**

On 2 October, PC Docherty and PC Baldwin were called to a disturbance at Hoxton. When they reached the scene, Baldwin was attacked by Ryan and stabbed four times with a pocket knife. He died in hospital soon afterwards.
The judge at the trial told Ryan that he had no hope of being reprieved. He received no visits from friends or relatives, and was sullen and morose to the end.
Hanged by James and Thomas Billington.

December 14th: Thomas DALEY (40)   **Maidstone**

A labourer who beat to death his paramour, Sarah Ann Penfold, at Chatham on 4 June.
They had been drinking in a public house and on returning home, they began to quarrel. A neighbour heard a thud followed by a moaning and a cry of 'Don't Tom, you'll kill me.' The disturbance lasted only a few minutes so she decided not to investigate.
The next morning, Daley called on his neighbour and told her he thought Sarah was dead, and when she went into the house, she found the woman lying naked on a chair, shockingly disfigured and covered in blood. Beside the body was a blood stained poker.
The police were summoned and Daley was taken into custody and charged with murder after he confessed.

1898

Sentenced to death at Kent Assizes and hanged by James Billington. The prisoner weighed 180 pounds so the hangman decided on a drop of six feet six inches.

December 21st: John COTTON (66) Derby

A boatman sentenced to death at Derby Assize Court for the murder of his thirty six year old third wife, whom he beat repeatedly over the head with a poker. He claimed that the motive was extreme provocation through jealousy but in the condemned cell he confessed to his guards that he had also murdered his first two wives.

Hanged by James and Thomas Billington.

1899

Cases where no executioner is recorded are multiple executions, and readers are asked to refer to the entries before or after for details of the hangman.

1899

January 3rd: John SCHNEIDER (36)   Newgate

Aka Richard Mandelov or Montague, sentenced to death at the Old Bailey on 14 December for the murder of Conrad Burndt, a bakery worker. Burndt's calcined remains had been found inside a baker's oven on William Street, close to Portland Station.

     Schneider, a Pole, was a former employee at the bakery, but since his dismissal he had been replaced by Burndt, a German immigrant. Being unable to find regular employment, he was forced to walk the streets looking for work.

     On 10 November he called at the bakery and spoke to the owner, a Mr Ross, but was unable to regain his old job. It was a cold wet evening and Ross allowed Schneider to spend the night in the warmth of the bakery.

     At 3am on the following morning Ross arrived at the bakery and found Schneider alone. He enquired after Burndt, and Schneider told him he was unwell and had gone home to bed. Ross replied by asking Schneider to work the shift, and when the Pole agreed, went about some other business.

     A few minutes later Ross returned to the bakery and while examining the furnace he received a blow to the back of the head. After regaining his footing, he saw Schneider brandishing a knife and during the ensuing struggle, Ross was badly cut on the hand. Fortunately, he was able to escape from the bakery and lock the door, trapping the crazed Pole on the premises.

     Police hurried to the scene and took Schneider into custody. When they checked his pockets, they found some money and a watch which belonged to Burndt. Detectives returned to the bakery and a search of the furnace revealed the charred remains of the German baker. It was later discovered that Burndt had been alive when he was thrown into the furnace.

     Schneider pleaded insanity but was convicted, and hanged by James Billington.

January 7th: Patrick HOLMES (24)   Kilkenny

A farm labourer from Paulstown, Kilkenny, convicted at his second trial of the murder of Ellen Lawlor (70) on 4 July 1898. The jury at the first trial had failed to reach a verdict.

     Mrs Lawlor lived alone in a secluded house from where she ran a huckster's business, and the local people thought her to be a wealthy woman. Holmes robbed her then battered her to death to prevent her identifying him.

The authorities had to erect a new scaffold as it was over fifty years since the last execution at Kilkenny. Scott was the hangman.

January 10th: Thomas KELLY　　　　　　　　　　　　　　　　　Armagh

Convicted of the murder of his father, Bernard Kelly, an innkeeper at Ballconnell, Co Cavan, in October 1898.

Relations between them had become strained, and on the day of the murder he was seen cleaning a gun in the kitchen. Later his father was found shot dead and Kelly was charged. He claimed it was an accident.

Hanged by Scott and Binns.

January 13th: Philip KING　　　　　　　　　　　　　　　　　　Armagh

Sentenced to death at Ulster Assizes on 13 December for the murder of his his wife Mary, their two children, and his mother-in-law Mary Reilly at Nolagh, Co Cavan on 30 January 1898.

The two women were found battered to death beside the children, a suffocated baby of two months, and a two year old who had been starved to death.

The motive was revenge after Mrs Reilly had issued a summons against King for making threats against her. As Lord Chief Justice O'Brien passed sentence, King interrupted him and declared: 'Lord have mercy on you! You will have more to answer for than me, I am not guilty.'

Hanged by Scott.

March 28th: George ROBERTSON (45)　　　　　　　　　　　　Newgate

A diminutive man convicted of the murder of Mary Kenealy (4), who was discovered in a house off Drury Lane with her throat cut. She had also been sexually assaulted. The girl's mother called at the house and found Robertson, whom she knew well, in an adjoining room cleaning up the bloodstains. He attacked her then fled, but was subsequently captured and charged with murder.

Hanged by James and Thomas Billington.

1899

May 3rd: Frederick James ANDREWS (45)   **Wandsworth**

Mrs Francis Short was a widow who lived with Andrews at Kensington. She was a hardworking woman who supported him by selling fruit and vegetables from a stall.

Andrews frequently ill-treated her and after a quarrel in March, he cut her throat and then stabbed her over forty times with a pen knife. He then went out and pawned her clothes.

Hanged by James and Thomas Billington.

July 11th: Joseph Cornelius PARKER (24)   **Northampton**

Parker was a blacksmith's striker who shot dead his girlfriend, Mary Elizabeth Meadows. He stated at his trial that they had arranged to die together, but after shooting her twice he claimed he 'hadn't the heart to kill himself.'

He pleaded insaity and it was revealed that he had tried to commit suicide at least three times. In the condemned cell, he confessed to a warder that he had planned the murder in advance, and that he had intended to kill her on a Friday night, but after they had been out drinking he postponed it until the next day.

Hanged by James Billington.

July 18th: Charles MAIDMENT (22)   **Winchester**

A labourer who murdered his ex-fiancee Dorcas Houghton at Swanwick, New Faversham, in April, after she had broken off their engagement. They had arranged a meeting to return gifts to him. After failing to persuade her to go out with him again, he shot her dead and gave himself up to the police.

He pleaded insanity at the trial but the prosecution called two doctors who refuted the claim and he was hanged by James Billington.

1899

July 19th: Mary Ann ANSELL (22)　　　　　　　　　　　　**St Albans**

On 9 March, Mary Ansell, a domestic servant, sent a cake to her younger sister, Caroline, who was in an asylum at Watford. The cake was shared out among the patients. Several of them became ill, and Caroline Ansell died.

Mary aroused suspicion when she refused to give permission for them to hold an autopsy. A doctor at the asylum had the contents of Caroline's stomach analysed and found she had died as a result of phosphorus poisoning.

She protested her innocence throughout the trial but allegedly confessed in the condemned cell.

Hanged by James Billington.

July 25th: Edward BELL　　　　　　　　　　　　　　　　**Lincoln**

Bell, a farm labourer, and his wife had an unhappy marriage, and during the spring he became enamoured with a younger woman, Mary Hodson. A few weeks after they met, Mrs Bell died.

Bell may have got away with murder if he had not aroused suspicion by becoming engaged two day's after his wife's funeral. When it came to the attention of police, they decided to have her remains exhumed and traces of strychnine were discovered. Bell was arrested and later confessed that he had allowed passion to drive him to commit murder.

He was hanged by William Billington, who was carrying out his first job as a chief executioner.

August 9th: Elias TORR (52)　　　　　　　　　　　　　**Nottingham**

A farmer convicted of the murder of his eldest daughter, Margaret Ann (21).

Torr was a violent man addicted to drink, and his family were constantly afraid of him. They lived in a farmhouse beside the main Nottingham to Melton railway line.

At the end of April, there was a fierce family quarrel after which his wife and daughter went to stay with a neighbouring farmer. Torr went to the farm to try and pacify his family but was refused entry. In a rage, he battered the door down with the butt of his gun and as his family fled through a back door, he opened fire and fatally wounded Margaret.

Convicted at Nottingham Assizes and hanged by James and William Billington.

October 3rd: Frederick PRESTON (22)   Newgate

A French polisher who murdered his girlfriend, Eliza Jane Mears, on 9 July at Hackney. They had been going out for a while but her mother urged her to give him up as he treated her in a brutal fashion. She did so, and he beat her to death with a blunt instrument.

Hanged by James Billington.

October 4th: Robert WARD (27)   Wandsworth

A bricklayer who murdered his two young daughters at Walworth on 20 July. He became jealous of the attention his wife was giving an old boyfriend who had returned to London after serving in India. Ward's reaction was to cut the throats of his children, before attempting to slit his own.

Hanged by James Billington.

November 15th: Thomas SKEFFINGTON (20)   Newgate

On the night of Monday 2 October, Skeffington, a well dressed young man, left the Upton Arms and met Florence Wells (24) on a Dalston street. They talked for several minutes and then, in front of startled onlookers, he withdrew a knife and stabbed her twice in the neck.

As she lay in a pool of blood on the kerb, Skeffington calmly walked into a local police station and said: 'I have killed a woman. I bought a knife to do it. I meant to do it.' The woman bled to death before she could be taken to hospital and Skeffington was charged with murder.

At his trial, it was revealed that he had discovered she was already married just before proposing to her; and that he had also lost his job in a Hackney public house. In a rage brought on by despair, he killed her.

Hanged by James Billington.

1899

November 21st: George NUNN (18)   Ipswich

A young labourer convicted of the murder of Mrs Eliza Dixon at Wrotham in July. He waylaid her as she returned home with some beer for her husband's supper, and made improper suggestions which she rejected. He then killed her by stabbing her in the throat.

     He was recommended to mercy on account of his age but hanged by James Billington.

November 28th: Charles SCOTT (28)   Reading

A glassblower from Windsor, who murdered his girlfriend Eliza O'Shea, a soldier's wife. They were both frequent drinkers, and after a quarrel on 2 September, he cut her throat from ear to ear. He then gave himself up to a local policeman.

     Hanged by James Billington and his assistant Robert Wade.

December 5th: Samuel CROZIER (35)   Chelmsford

On Monday 25 June, Crozier, the landlord of the Admiral Ross Inn, Galleywood Common, Chelmsford, was seen by witnesses to assault his wife Ann (31) in a room above the pub. They had only recently married and he was seen to knock her off a sofa, then kick and beat her.

     The next morning, she died from her injuries, but with the doctor unaware of the fight on the previous day, he stated that death was from natural causes as a result of a fall.

     Word soon reached police about the fight and less than an hour after Mrs Crozier's funeral, her husband was in custody on a murder charge.

     He was convicted at Essex Assizes and hanged by James and William Billington. When asked by the Governor, moments before being led to the drop, if he had anything to say, Crozier replied in a firm voice: 'No sir, nothing than I have already said at the trial.'

December 6th: Michael DOWDLE (40)   Manchester

A pensioned Irish soldier who worked as a quarryman, convicted at Manchester Assizes for the murder of his wife at Whitworth, near Rochdale.

Ellen Dowdle had left her husband in the summer of 1899 due to his increasingly quarrelsome and brutal behaviour. On 12 August, she went to stay with friends who lived less than a quarter of a mile away.

On 19 August, Dowdle called at the house and found his wife alone. He made a passionate plea for her to return home and promised to mend his ways. She refused and after repeated attempts also failed, his temper got the better of him and he attacked her. At that moment, one of their friends' children came home and witnessed the attack. He rushed out into the street and found a policeman to whom he pleaded: 'Come quick, Mr Dowdle is hacking up his wife's throat with a carving knife.'

The officer hurried to the house where he found Dowdle walking towards the police station, followed by a crowd of children.

Dowdle had served with gallantry in the Zulu war but was sentenced to death in November. Hanged by James Billington and William Warbrick.

Victim Index

*= *christian name unknown*

Victim Index

Abrahams, John
1869, November 15th: Joseph WELSH

Adams, Caroline
1880, July 27th: Thomas BERRY

Addington, Margaret
1871, July 31st: Richard ADDINGTON

Addison, Martha Jane
1874, January 5th: Charles DAWSON

Addison, Mary
1891, December 22nd: John William JOHNSON

Allchin, Esther
1897, February 9th: Robert HAYMAN

Allcock, *
1896, December 23rd: Joseph ALLCOCK

Allen, Henry
1887, February 17th: Edward PRITCHARD

Allen, Mary Ann
1894, July 31st: William CROSSLEY

Allen, Mary Hannah
1878, April 1st: Henry ROWLES

Alston, Elizabeth
1883, November 26th: Thomas RILEY

Anderson, *
1875, December 22nd: John William ANDERSON

Anderson, *
1883, February 19th: James ANDERSON

Angel, Miriam
1877, August 22nd: Israel LIPSKI

Ansell, Caroline
1899, July 19th: Mary Ann ANSELL

Anstree, Edward
1880, November 26th: Thomas WHEELER

Askins, Margaret
1885, December 9th: George THOMAS

Austwick, Police Constable *
1886, November 29th: James MURPHY

Bagnall, Edith
1881, February 22nd: James WILLIAMS

Bains, *
1886, February 9th: John BAINS

Bakewell, Fred
1895, August 20th: Thomas BOND

Baldey, David
1869, January 19th: Martin Henry VINALL

Baldwin, Police Constable *
1898, November 15th: John RYAN

Ballard, Phillip
1888, March 20th: James JONES & Alfred SCANDRETT

Bannister, *
1877, April 2nd: James BANNISTER

Barber, Maria
1878, February 11th: James CAFFYN

Barnes, Alice
1893, January 3rd: Cross DUCKWORTH

Barr, *
1876, May 31st: Thomas BARR

Barrett, Police Constable *
1886, November 30th: James BARTON

Bartlett, *
1888, November 13th: Leir Richard BARTLETT

Beetmore, Jane
1888, December 18th: William WADDELL

Bell, *
1899, July 25th: Edward BELL

Bellamy, Emma
1875, January 4th: James CRANWELL

Bernard, Frederick
1877, January 2nd: Isaac MARKS

Berridge, William
1888, May 22nd: James William RICHARDSON

Berry, Edith
1887, March 14th: Elizabeth BERRY

Betts, William
1897, December 16th: William BETTS

Bidwell, Henry
1877, November 20th: Henry MARSH

Biggadyke, Richard
1868, December 28th: Priscilla BIGGADYKE

Bird, Captain *
1874, November 16th: Thomas SMITH

Bloxham, Thomas
1887, February 14th: Thomas BLOXHAM

Blundell, John
1876, August 14th: Richard THOMPSON

Bly, Edward
1870, August 15th: Thomas RADCLIFFE

Boot, Elizabeth
1896, August 5th: William PUGH

Boss, Ann
1870, August 1st: Walter MILLAR

Boughen, Alice
1875, March 29th: Richard COATES

Bovell, Mary Jane
1889, January 1st: Thomas CLEWES

Bowser, Susan
1897, July 27th: Joseph BOWSER

Boyd, William
1869, December 13th: Frederick HINSON

Boyle, *
1893, January 6th: John BOYLE

Bradshaw, *
1891, August 19th: Robert BRADSHAW

Brehaney, Michael
1880, January 16th: Martin McHUGO

Brett, *
1889, December 31st: Frederick BRETT

Bridge, Mary Ann
1876, April 4th: Thomas FORDRED

Britland, * (husband & daughter)
1886, August 9th: Mary Ann BRITLAND

Briton, John
1883, November 6th: Henry POWELL

Brooks, Paymaster Sergeant *
1878, November 12th: Patrick John BYRNE

Brown, *
1897, January 5th: Henry BROWN

Brown, Thomas
1883, January 23rd: Sylvester POFF & James BARRETT

Bulmer, *
1889, January 1st: Charles BULMER

Bunting, Elizabeth
1885, August 17th: Thomas BOULTON

Burdey, Phillip
1874, December 28th: Hugh DALEY

Burgen, Effie
1895, December 3rd: Arthur COVINGTON

Burke, Harry
1883, May 14th: Joseph BRADY
1883, May 18th: Daniel CURLEY
1883, May 28th: Michael FAGAN
1883, June 2nd: Thomas CAFFREY
1883, June 9th: Timothy KELLY

Burndt, Conrad
1899, January 3rd: John SCHNEIDER

Burns, *
1885, January 20th: Thomas PARRY

Burton, Mary
1898, August 3rd: Thomas JONES

Bury, *
1889, April 24th: William Henry BURY

Byrne, Police Constable *
1886, February 8th: Anthony Ben RUDGE, James BAKER, James MARTIN

Calder, Jane
1898, March 12th: John HERDMAN

Caldwell, Eliza
1881, August 15th: Thomas BROWN

Campbell, John
1877, August 21st: Patrick McGOVERN

Carey, James
1883, December 17th: Patrick O'DONNELL

Carlam, Samuel
1883, May 8th: Patrick CAREY

Carter, *
1893, December 5th: John CARTER

Cassidy, *
1880, February 17th: William CASSIDY

Cassidy, *
1884, August 19th: Peter CASSIDY

Cavendish, Lord Frederick
1883, May 14th: Joseph BRADY
1883, May 18th: Daniel CURLEY
1883, May 28th: Michael FAGAN
1883, June 2nd: Thomas CAFFREY
1883, June 9th: Timothy KELLY

Chantrelle, Elizabeth
1878, May 31st: Eugene Marie CHANTRELLE

Charlton, *
1875, December 23rd: Richard CHARLTON

Chipperfield, *
1896, February 25th: Alfred CHIPPERFIELD

Churchill, *
1879, May 26th: Catherine CHURCHILL

Clifford, Florence
1894, January 2nd: William HARRIS

Clover, Matilda
1892, November 15th: Thomas CREAM

Cock, Police Constable Nicholas
1879, February 25th: Charles Frederick PEACE

Coe, John
1880, May 11th: John Henry WOOD

Cole, Police Constable *
1884, October 6th: Thomas Henry ORROCK

Coleman, Stephen
1882, January 31st: Charles GERRISH

Connely, Mary
1892, December 22nd: Thomas EDWARDS

Connor, Elizabeth
1893, January 18th: William McKEOWN

Coppen, Emma Skevington
1874, October 13th: John Walter COPPEN

Corrigan, *
1874, January 5th: Thomas CORRIGAN

Cotton, *
1898, December 21st: John COTTON

Cotton, Joanna
1875, April 19th: William TOBIN

Cox, Bernard
1893, September 2nd: James REILLY

Cox, Mark
1883, May 21st: Joseph WEDLAKE

Crawley, Joseph
1892, March 17th: Charles RAYNOR & Frederick EGGLESTON

Crawley, Patrick
1889, April 8th: Peter STAFFORD

Cronin, Thomas
1886, January 12th: John CRONIN

Cross, *
1888, January 10th: Phillip Henry Eustace CROSS

Cross, Catherine
1894, March 27th: Walter SMITH

Crossman, Maria
1892, March 22nd: Joseph WILSON

Crouch, William
1876, August 1st: James PARRIS

Crozier, *
1899, December 5th: Samuel CROZIER

Cruise, Tom
1882, December 4th: Bernard MULLARKEY

Cudworth, *
1892, August 18th: Moses CUDWORTH

Dainton, *
1891, December 15th: Henry DAINTON

Daly, Dennis
1889, August 7th: Lawrence Maurice HICKEY

Daniels, Eliza
1880, November 27th: William Joseph DISTON

Davies, *
1890, August 26th: Frederick DAVIES

Davies, Emma
1889, March 13th: Samuel RYLANDS

Davies, Richard
1890, April 8th: Richard DAVIES

Davies, Thomas
1888, March 13th: David REES

Davies, Walter
1890, April 15th: William Matthew CHADWICK

Davis, Police Constable *
1885, May 25th: Moses SHRIMPTON

Davis, Mary
1894, November 29th: Thomas RICHARDS

Deacon, *
1876, April 24th: Edward DEACON

Death, Maria
1869, December 13th: Frederick HINSON

De Grave, Francois
1890, August 27th: Francois MONTEAU

Delaney, *
1888, August 10th: Arthur James DELANEY

Delvin, *
1890, September 23rd: Henry DELVIN

Dennis, Catherine
1892, January 5th: James STOCKWELL

Dennis, Florence
1894, December 4th: James Canham READ

Derrick, Lucy
1879, May 12th: Edwin SMART

Dews, *
1894, August 21st: Alfred DEWS

Dickson, Anne
1885, November 23rd: John HILL & John WILLIAMS

Dixon, Eliza
1899, November 21st: George NUNN

Dixon, Mary
1886, August 9th: Mary Ann BRITLAND

Dockerty, Margaret
1876, December 21st: William FLANAGAN

Dodge, Emma Holmes
1893, March 28th: William WILLIAMS

Doloughty, John
1882, September 11th: Francis HYNES

Donahoe, Daniel
1872, August 13th: Francis BRADFORD

Donovan, James
1895, February 9th: John TWISS

Donworth, Ellen
1892, November 15th: Thomas CREAM

Dowdle, *
1899, December 6th: Michael DOWDLE

Drewatt, Inspector *
1877, March 12th: Francis TIDBURY & Henry TIDBURY

Dugdale, Richard
1884, November 24th: Kay HOWARTH

Dunne, Patrick
1870, May 27th: Lawrence SHEILD & Margaret SHEILD

Dyson, *
1879, February 25th: Charles Frederick PEACE

Eagle, Jane
1895, November 13th: Richard WINGROVE

Eblethrift, Emma
1876, August 29th: John EBLETHRIFT

Edmunds, John
1880, May 10th: William DUMBLETON

Edwards, Rosanna
1872, August 12th: Christopher EDWARDS

Elbrough, Florence
1894, April 4th: Frederick William FENTON

Ellis, *
1896, August 25th: Joseph Robert ELLIS

Evans, Annie Seabrook
1873, August 4th: Henry EVANS

Evans, Elizabeth Hannah
1887, November 28th: Enoch WADELY

Eves, Police Constable Adam John
1893, August 16th: John DAVIS

Faithful, Angelina
1896, July 21st: Frederick BURDEN

Fawcett, *
1891, August 25th: Edward Henry FAWCETT

Ferguson, Edward
1875, March 24th: John McDAID

Fiddler, Dorothy
1875, August 16th: Mark FIDDLER

Firth, Elizabeth
1875, December 21st: William SMEDLEY

Fishive, Patrick
1891, February 2nd: Bartholomew SULLIVAN

Fitzsimmons, James
1888, April 29th: Daniel HAYES & Daniel MORIARTY

Fitzsimmons, Maria
1882, May 16th: Thomas FURY

Flanagan, Henry
1874, August 31st: Henry FLANAGAN

Flew, *
1893, March 16th: Albert MANNING

Fortune, John
1884, March 31st: William INNES & Robert Flockheart VICKERS

Foulson, John
1875, March 30th: John MORGAN

Furlonger, Thomas
1890, June 10th: Daniel Stewart GORRIE

Gaffrey, James
1873, September 8th: James CONNOR

Gale, Annie Sarah
1896, June 9th: William SEAMAN

Galloway, Florence
1878, February 4th: George PIGGOTT

Galloway, Samuel
1871, April 24th: Michael CAMPBELL

Gardner, Emily
1872, January 8th: Frederick JONES

Gardner, Lyle
1894, August 17th: John GILMOUR

Gardner, Mary Ann
1891, July 28th: Arthur SPENCER

Garner, *
1894, April 3rd: Philip GARNER

Gibbons, *
1892, August 17th: Patrick GIBBONS

Gibbs, *
1874, August 24th: James Henry GIBBS

Gillow, Arthur
1879, February 4th: Stephen GAMBRILL

Glass, William
1873, August 26th: Thomas Hartley MONTGOMERY

Godwin, Louisa
1874, May 25th: John GODWIN

Gold, Isaac
1881, November 29th: Percy LEFROY

Goodale, *
1885, November 30th: Robert GOODALE

Goodwin, Private *
1898, April 5th: Wilfrid F KENNY

Gordon, George
1889, December 24th: William DUKES

Graham, Lucy
1879, March 24th: James SIMMS

Green, Emma
1876, December 20th: John GREEN

Green, Lydia
1887, April 18th: Thomas William CURRELL

Gregson, *
1870, January 10th: John GREGSON

Griffiths, Quartermaster Sergeant *
1878, November 12th: Patrick John BYRNE

Griffiths, Sarah
1887, August 16th: Thomas Henry BEVAN

Grossmith, Emma
1868, September 8th: Alexander Arthur MACKAY

Hackett, George
1895, August 20th: Thomas BOND

Hale, *
1875, April 26th: William HALE

Hall, Polly
1881, May 23rd: James HALL

Halton, Alice
1877, August 13th: Henry LEIGH

Hamblin, Elizabeth
1884, December 8th: Ernest EWERSTADT

Hancock, *
1873, January 7th: Edward HANCOCK

Harris, *
1884, October 6th: Thomas HARRIS

Harris, Florence
1888, August 28th: Harry Benjamin JONES

Harrison, Hannah
1890, August 26th: James HARRISON

Hassell, *
1877, November 19th: William HASSELL

Hastings, Emma
1888, August 28th: George Nathaniel DANIELS

Haynes, Ellen
1882, August 22nd: Thomas HAYNES

Heaney, *
1892, January 12th: James HEANEY

Hemmings, *
1893, April 4th: Edward HEMMINGS

Henshaw, Hannah
1883, December 3rd: Henry DUTTON

Hewitt, Sarah
1886, June 15th: Edward HEWITT

Hickey, James
1891, July 21st: Franz Joseph MUNCH

Hide, Reginald
1879, August 11th: Annie TOOKE

Higgins, Thomas
1884, March 5th: Catherine FLANAGAN & Margaret HIGGINS

Hodgson, Louisa
1875, August 9th: Peter BLANCHARD

Hogan, Hannah (& child)
1879, January 10th: Thomas CUNCEEN

Hogg, Phoebe (& child)
1890, December 23rd: Mary Eleanor WHEELER

Holland, Emily
1876, August 14th: William FISH

Holmes, *
1872, August 12th: Charles HOLMES

Holmes, Annie
1898, June 28th: William HORSFORD

Holmes, Elizabeth
1880, November 16th: William BROWNLESS

Holt, Elizabeth Ann
1890, December 30th: Thomas McDONALD

Hook, Julia
1889, December 31st: William Thomas HOOK

Horry, Jane
1872, April 1st: William Frederick HORRY

Horton, *
1886, February 1st: John HORTON

Horton, *
1889, August 21st: George HORTON

Houghton, Dorcas
1899, July 18th: Charles MAIDMENT

Howard, Charles
1885, July 13th: Henry ALT

Huddy, John
1883, January 15th: Patrick HIGGINS
1883, January 17th: Michael FLYNN & Thomas HIGGINS

Huddy, Joseph
1883, January 15th: Patrick HIGGINS
1883, January 17th: Michael FLYNN & Thomas HIGGINS

Hudson, Elizabeth
1873, August 4th: Benjamin HUDSON

Hudson, Heseltine
1895, August 13th: Robert Heseltine HUDSON

Hudson, Kate
1895, August 13th: Robert Heseltine HUDSON

Huelin, Rev Elias
1870, August 1st: Walter MILLAR

Hughes, Peter
1882, November 28th: Edward WHEATFALL

Hughes, Sarah
1877, November 23rd: Cadwaller JONES

Hyland, John
1876, August 25th: Thomas CROWE

Ings, Percival John
1887, May 16th: Henry William YOUNG

Insole, *
1887, February 21st: Richard INSOLE

Jackson, Elizabeth
1874, August 18th: William JACKSON

Jeal, Edith
1892, April 26th: George Henry WOOD

Jenkins, *
1874, January 12th: Edwin BAILEY & Ann BERRY

Jennings, Mary
1884, March 5th: Catherine FLANAGAN & Margaret HIGGINS

Jimenez, Jose
1884, March 10th: Michael McLEAN

Johnson, Louisa
1893, July 18th: Richard SABEY

Jones, Edward
1875, September 6th: Edward COOPER

Jones, Mary Jane
1894, February 13th: George THOMAS

Joyce, Detective *
1892, August 16th: John George WENZEL

Joyce, Bridget
1882, December 15th: Pat CASEY, Miles JOYCE, Pat JOYCE

Joyce, John
1882, December 15th: Pat CASEY, Miles JOYCE, Pat JOYCE

Joyce, Michael
1882, December 15th: Pat CASEY, Miles JOYCE, Pat JOYCE

Joyce, Peggy (Miss)
1882, December 15th: Pat CASEY, Miles JOYCE, Pat JOYCE

Joyce, Peggy (Mrs)
1882, December 15th: Pat CASEY, Miles JOYCE, Pat JOYCE

Judge, Amy
1878, October 8th: Thomas SMITHERS

Judge, Jane
1886, November 16th: Patrick JUDGE

Jupe, Sarah
1894, December 12th: William ROGERS

Kay, Mary
1896, August 11th: Samuel WILKINSON

Keegan, Bernard
1898, January 14th: Patrick HESTOR

Keenan, Mary Kate
1892, April 4th: James CAMPBELL

Kelly, Annie
1887, August 1st: Alfred SOWERY

Kelly, Bernard
1899, January 10th: Thomas KELLY

Kemp, Florence
1885, January 13th: Horace Robert JAY

Kenealy, Mary
1899, March 28th: George ROBERTSON

Kennedy, Ann
1872, December 30th: Michael KENNEDY

Kenny, John
1883, December 18th: Joseph POOLE

Kent, Frederick
1889, April 10th: Thomas ALLEN

Kewish Snr, John
1872, August 1st: John KEWISH

Kidd, Mary
1874, December 29th: Robert TAYLOR

Kidd, Detective Sergeant Robert
1895, December 17th: Elijah WINSTANLEY

Kiegoam, John
1875, August 2nd: Michael GILLINGHAM

King, Mary (& her two children)
1899, January 13th: Philip KING

Knight, *
1894, December 12th: Cyrus KNIGHT

Knight, Bridget
1893, July 10th: Edward LEIGH

Lace, *
1872, August 26th: William LACE

Lane, Harriet
1875, December 21st: Henry WAINWRIGHT

Langan, Charles
1875, September 6th: William BAKER

Last, Henry
1886, December 13th: George HARMER

Lawlor, Ellen
1899, January 7th: Patrick HOLMES

Lawrence, Bensley Cyrus
1889, January 2nd: Charles DOBELL & William GOWER

Laycock, Maria (& four children)
1884, August 26th: Joseph LAYCOCK

Le Brun, Nancy
1875, August 11th: Joseph Phillip LE BRUN

Lefley, *
1884, May 26th: Mary LEFLEY

Leigh, Christina
1883, February 12th: Abraham THOMAS

Levy, Jonathon Goodman
1896, June 9th: William SEAMAN

Lewis, May
1896, August 18th: Frank TAYLOR

Lindsay, Charlotte
1886, February 1st: John HORTON

Lines, Police Constable *
1875, July 27th: Jeremiah CORKERY

Lloyd, *
1897, August 18th: Thomas LLOYD

Lord, Daniel
1877, August 21st: John GOLDING

Lyden, *
1882, September 22nd: Patrick WALSH

Lyden, Martin
1882, September 22nd: Patrick WALSH

Lynch, Bridget
1877, October 15th: John LYNCH

Lynch, Patrick
1873, August 20th: Laurence SMITH

Lyons, Mary Ann
1892, April 19th: Daniel HANDLEY

Mabbotts, William
1886, July 27th: William SAMUELS

Malcolm, Percy John
1882, April 28th: George Henry LAMSON

Manning, Nicholas
1874, August 31st: Mary WILLIAMS

Marmon, Doris
1896, June 10th: Amelia Elizabeth DYER

Marsh, Alice
1892, November 15th: Thomas CREAM

Marsh, Mary Ann
1881, May 17th: Albert MOORE

Marshall, Emmanuel (& family)
1870, August 8th: John OWEN

Marshall, Mary Ann
1894, December 11th: Samuel George EMERY

Marshall, Sally
1871, April 3rd: William BULL

Martin, Nicholas
1891, August 20th: John CONWAY

Masfen, William
1893, August 15th: John Thomas HEWITT

Mather, Ellen
1879, May 20th: William COOPER

Matthews, *
1896, July 21st: Philip MATTHEWS

McDiarmid, John
1884, March 31st: William INNES &
Robert Flockheart VICKERS

McDonald, *
1878, October 3rd: William McDONALD

McEntire, Ellen
1881, May 31st: Joseph Patrick McENTIRE

McGill, Mary
1886, February 22nd: Owen McGILL

McGowan, *
1878, November 19th: James McGOWAN

McGuiness, Ann
1879, February 11th: William McGUINESS

McGuire, Mary
1897, June 7th: George PATERSON

McKenna, Annie
1877, March 27th: John McKENNA

McKivett, Margaret
1875, April 19th: Alfred Thomas HEAP

McShane, Mary
1876, August 21st: Steven McKEOWN

Meadows, Mary Elizabeth
1899, July 11th: Joseph Cornelius PARKER

Mears, Eliza Jane
1899, October 3rd: Frederick PRESTON

Mellor, Ann
1877, November 21st: Thomas GREY

Mellor, Ann
1881, February 21st: William STANWAY

Mellor, Mary Jane
1892, December 20th: James MELLOR

Meredith, Alfred
1879, February 10th: Enoch WHISTON

Messenger, Jane
1880, December 13th: William HERBERT

Metcalfe, William
1879, May 27th: John D'ARCY

Meyrick, Ann
1872, March 18th: Edward ROBERTS

Miles, Albert
1884, February 25th: Charles KITE

Miller, James
1880, April 14th: Peter CONWAY

Miller, John
1870, October 4th: George CHALMERS

Miller, John
1875, October 5th: Patrick DOCHERTY

Miller, Mary
1888, May 15th: John Alfred GELL

Minahan, Bridget
1885, December 7th: Daniel MINAHAN

Mitchell, William
1894, July 18th: Samuel ELKINS

Mohan, Mary
1883, May 8th: Patrick CAREY

Mooney, Thomas
1875, August 2nd: William McHUGH

Moore, *
1872, August 13th: Thomas MOORE

Moore, Elizabeth
1884, August 24th: James TOBIN

Moore, Ellen
1872, December 9th: Augustus ELLIOT

Moran, Mary Ellen
1891, May 19th: Alfred William TURNER

Morgan, *
1896, February 4th: William James
MORGAN

Morgan, Richard
1875, January 4th: John McGRAVE &
Michael MULLEN

Morley, Elizabeth
1895, December 31st: Patrick MORLEY

Moulden, Sergeant *
1892, July 26th: John GURD

Moylan, John
1885, January 16th: Michael DOWNEY

Moyse, Edward
1895, June 4th: William MILLER

Murphy, Margaret
1870, July 28th: Andrew CARR

Musson, Fanny
1881, August 23rd: George DURLING

Nash, *
1886, March 1st: Thomas NASH

Neal, Theresa
1890, March 26th: John NEAL

Newell, Isabella
1894, December 10th: John William
NEWELL

Newitt, John Cox
1874, March 31st: Thomas
CHAMBERLAIN

Newton, John
1883, May 7th: Thomas GARRY

Nicholson, *
1889, January 8th: George NICHOLSON

Nield, Thomas
1875, March 30th: John STANTON

Nightingale, Elizabeth
1890, July 29th: George BOWLING

Norman, *
1885, October 5th: Henry NORMAN

Nurney, Patrick
1869, March 29th: Michael James JOHNSON

Oakley, Annie Emma
1892, October 11th: John James BANBURY

O'Donnell, Elizabeth
1876, December 11th: Charles O'DONNELL

O'Keefe, John
1883, April 30th: Timothy O'KEEFE

Oldham, Sarah Ann
1895, March 26th: Edmund KESTEVEN

Osbourne, Emma Elizabeth
1877, August 14th: Caleb SMITH

O'Shea, Eliza
1899, November 28th: Charles SCOTT

Palmer, Emma
1885, March 17th: Henry KIMBERLEY

Parker, James Stanley
1886, May 31st: Albert Edward BROWN

Parton, Eliza
1879, May 28th: Thomas JOHNSON

Partridge, James
1874, January 5th: Edward GOUGH

Pastor, Lizzie
1891, January 11th: Frederick Thomas STOREY

Payne, Corporal *
1896, July 21st: Samuel Edward SMITH

Pearcey, Charlotte
1893, July 19th: Amie Holman MEUNIER

Penfold, Sarah Ann
1898, December 14th: Thomas DALEY

Pepper, William
1882, May 23rd: Osmond Otto BRAND

Phillips, Amelia
1874, January 12th: Charles Edward BUTT

Phillips, Mary Jane
1889, January 14th: Arthur McKEOWN

Phillips, Winifred Whittaker
1890, January 7th: Charles Lister HIGGENBOTHAM

Pickerill, George
1888, March 28th: William ARROWSMITH

Pickering, *
1892, June 14th: Henry PICKERING

Pickles, Sarah
1897, August 17th: Walter ROBINSON

Pickup, John Kirkby
1898, February 22nd: George William HOWE

Plunkett/Abigail, Jane
1882, May 22nd: William George ABIGAIL

Pritchard, Annie
1893, January 10th: Andrew George McCRAE

Puddipant, William
1892, March 17th: Charles RAYNOR & Frederick EGGLESTON

Purcell, Emily
1889, December 9th: Benjamin PURCELL

Pyle, Thomas
1883, November 19th: Peter BRAY

Quinn, Kate
1887, February 15th: Thomas LEATHERBARROW

Quinn, Patrick
1884, January 15th: Peter WADE

Quirke, Patrick
1888, May 7th: James KIRBY

Radcliffe, Annie
1881, November 28th: John Aspinall SIMPSON

Rasch, *
1894, August 14th: Paul KOEZULA

Reilly, Mary
1899, January 13th: Philip KING

Relfe, Emma
1876, December 14th: Robert BROWNING

Revell, Hester
1878, July 29th: Charles Joseph REVELL

Reynolds, *
1895, December 24th: Henry WRIGHT

Richards, Henry
1892, July 26th: John GURD

Richardson, George
1886, May 31st: James WHELAN

Robinson, *
1881, February 28th: Albert ROBINSON

Robinson, *
1897, August 17th: Joseph ROBINSON

Robinson, Sergeant James
1893, December 6th: George MASON

Rockington, Eliza Francis
1877, November 12th: Thomas Benjamin PRATT

Rodden, Eliza
1879, December 3rd: Henry BEDINGFIELD

Rodgers, *
1887, November 21st: Joseph MORLEY

Rogers, Sarah
1877, July 31st: Henry ROGERS

Rose, Mary
1896, August 11th: John ROSE

Rowe, William
1893, March 28th: William WILLIAMS

Rushy, *
1893, December 19th: Henry RUMBOLD

Ryan, John
1871, August 17th: William COLLINS

Sandford, William
1875, April 9th: John RUSSELL

Sargent, Annie
1888, August 15th: George SARGENT

Saunders, *
1886, February 16th: George SAUNDERS

Saunders, Maria
1877, April 17th: Frederick Edwin BAKER

Scott, Betty
1882, February 13th: Richard TEMPLETON

Scott, Robert
1898, August 30th: Joseph LEWIS

Scrivener, Henry Ernest
1874, June 29th: Frances STEWART

Sharpe, Elizabeth
1883, August 6th: James BURTON

Shaw, Ellen
1884, December 8th: Arthur SHAW

Sheehan, Christine
1886, January 20th: William SHEEHAN

Sheehan, Hannah
1886, January 20th: William SHEEHAN

Sheehan, Thomas
1886, January 20th: William SHEEHAN

Shepherd, Ada
1880, December 13th: George PAVEY

Sheward, Martha
1869, April 20th: William SHEWARD

Short, Francis
1899, May 3rd: Frederick James ANDREWS

Shorter, Police Constable *
1877, March 12th: Francis TIDBURY & Henry TIDBURY

Shrivell, Emma
1892, November 15th: Thomas CREAM

Simmons, Inspector *
1885, May 18th: James LEE

Skullen, Corporal Arthur
1869, October 11th: William TAYLOR

Sloan, Margaret
1876, May 31st: Thomas BARR

Sloper, *
1876, December 19th: Silas BARLOW

Sloper, Ellen
1876, December 19th: Silas BARLOW

Smith, *
1887, May 9th: Charles SMITH

Smith, *
1898, March 22nd: Charles SMITH

Smith, Bridget
1891, March 13th: John PURCELL

Smith, Henry
1896, June 9th: Henry FOWLER & Albert MILSOM

Smith, Jane
1878, August 12th: Thomas CHOLERTON

Smith, Maud
1893, July 25th: George Samuel COOK

Smith, William
1884, May 27th: Joseph LAWSON

Spicer, * (two children)
1890, August 22nd: Felix SPICER

Springhall, Harry
1886, February 10th: John THURSTON

Starkey, *
1877, July 31st: John Henry STARKEY

Steele, Isabella
1887, November 14th: William HUNTER

Steers, Walter Charles
1891, December 23rd: Charles SAUNDERS

Stelfox, Edward
1876, April 25th: Joseph WEBBER

Stephens, Frank
1890, March 11th: Joseph BOSWELL & Samuel BOSWELL

Stevens, Elizabeth
1894, May 22nd: John LANGFORD

Stock, George
1872, August 13th: James TOOTH

Stodhart, Ada
1887, August 22nd: Henry HOBSON

Sullivan, Abigail
1892, March 1st: James MUIR

Sutton, Annie
1887, March 21st: Joseph KING

Sutton, Henry
1887, March 21st: Joseph KING

Swift, Mary Elizabeth
1892, March 29th: John NOBLE

Taylor, *
1882, December 12th: Charles TAYLOR

Taylor, *
1892, August 16th: James TAYLOR

Taylor, Charlotte
1887, December 6th: Thomas PAYNE

Terry, *
1887, February 22nd: Benjamin TERRY

Thomas, David
1886, March 2nd: David ROBERTS

Thomas, Julia
1879, July 29th: Catherine WEBSTER

Thompson, Jane
1874, January 5th: William THOMPSON

Thrussel, William
1876, April 10th: George HILL

Tickner, *
1895, July 2nd: Henry TICKNER

Torr, Margaret Ann
1899, August 9th: Elias TORR

Tracey, Patrick
1880, March 2nd: Hugh BURNS & Patrick KEARNS

Trainer, Philip
1869, March 23rd: John McCONVILLE

Tregillis, Mary
1883, January 2nd: Louisa Jane TAYLOR

Trevett, James
1869, August 12th: Jonah DETHERIDGE

Trickett, *
1878, February 12th: James TRICKETT

Tugby, Joseph
1877, November 27th: John SWIFT, John UPTON, James SATCHELL

Turner, *
1882, August 21st: William TURNER

Tyrer, *
1893, November 28th: Emanuel HAMER

Upton, *
1888, July 17th: Robert UPTON

Vaughan, Annie
1888, March 27th: George CLARKE

Vernon, Sarah Alice
1879, August 26th: John RALPH

Wadge, *
1878, August 15th: Selina WADGE

Waine, Joseph
1873, January 13th: Hugh SLANE & John HAYES

Walber, James
1894, April 2nd: Margaret WALBER

Wales, John
1876, July 26th: John WILLIAMS

Walker, Henrietta
1887, November 15th: Joseph WALKER

Walker, Henry
1877, March 26th: William CLARK

Wallace, William John
1878, July 30th: Robert VEST

Walsh, *
1873, August 19th: Edward WALSH

Walsh, Bridget
1874, August 10th: John MacDONALD

Walshe, Edward
1868, August 13th: Thomas WELLS

Ward, * (two daughters)
1899, October 4th: Robert WARD

Ward, Hugh John
1869, March 23rd: John DOLAN

Wardlaw, *
1875, October 19th: David WARDLAW

Wass, William
1891, August 18th: Thomas SADLER

Waterhouse, Barbara
1891, August 18th: Walter Lewis TURNER

Watkins, Alice
1878, November 18th: Joseph GARCIA

Watkins, Charlotte
1878, November 18th: Joseph GARCIA

Watkins, Elizabeth
1878, November 18th: Joseph GARCIA

Watkins, Frederick
1878, November 18th: Joseph GARCIA

Watkins, William
1878, November 18th: Joseph GARCIA

Watson, James
1875, August 2nd: Elizabeth PEARSON

Watson, William
1875, August 16th: William McCULLOUGH

Watt, *
1898, July 12th: James WATT

Webb, Ralph
1888, August 7th: John JACKSON

Weedey, Police Constable
1890, December 30th: Robert KITCHING

Wells, Florence
1899, November 15th: Thomas SKEFFINGTON

Wendle, Eleanor
1881, November 24th: Alfred GOUGH

West, *
1889, December 31st: Robert WEST

Wharton, Elizabeth
1873, January 8th: Richard SPENCER

White, *
1883, May 21st: George WHITE

White, Amos
1877, April 3rd: John Henry JOHNSON

White, Edward
1896, October 6th: James JONES

White, Lydia Wills
1878, April 15th: Vincent Knowles WALKER

Whitehead, *
1894, November 27th: James Wilshaw WHITEHEAD

Whiteley, Margaret
1876, April 26th: John DALY

Wild, James
1884, November 24th: Harry Hammond SWINDELLS

Wilkes, *
1898, July 19th: William WILKES

Wilkinson, Eliza
1880, August 16th: John WAKEFIELD

Williams, Elizabeth
1885, August 3rd: Joseph TUCKER

Willis, John
1888, December 11th: Samuel CROWTHER

Wilson, Lily McClaren
1890, March 12th: William ROW

Wilton, Sarah
1887, August 29th: William WILTON

Wingfield, Margaret
1880, March 22nd: John WINGFIELD

Withey, Jane
1889, April 11th: John WITHEY

Wood, Emma
1887, May 30th: Walter WOOD

Wood, Juliet
1896, December 22nd: August CARLSEN

Woodhead, Caroline
1878, February 13th: John BROOKS

Woods, William
1876, March 28th: George HUNTER

Wooldridge, Laura
1896, July 7th: Charles Thomas WOOLDRIDGE

Worthington, *
1875, January 4th: William WORTHINGTON

Wright, Sarah
1876, December 19th: James DALGLEISH

Wyndham, James
1893, December 21st: Frederick WYNDHAM

Wyre, *
1888, July 18th: Thomas WYRE

Youell, Jane
1895, June 18th: James CANNING

Method Index

Method Index

Abortion
1875, April 19th: Alfred Thomas HEAP

Axe
1869, August 12th: Jonah DETHERIDGE
1872, March 18th: Edward ROBERTS
1876, April 24th: Edward DEACON
1878, February 11th: James CAFFYN
1878, November 18th: Joseph GARCIA
1879, July 29th: Catherine WEBSTER
1881, May 23rd: James HALL
1883, May 21st: Joseph WEDLAKE
1888, March 20th: James JONES & Alfred SCANDRETT
1888, May 15th: John Alfred GELL
1889, January 1st: Thomas CLEWES
1889, January 8th: George NICHOLSON
1889, December 9th: Benjamin PURCELL
1893, April 4th: Edward HEMMINGS
1893, July 19th: Amie Holman MEUNIER
1894, January 2nd: William HARRIS
1894, July 31st: William CROSSLEY
1897, August 18th: Thomas LLOYD
1897, December 16th: William BETTS

Beatings
1869, December 13th: Frederick HINSON
1870, January 10th: John GREGSON
1870, August 8th: John OWEN
1870, August 15th: Thomas RADCLIFFE
1870, October 4th: George CHALMERS
1871, April 3rd: William BULL
1872, August 26th: William LACE
1873, January 13th: Hugh SLANE & John HAYES
1874, January 5th: Thomas CORRIGAN
1874, January 5th: Charles DAWSON
1875, January 4th: John McGRAVE & Michael MULLEN
1875, March 29th: Richard COATES
1876, April 4th: Thomas FORDRED
1876, May 23rd: George KADI, Pascaler CALADIS, Matteo CORGALIS, Giovanni CACCARIS
1876, May 31st: Thomas BARR
1876, April 26th: John DALY
1877, March 27th: John McKENNA
1877, August 13th: Henry LEIGH
1877, November 27th: John SWIFT, John UPTON, James SATCHELL
1878, February 12th: James TRICKETT
1878, November 25th: Henry GILBERT
1879, February 4th: Stephen GAMBRILL
1879, February 11th: William McGUINESS
1879, August 25th: James DILLEY
1880, January 5th: Charles SURETY
1882, August 21st: William TURNER
1882, August 22nd: Thomas HAYNES
1883, May 21st: George WHITE
1884, March 10th: Michael McLEAN
1884, May 27th: Joseph LAWSON
1884, January 15th: Peter WADE
1886, February 1st: John HORTON
1886, February 10th: John THURSTON
1886, February 22nd: Owen McGILL
1886, March 2nd: David ROBERTS
1886, June 15th: Edward HEWITT
1887, February 15th: Thomas LEATHERBARROW
1887, August 16th: Thomas Henry BEVAN
1888, March 13th: David REES
1888, August 7th: John JACKSON
1888, August 10th: Arthur James DELANEY
1889, December 31st: William Thomas HOOK
1891, December 23rd: Charles SAUNDERS
1892, March 17th: Charles RAYNOR & Frederick EGGLESTON
1893, January 6th: John BOYLE
1895, February 9th: John TWISS
1896, August 5th: William PUGH
1897, February 9th: Robert HAYMAN
1898, March 12th: John HERDMAN
1898, July 19th: William WILKES
1898, August 3rd: Thomas JONES
1899, December 5th: Samuel CROZIER

Billhook
1876, December 19th: James DALGLEISH
1879, May 26th: Catherine CHURCHILL
1895, July 2nd: Henry TICKNER

Blunt instrument
1868, September 8th: Alexander Arthur MACKAY
1870, August 1st: Walter MILLAR
1871, April 24th: Michael CAMPBELL
1872, August 12th: Christopher EDWARDS
1873, August 4th: Benjamin HUDSON
1873, August 4th: Henry EVANS
1873, August 19th: Edward WALSH
1873, August 26th: Thomas Hartley MONTGOMERY
1874, May 25th: John GODWIN
1874, August 10th: John MacDONALD
1874, December 28th: Hugh DALEY
1875, January 4th: James CRANWELL
1875, January 4th: William WORTHINGTON

Blunt instrument   Method Index   Firearms

1875, October 5th: Patrick DOCHERTY
1875, October 19th: David WARDLAW
1875, March 24th: John McDAID
1875, April 9th: John RUSSELL
1876, April 10th: George HILL
1876, August 1st: James PARRIS
1876, December 11th: Charles O'DONNELL
1876, August 21st: Steven McKEOWN
1877, April 2nd: James BANNISTER
1877, August 21st: John GOLDING
1877, November 20th: Henry MARSH
1877, November 23rd: Cadwaller JONES
1879, May 27th: John D'ARCY
1879, August 11th: Annie TOOKE
1879, January 10th: Thomas CUNCEEN
1880, May 11th: John Henry WOOD
1880, January 16th: Martin McHUGO
1880, April 14th: Peter CONWAY
1881, May 31st: Joseph Patrick McENTIRE
1881, August 23rd: George DURLING
1882, December 15th: Pat CASEY, Miles JOYCE, Pat JOYCE
1883, May 8th: Patrick CAREY
1883, August 6th: James BURTON
1883, November 6th: Henry POWELL
1883, November 19th: Peter BRAY
1883, January 15th: Patrick HIGGINS
1883, January 17th: Michael FLYNN & Thomas HIGGINS
1884, August 19th: Peter CASSIDY
1884, August 24th: James TOBIN
1885, August 17th: Thomas BOULTON
1885, November 23rd: John HILL & John WILLIAMS
1885, December 7th: Daniel MINAHAN
1886, May 31st: Albert Edward BROWN
1886, November 30th: James BARTON
1886, December 13th: George HARMER
1886, January 20th: William SHEEHAN
1887, February 17th: Edward PRITCHARD
1887, February 22nd: Benjamin TERRY
1887, May 9th: Charles SMITH
1888, July 17th: Robert UPTON
1888, November 13th: Leir Richard BARTLETT
1889, March 13th: Samuel RYLANDS
1889, December 9th: Benjamin PURCELL
1889, December 24th: William DUKES
1889, January 14th: Arthur McKEOWN
1890, April 8th: Richard DAVIES
1890, June 10th: Daniel Stewart GORRIE
1890, July 29th: George BOWLING
1890, August 26th: James HARRISON
1890, September 23rd: Henry DELVIN
1890, December 23rd: Mary Eleanor WHEELER
1891, March 13th: John PURCELL

1892, August 16th: James TAYLOR
1892, August 18th: Moses CUDWORTH
1892, April 19th: Daniel HANDLEY
1893, July 25th: George Samuel COOK
1893, September 2nd: James REILLY
1894, April 3rd: Philip GARNER
1894, December 10th: John William NEWELL
1896, June 9th: Henry FOWLER & Albert MILSOM
1896, June 9th: William SEAMAN
1896, August 11th: Samuel WILKINSON
1896, August 18th: Frank TAYLOR
1897, January 5th: Henry BROWN
1897, June 7th: George PATERSON
1898, February 22nd: George William HOWE
1898, March 22nd: Charles SMITH
1898, December 14th: Thomas DALEY
1898, December 21st: John COTTON
1899, October 3rd: Frederick PRESTON
1899, January 7th: Patrick HOLMES
1899, January 13th: Philip KING

Burnings
1880, February 17th: William CASSIDY
1882, December 4th: Bernard MULLARKEY
1885, August 3rd: Joseph TUCKER
1899, January 3rd: John SCHNEIDER

Chain
1894, April 2nd: Margaret WALBER

Drowning
1874, June 29th: Frances STEWART
1875, August 2nd: William McHUGH
1878, August 15th: Selina WADGE
1879, August 26th: John RALPH
1881, February 22nd: James WILLIAMS
1882, May 23rd: Osmond Otto BRAND
1882, November 28th: Edward WHEATFALL
1886, March 1st: Thomas NASH
1886, May 31st: James WHELAN
1888, July 18th: Thomas WYRE
1891, December 15th: Henry DAINTON
1896, June 10th: Amelia Elizabeth DYER

Falls
1881, November 29th: Percy LEFROY
1893, November 28th: Emanuel HAMER

Firearms
1868, August 13th: Thomas WELLS
1869, January 19th: Martin Henry VINALL
1869, March 23rd: John McCONVILLE
1869, October 11th: William TAYLOR
1869, December 13th: Frederick HINSON
1870, May 27th: Lawrence SHEILD & Margaret SHEILD

Firearms — Method Index

1872, April 1st: William Frederick HORRY
1872, August 1st: John KEWISH
1872, December 9th: Augustus ELLIOT
1872, December 30th: Michael KENNEDY
1873, January 8th: Richard SPENCER
1874, January 12th: Charles Edward BUTT
1874, August 31st: Mary WILLIAMS
1874, November 16th: Thomas SMITH
1875, August 11th: Joseph Phillip LE BRUN
1875, September 6th: William BAKER
1875, September 6th: Edward COOPER
1875, December 21st: Henry WAINWRIGHT
1875, December 23rd: Richard CHARLTON
1876, March 28th: George HUNTER
1876, April 25th: Joseph WEBBER
1876, May 23rd: George KADI, Pascaler CALADIS, Matteo CORGALIS, Giovanni CACCARIS
1876, July 26th: John WILLIAMS
1876, December 20th: John GREEN
1876, August 25th: Thomas CROWE
1877, January 2nd: Isaac MARKS
1877, March 12th: Francis TIDBURY & Henry TIDBURY
1877, March 26th: William CLARK
1877, April 3rd: John Henry JOHNSON
1878, February 4th: George PIGGOTT
1878, April 1st: Henry ROWLES
1878, October 3rd: William McDONALD
1878, November 12th: Patrick John BYRNE
1879, February 10th: Enoch WHISTON
1879, February 25th: Charles Frederick PEACE
1880, March 2nd: Hugh BURNS & Patrick KEARNS
1880, November 26th: Thomas WHEELER
1880, December 13th: William HERBERT
1881, November 29th: Percy LEFROY
1882, May 22nd: William George ABIGAIL
1882, September 11th: Francis HYNES
1882, September 22nd: Patrick WALSH
1882, December 15th: Pat CASEY, Miles JOYCE, Pat JOYCE
1883, February 12th: Abraham THOMAS
1883, May 7th: Thomas GARRY
1883, May 23rd: Henry MULLEN & Martin SCOTT
1883, December 17th: Patrick O'DONNELL
1883, January 15th: Patrick HIGGINS
1883, January 17th: Michael FLYNN & Thomas HIGGINS
1883, January 23rd: Sylvester POFF & James BARRETT
1883, April 30th: Timothy O'KEEFE

1883, December 18th: Joseph POOLE
1884, March 31st: William INNES & Robert Flockheart VICKERS
1884, October 6th: Thomas Henry ORROCK
1884, November 24th: Harry Hammond SWINDELLS
1885, March 17th: Henry KIMBERLEY
1885, May 18th: James LEE
1885, December 9th: George THOMAS
1885, January 16th: Michael DOWNEY
1885, January 20th: Thomas PARRY
1886, February 8th: Anthony Ben RUDGE, James BAKER, James MARTIN
1886, November 16th: Patrick JUDGE
1886, November 29th: James MURPHY
1887, February 21st: Richard INSOLE
1887, April 18th: Thomas William CURRELL
1887, August 1st: Alfred SOWERY
1888, May 22nd: James William RICHARDSON
1888, August 28th: George Nathaniel DANIELS
1888, August 28th: Harry Benjamin JONES
1888, April 29th: Daniel HAYES & Daniel MORIARTY
1888, May 7th: James KIRBY
1889, January 2nd: Charles DOBELL & William GOWER
1889, April 8th: Peter STAFFORD
1889, August 7th: Lawrence Maurice HICKEY
1890, March 11th: Joseph BOSWELL & Samuel BOSWELL
1890, August 26th: Frederick DAVIES
1890, August 27th: Francois MONTEAU
1890, December 30th: Robert KITCHING
1891, July 21st: Franz Joseph MUNCH
1891, July 28th: Arthur SPENCER
1891, August 25th: Edward Henry FAWCETT
1891, December 22nd: John William JOHNSON
1892, March 22nd: Joseph WILSON
1892, July 26th: John GURD
1892, August 16th: John George WENZEL
1892, October 11th: John James BANBURY
1893, March 16th: Albert MANNING
1893, March 28th: William WILLIAMS
1893, August 15th: John Thomas HEWITT
1893, December 6th: George MASON
1893, December 19th: Henry RUMBOLD
1893, December 21st: Frederick WYNDHAM
1894, March 27th: Walter SMITH

Firearms

1894, April 4th: Frederick William FENTON
1894, July 18th: Samuel ELKINS
1894, December 4th: James Canham READ
1894, December 12th: William ROGERS
1894, August 17th: John GILMOUR
1895, August 20th: Thomas BOND
1895, December 3rd: Arthur COVINGTON
1895, December 31st: Patrick MORLEY
1896, July 21st: Samuel Edward SMITH
1897, July 27th: Joseph BOWSER
1897, August 17th: Joseph ROBINSON
1898, July 12th: James WATT
1898, August 30th: Joseph LEWIS
1898, April 5th: Wilfrid F KENNY
1899, July 11th: Joseph Cornelius PARKER
1899, July 18th: Charles MAIDMENT
1899, August 9th: Elias TORR
1899, January 10th: Thomas KELLY

Poisonings

1868, December 28th: Priscilla BIGGADYKE
1873, March 24th: Mary Ann COTTON
1874, January 12th: Edwin BAILEY & Ann BERRY
1875, August 2nd: Elizabeth PEARSON
1876, December 19th: Silas BARLOW
1878, May 31st: Eugene Marie CHANTRELLE
1879, August 25th: James DILLEY
1882, April 28th: George Henry LAMSON
1883, January 2nd: Louisa Jane TAYLOR
1884, March 5th: Catherine FLANAGAN & Margaret HIGGINS
1884, May 26th: Mary LEFLEY
1886, July 27th: William SAMUELS
1886, August 9th: Mary Ann BRITLAND
1887, March 14th: Elizabeth BERRY
1877, August 22nd: Israel LIPSKI
1888, January 10th: Phillip Henry Eustace CROSS
1889, August 21st: George HORTON
1892, November 15th: Thomas CREAM
1894, August 21st: Alfred DEWS
1898, June 28th: William HORSFORD
1899, July 19th: Mary Ann ANSELL
1899, July 25th: Edward BELL

Sharp-edged instrument

1870, May 27th: Lawrence SHEILD & Margaret SHEILD
1870, July 28th: Andrew CARR
1871, July 31st: Richard ADDINGTON
1871, August 17th: William COLLINS
1872, January 8th: Frederick JONES
1872, August 12th: Charles HOLMES
1873, August 20th: Laurence SMITH
1874, January 5th: William THOMPSON
1874, March 31st: Thomas CHAMBERLAIN
1874, August 18th: William JACKSON
1874, August 24th: James Henry GIBBS
1875, January 4th: James CRANWELL
1875, August 16th: Mark FIDDLER
1875, December 21st: William SMEDLEY
1875, December 21st: Henry WAINWRIGHT
1875, April 19th: William TOBIN
1876, August 14th: William FISH
1876, December 14th: Robert BROWNING
1877, April 17th: Frederick Edwin BAKER
1877, July 31st: Henry ROGERS
1877, July 31st: John Henry STARKEY
1877, August 14th: Caleb SMITH
1877, October 15th: John LYNCH
1877, November 21st: Thomas GREY
1878, February 13th: John BROOKS
1878, July 29th: Charles Joseph REVELL
1878, August 12th: Thomas CHOLERTON
1878, November 19th: James McGOWAN
1879, March 24th: James SIMMS
1879, May 12th: Edwin SMART
1879, May 20th: William COOPER
1879, December 3rd: Henry BEDINGFIELD
1880, May 10th: William DUMBLETON
1880, August 16th: John WAKEFIELD
1880, November 16th: William BROWNLESS
1880, December 13th: George PAVEY
1881, May 17th: Albert MOORE
1881, August 15th: Thomas BROWN
1881, November 28th: John Aspinall SIMPSON
1882, February 13th: Richard TEMPLETON
1882, December 12th: Charles TAYLOR
1883, February 19th: James ANDERSON
1883, November 13th: Thomas Lyons DAY
1883, November 26th: Thomas RILEY
1883, December 3rd: Henry DUTTON
1883, June 9th: Timothy KELLY
1884, August 19th: Peter CASSIDY
1884, August 26th: Joseph LAYCOCK
1884, October 6th: Thomas HARRIS
1884, November 24th: Kay HOWARTH
1885, January 13th: Horace Robert JAY
1885, November 30th: Robert GOODALE
1886, February 1st: John HORTON
1886, February 16th: George SAUNDERS
1886, May 31st: Albert Edward BROWN
1887, February 14th: Thomas BLOXHAM
1887, March 21st: Joseph KING
1887, May 30th: Walter WOOD
1887, August 22nd: Henry HOBSON
1887, August 29th: William WILTON

1887, November 14th: William HUNTER
1887, November 15th: Joseph WALKER
1887, November 21st: Joseph MORLEY
1887, November 28th: Enoch WADELY
1887, December 6th: Thomas PAYNE
1888, March 27th: George CLARKE
1888, March 28th: William ARROWSMITH
1888, August 15th: George SARGENT
1889, December 31st: Frederick BRETT
1889, December 31st: Robert WEST
1890, January 7th: Charles Lister HIGGENBOTHAM
1890, March 12th: William ROW
1890, August 22nd: Felix SPICER
1891, August 18th: Walter Lewis TURNER
1891, August 19th: Robert BRADSHAW
1891, August 20th: John CONWAY
1892, March 29th: John NOBLE
1892, June 14th: Henry PICKERING
1892, August 17th: Patrick GIBBONS
1892, December 22nd: Thomas EDWARDS
1892, January 12th: James HEANEY
1893, January 10th: Andrew George McCRAE
1893, January 18th: William McKEOWN
1893, April 4th: Edward HEMMINGS
1893, July 18th: Richard SABEY
1893, August 16th: John DAVIS
1894, February 13th: George THOMAS
1894, November 27th: James Wilshaw WHITEHEAD
1894, December 12th: Cyrus KNIGHT
1895, March 26th: Edmund KESTEVEN
1895, June 18th: James CANNING
1895, November 13th: Richard WINGROVE
1895, December 24th: Henry WRIGHT
1896, February 25th: Alfred CHIPPERFIELD
1896, July 7th: Charles Thomas WOOLDRIDGE
1896, July 21st: Frederick BURDEN
1896, August 11th: John ROSE
1896, December 22nd: August CARLSEN
1896, December 23rd: Joseph ALLCOCK
1897, August 17th: Walter ROBINSON
1899, March 28th: George ROBERTSON
1899, May 3rd: Frederick James ANDREWS
1899, October 4th: Robert WARD
1899, November 28th: Charles SCOTT
1899, December 6th: Michael DOWDLE

Stabbings
1869, March 23rd: John DOLAN
1869, March 29th: Michael James JOHNSON

1869, April 20th: William SHEWARD
1869, November 15th: Joseph WELSH
1870, March 28th: William MOBBS
1872, August 13th: Francis BRADFORD
1873, January 7th: Edward HANCOCK
1873, September 8th: James CONNOR
1874, January 5th: Edward GOUGH
1874, October 13th: John Walter COPPEN
1874, December 29th: Robert TAYLOR
1875, March 30th: John STANTON
1875, March 30th: John MORGAN
1875, April 26th: William HALE
1875, July 27th: Jeremiah CORKERY
1875, August 2nd: Michael GILLINGHAM
1875, August 9th: Peter BLANCHARD
1875, August 16th: William McCULLOUGH
1875, December 22nd: John William ANDERSON
1876, May 23rd: George KADI, Pascaler CALADIS, Matteo CORGALIS, Giovanni CACCARIS
1876, August 14th: Richard THOMPSON
1876, August 29th: John EBLETHRIFT
1877, August 21st: Patrick McGOVERN
1877, November 12th: Thomas Benjamin PRATT
1877, November 19th: William HASSELL
1878, April 15th: Vincent Knowles WALKER
1878, July 30th: Robert VEST
1878, October 8th: Thomas SMITHERS
1878, November 18th: Joseph GARCIA
1879, May 28th: Thomas JOHNSON
1879, August 25th: Joseph PRISTORIA
1880, March 22nd: John WINGFIELD
1880, November 27th: William Joseph DISTON
1880, July 27th: Thomas BERRY
1881, February 21st: William STANWAY
1881, February 28th: Albert ROBINSON
1881, November 29th: Percy LEFROY
1882, January 31st: Charles GERRISH
1882, May 16th: Thomas FURY
1883, May 14th: Joseph BRADY
1884, February 25th: Charles KITE
1884, December 8th: Ernest EWERSTADT
1885, May 25th: Moses SHRIMPTON
1885, July 13th: Henry ALT
1885, October 5th: Henry NORMAN
1886, February 9th: John BAINS
1887, February 14th: Thomas BLOXHAM
1888, December 11th: Samuel CROWTHER
1888, December 18th: William WADDELL
1889, January 1st: Charles BULMER
1889, April 10th: Thomas ALLEN
1889, April 11th: John WITHEY
1890, March 26th: John NEAL

Stabbings

1890, April 15th: William Matthew CHADWICK
1890, December 30th: Thomas McDONALD
1891, January 11th: Frederick Thomas STOREY
1891, May 19th: Alfred William TURNER
1891, August 18th: Thomas SADLER
1892, January 5th: James STOCKWELL
1892, March 1st: James MUIR
1892, April 26th: George Henry WOOD
1892, December 20th: James MELLOR
1893, July 10th: Edward LEIGH
1894, May 22nd: John LANGFORD
1894, December 11th: Samuel George EMERY
1895, June 4th: William MILLER
1895, August 13th: Robert Heseltine HUDSON
1895, December 17th: Elijah WINSTANLEY
1896, February 4th: William James MORGAN
1896, August 25th: Joseph Robert ELLIS
1896, October 6th: James JONES
1898, March 12th: John HERDMAN
1898, November 15th: John RYAN
1899, May 3rd: Frederick James ANDREWS
1899, November 15th: Thomas SKEFFINGTON
1899, November 21st: George NUNN

Starvation

1870, October 11th: Margaret WATERS
1899, January 13th: Philip KING

Strangulation

1870, October 11th: Margaret WATERS
1872, August 13th: Thomas MOORE
1874, August 31st: Henry FLANAGAN
1881, November 24th: Alfred GOUGH
1882, November 13th: William Meager BARTLETT
1884, December 8th: Arthur SHAW
1886, January 20th: William SHEEHAN
1887, May 16th: Henry William YOUNG
1889, March 6th: Ebeneezer Samuel JENKINS
1889, March 11th: Jessie KING
1889, April 24th: William Henry BURY
1890, December 23rd: Mary Eleanor WHEELER
1892, April 4th: James CAMPBELL
1894, August 14th: Paul KOEZULA
1896, July 21st: Philip MATTHEWS
1896, August 4th: Joseph HIRST

Suffocation

1870, October 11th: Margaret WATERS
1889, March 11th: Jessie KING
1893, January 3rd: Cross DUCKWORTH
1893, August 10th: Charles SQUIRES
1894, November 29th: Thomas RICHARDS
1899, January 13th: Philip KING

Executioner Index

*=*christian name unknown*

Executioners Index

Anderson, *
1874, January 12th: Charles Edward BUTT
1874, January 12th: Edwin BAILEY & Ann BERRY
1875, January 4th: John McGRAVE & Michael MULLEN
1875, January 4th: William WORTHINGTON

Anderson, * (asst)
1874, May 25th: John GODWIN

Archer, Alfred (asst)
1883, December 17th: Patrick O'DONNELL

Askern, Thomas
1868, December 28th: Priscilla BIGGADYKE
1874, August 18th: William JACKSON
1875, December 21st: William SMEDLEY
1876, December 19th: James DALGLEISH
1877, April 3rd: John Henry JOHNSON

Berry, James
1884, March 31st: William INNES & Robert Flockheart VICKERS
1884, May 26th: Mary LEFLEY
1884, May 27th: Joseph LAWSON
1884, August 19th: Peter CASSIDY
1884, October 6th: Thomas Henry ORROCK
1884, October 6th: Thomas HARRIS
1884, November 24th: Kay HOWARTH
1884, November 24th: Harry Hammond SWINDELLS
1884, December 8th: Ernest EWERSTADT
1884, December 8th: Arthur SHAW
1884, August 24th: James TOBIN
1885, January 13th: Horace Robert JAY
1885, March 17th: Henry KIMBERLEY
1885, May 18th: James LEE
1885, May 25th: Moses SHRIMPTON
1885, July 13th: Henry ALT
1885, August 3rd: Joseph TUCKER
1885, August 17th: Thomas BOULTON
1885, October 5th: Henry NORMAN
1885, November 23rd: John HILL & John WILLIAMS
1885, November 30th: Robert GOODALE
1885, December 7th: Daniel MINAHAN
1885, December 9th: George THOMAS
1885, January 16th: Michael DOWNEY
1885, January 20th: Thomas PARRY
1886, February 1st: John HORTON
1886, February 8th: Anthony Ben RUDGE, James BAKER, James MARTIN

1886, February 9th: John BAINS
1886, February 10th: John THURSTON
1886, February 16th: George SAUNDERS
1886, February 22nd: Owen McGILL
1886, March 1st: Thomas NASH
1886, March 2nd: David ROBERTS
1886, May 31st: Albert Edward BROWN
1886, May 31st: James WHELAN
1886, June 15th: Edward HEWITT
1886, July 27th: William SAMUELS
1886, August 9th: Mary Ann BRITLAND
1886, November 16th: Patrick JUDGE
1886, November 29th: James MURPHY
1886, November 30th: James BARTON
1886, December 13th: George HARMER
1886, January 12th: John CRONIN
1886, January 20th: William SHEEHAN
1887, February 14th: Thomas BLOXHAM
1887, February 15th: Thomas LEATHERBARROW
1887, February 17th: Edward PRITCHARD
1887, February 21st: Richard INSOLE
1887, February 22nd: Benjamin TERRY
1887, March 14th: Elizabeth BERRY
1887, March 21st: Joseph KING
1887, April 18th: Thomas William CURRELL
1887, May 9th: Charles SMITH
1887, May 16th: Henry William YOUNG
1887, May 30th: Walter WOOD
1887, August 1st: Alfred SOWERY
1887, August 16th: Thomas Henry BEVAN
1877, August 22nd: Israel LIPSKI
1887, August 29th: William WILTON
1887, November 14th: William HUNTER
1887, November 15th: Joseph WALKER
1887, November 21st: Joseph MORLEY
1887, November 28th: Enoch WADELY
1887, December 6th: Thomas PAYNE
1888, March 13th: David REES
1888, March 20th: James JONES & Alfred SCANDRETT
1888, March 27th: George CLARKE
1888, March 28th: William ARROWSMITH
1888, May 15th: John Alfred GELL
1888, July 17th: Robert UPTON
1888, July 18th: Thomas WYRE
1888, August 7th: John JACKSON
1888, August 10th: Arthur James DELANEY
1888, August 15th: George SARGENT
1888, August 28th: George Nathaniel DANIELS

1888, August 28th: Harry Benjamin JONES
1888, November 13th: Leir Richard BARTLETT
1888, December 11th: Samuel CROWTHER
1888, December 18th: William WADDELL
1888, January 10th: Phillip Henry Eustace CROSS
1888, April 29th: Daniel HAYES & Daniel MORIARTY
1888, May 7th: James KIRBY
1889, January 1st: Thomas CLEWES
1889, January 2nd: Charles DOBELL & William GOWER
1889, January 8th: George NICHOLSON
1889, March 6th: Ebeneezer Samuel JENKINS
1889, March 11th: Jessie KING
1889, March 13th: Samuel RYLANDS
1889, April 10th: Thomas ALLEN
1889, April 11th: John WITHEY
1889, April 24th: William Henry BURY
1889, August 21st: George HORTON
1889, December 9th: Benjamin PURCELL
1889, December 24th: William DUKES
1889, December 31st: William Thomas HOOK
1889, January 14th: Arthur McKEOWN
1889, April 8th: Peter STAFFORD
1889, August 7th: Lawrence Maurice HICKEY
1890, January 7th: Charles Lister HIGGENBOTHAM
1890, March 11th: Joseph BOSWELL & Samuel BOSWELL
1890, March 12th: William ROW
1890, March 26th: John NEAL
1890, April 8th: Richard DAVIES
1890, April 15th: William Matthew CHADWICK
1890, June 10th: Daniel Stewart GORRIE
1890, July 29th: George BOWLING
1890, August 22nd: Felix SPICER
1890, August 26th: Frederick DAVIES
1890, August 27th: Francois MONTEAU
1890, September 23rd: Henry DELVIN
1890, December 23rd: Mary Eleanor WHEELER
1890, December 30th: Thomas McDONALD
1891, January 11th: Frederick Thomas STOREY
1891, May 19th: Alfred William TURNER
1891, July 21st: Franz Joseph MUNCH
1891, July 28th: Arthur SPENCER
1891, August 18th: Thomas SADLER
1891, August 19th: Robert BRADSHAW
1891, August 20th: John CONWAY

1891, August 25th: Edward Henry FAWCETT
1891, February 2nd: Bartholomew SULLIVAN
1891, March 13th: John PURCELL

Billington, James
1884, August 26th: Joseph LAYCOCK
1887, August 22nd: Henry HOBSON
1888, May 22nd: James William RICHARDSON
1889, January 1st: Charles BULMER
1889, December 31st: Frederick BRETT
1889, December 31st: Robert WEST
1890, August 26th: James HARRISON
1890, December 30th: Robert KITCHING
1891, August 18th: Walter Lewis TURNER
1891, December 15th: Henry DAINTON
1891, December 22nd: John William JOHNSON
1891, December 23rd: Charles SAUNDERS
1892, January 5th: James STOCKWELL
1892, March 1st: James MUIR
1892, March 17th: Charles RAYNOR & Frederick EGGLESTON
1892, March 22nd: Joseph WILSON
1892, March 29th: John NOBLE
1892, April 26th: George Henry WOOD
1892, June 14th: Henry PICKERING
1892, July 26th: John GURD
1892, August 16th: John George WENZEL
1892, August 16th: James TAYLOR
1892, August 17th: Patrick GIBBONS
1892, August 18th: Moses CUDWORTH
1892, October 11th: John James BANBURY
1892, November 15th: Thomas CREAM
1892, December 20th: James MELLOR
1892, December 22nd: Thomas EDWARDS
1893, January 3rd: Cross DUCKWORTH
1893, January 10th: Andrew George McCRAE
1893, January 18th: William McKEOWN
1893, March 16th: Albert MANNING
1893, March 28th: William WILLIAMS
1893, April 4th: Edward HEMMINGS
1893, July 18th: Richard SABEY
1893, July 19th: Amie Holman MEUNIER
1893, July 25th: George Samuel COOK
1893, August 10th: Charles SQUIRES
1893, August 16th: John DAVIS
1893, November 28th: Emanuel HAMER
1893, December 5th: John CARTER
1893, December 6th: George MASON
1893, December 19th: Henry RUMBOLD
1893, December 21st: Frederick WYNDHAM
1894, January 2nd: William HARRIS

Billington, James

1894, February 13th: George THOMAS
1894, March 27th: Walter SMITH
1894, April 2nd: Margaret WALBER
1894, April 3rd: Philip GARNER
1894, April 4th: Frederick William FENTON
1894, May 22nd: John LANGFORD
1894, July 18th: Samuel ELKINS
1894, July 31st: William CROSSLEY
1894, August 14th: Paul KOEZULA
1894, August 21st: Alfred DEWS
1894, November 27th: James Wilshaw WHITEHEAD
1894, November 29th: Thomas RICHARDS
1894, December 4th: James Canham READ
1894, December 10th: John William NEWELL
1894, December 11th: Samuel George EMERY
1894, December 12th: Cyrus KNIGHT
1894, December 12th: William ROGERS
1895, March 26th: Edmund KESTEVEN
1895, June 4th: William MILLER
1895, June 18th: James CANNING
1895, July 2nd: Henry TICKNER
1895, August 13th: Robert Heseltine HUDSON
1895, November 13th: Richard WINGROVE
1895, December 3rd: Arthur COVINGTON
1895, December 17th: Elijah WINSTANLEY
1895, December 24th: Henry WRIGHT
1895, December 31st: Patrick MORLEY
1895, February 9th: John TWISS
1896, February 4th: William James MORGAN
1896, February 25th: Alfred CHIPPERFIELD
1896, June 9th: Henry FOWLER & Albert MILSOM
1896, June 9th: William SEAMAN
1896, June 10th: Amelia Elizabeth DYER
1896, July 7th: Charles Thomas WOOLDRIDGE
1896, July 21st: Philip MATTHEWS
1896, July 21st: Frederick BURDEN
1896, July 21st: Samuel Edward SMITH
1896, August 4th: Joseph HIRST
1896, August 5th: William PUGH
1896, August 11th: John ROSE
1896, August 11th: Samuel WILKINSON
1896, August 18th: Frank TAYLOR
1896, August 25th: Joseph Robert ELLIS
1896, October 6th: James JONES
1896, December 22nd: August CARLSEN
1896, December 23rd: Joseph ALLCOCK
1897, January 5th: Henry BROWN

Billington, William (asst)

1897, February 9th: Robert HAYMAN
1897, June 7th: George PATERSON
1897, July 27th: Joseph BOWSER
1897, August 17th: Joseph ROBINSON
1897, August 17th: Walter ROBINSON
1897, August 18th: Thomas LLOYD
1897, December 16th: William BETTS
1898, February 22nd: George William HOWE
1898, March 12th: John HERDMAN
1898, March 22nd: Charles SMITH
1898, June 28th: William HORSFORD
1898, July 12th: James WATT
1898, July 19th: William WILKES
1898, August 3rd: Thomas JONES
1898, August 30th: Joseph LEWIS
1898, November 15th: John RYAN
1898, December 14th: Thomas DALEY
1898, December 21st: John COTTON
1899, January 3rd: John SCHNEIDER
1899, March 28th: George ROBERTSON
1899, May 3rd: Frederick James ANDREWS
1899, July 11th: Joseph Cornelius PARKER
1899, July 18th: Charles MAIDMENT
1899, July 19th: Mary Ann ANSELL
1899, August 9th: Elias TORR
1899, October 3rd: Frederick PRESTON
1899, October 4th: Robert WARD
1899, November 15th: Thomas SKEFFINGTON
1899, November 21st: George NUNN
1899, November 28th: Charles SCOTT
1899, December 5th: Samuel CROZIER
1899, December 6th: Michael DOWDLE

Billington, Thomas (asst)

1897, July 27th: Joseph BOWSER
1897, August 17th: Joseph ROBINSON
1897, August 17th: Walter ROBINSON
1897, August 18th: Thomas LLOYD
1898, February 22nd: George William HOWE
1898, August 3rd: Thomas JONES
1898, August 30th: Joseph LEWIS
1898, November 15th: John RYAN
1898, December 21st: John COTTON
1899, March 28th: George ROBERTSON
1899, May 3rd: Frederick James ANDREWS

Billington, William

1899, July 25th: Edward BELL
1899, December 5th: Samuel CROZIER

Billington, William (asst)

1898, July 12th: James WATT
1899, August 9th: Elias TORR

Binns, Bartholomew
1883, November 6th: Henry POWELL
1883, November 13th: Thomas Lyons DAY
1883, November 19th: Peter BRAY
1883, November 26th: Thomas RILEY
1883, December 3rd: Henry DUTTON
1883, December 17th: Patrick O'DONNELL
1884, February 25th: Charles KITE
1884, March 5th: Catherine FLANAGAN & Margaret HIGGINS
1884, March 10th: Michael McLEAN
1884, January 15th: Peter WADE

Binns, Bartholomew (asst)
1899, January 10th: Thomas KELLY

Calcraft, William
1868, August 13th: Thomas WELLS
1868, September 8th: Alexander Arthur MACKAY
1869, January 19th: Martin Henry VINALL
1869, March 23rd: John DOLAN
1869, March 23rd: John McCONVILLE
1869, March 29th: Michael James JOHNSON
1869, April 20th: William SHEWARD
1869, August 12th: Jonah DETHERIDGE
1869, October 11th: William TAYLOR
1869, November 15th: Joseph WELSH
1869, December 13th: Frederick HINSON
1870, January 10th: John GREGSON
1870, March 28th: William MOBBS
1870, August 1st: Walter MILLAR
1870, August 8th: John OWEN
1870, August 15th: Thomas RADCLIFFE
1870, October 4th: George CHALMERS
1870, October 11th: Margaret WATERS
1871, April 3rd: William BULL
1871, April 24th: Michael CAMPBELL
1871, July 31st: Richard ADDINGTON
1871, August 17th: William COLLINS
1872, January 8th: Frederick JONES
1872, March 18th: Edward ROBERTS
1872, August 1st: John KEWISH
1872, August 12th: Charles HOLMES
1872, August 13th: Thomas MOORE
1872, August 13th: James TOOTH
1872, August 13th: Francis BRADFORD
1872, August 26th: William LACE
1872, December 9th: Augustus ELLIOT
1872, December 30th: Michael KENNEDY
1873, January 8th: Richard SPENCER
1873, January 13th: Hugh SLANE & John HAYES
1873, March 24th: Mary Ann COTTON
1873, August 4th: Benjamin HUDSON
1873, September 8th: James CONNOR
1874, January 5th: Thomas CORRIGAN

1874, March 31st: Thomas CHAMBERLAIN
1874, May 25th: John GODWIN

Chester, Richard (asst)
1884, March 31st: William INNES & Robert Flockheart VICKERS
1884, May 26th: Mary LEFLEY
1884, October 6th: Thomas Henry ORROCK
1884, October 6th: Thomas HARRIS
1884, November 24th: Kay HOWARTH
1884, November 24th: Harry Hammond SWINDELLS
1885, January 16th: Michael DOWNEY
1885, January 20th: Thomas PARRY

Heath, Samuel (asst)
1884, March 5th: Catherine FLANAGAN & Margaret HIGGINS

Incher, George
1875, March 30th: John STANTON
1876, May 23rd: George KADI, Pascaler CALADIS, Matteo CORGALIS, Giovanni CACCARIS
1877, July 31st: Henry ROGERS
1881, February 22nd: James WILLIAMS

Jones, *
1883, December 18th: Joseph POOLE

Maldon, Charles (asst)
1886, February 8th: Anthony Ben RUDGE, James BAKER, James MARTIN

Marwood, William
1872, April 1st: William Frederick HORRY
1874, January 5th: Charles DAWSON
1874, January 5th: Edward GOUGH
1874, January 5th: William THOMPSON
1874, June 29th: Frances STEWART
1874, August 10th: John MacDONALD
1874, August 24th: James Henry GIBBS
1874, August 31st: Henry FLANAGAN
1874, August 31st: Mary WILLIAMS
1874, October 13th: John Walter COPPEN
1874, November 16th: Thomas SMITH
1874, December 28th: Hugh DALEY
1874, December 29th: Robert TAYLOR
1875, January 4th: James CRANWELL
1875, March 29th: Richard COATES
1875, March 30th: John MORGAN
1875, April 19th: Alfred Thomas HEAP
1875, April 26th: William HALE
1875, July 27th: Jeremiah CORKERY
1875, August 2nd: Michael GILLINGHAM
1875, August 2nd: Elizabeth PEARSON
1875, August 2nd: William McHUGH
1875, August 9th: Peter BLANCHARD

1875, August 11th: Joseph Phillip LE BRUN
1875, August 16th: Mark FIDDLER
1875, August 16th: William McCULLOUGH
1875, September 6th: William BAKER
1875, September 6th: Edward COOPER
1875, October 5th: Patrick DOCHERTY
1875, October 19th: David WARDLAW
1875, December 21st: Henry WAINWRIGHT
1875, December 22nd: John William ANDERSON
1875, December 23rd: Richard CHARLTON
1875, March 24th: John McDAID
1875, April 9th: John RUSSELL
1876, March 28th: George HUNTER
1876, April 4th: Thomas FORDRED
1876, April 10th: George HILL
1876, April 24th: Edward DEACON
1876, April 25th: Joseph WEBBER
1876, May 23rd: George KADI, Pascaler CALADIS, Matteo CORGALIS, Giovanni CACCARIS
1876, May 31st: Thomas BARR
1876, July 26th: John WILLIAMS
1876, August 1st: James PARRIS
1876, August 14th: William FISH
1876, August 14th: Richard THOMPSON
1876, August 29th: John EBLETHRIFT
1876, December 11th: Charles O'DONNELL
1876, December 14th: Robert BROWNING
1876, December 19th: Silas BARLOW
1876, December 20th: John GREEN
1876, December 21st: William FLANAGAN
1876, August 21st: Steven McKEOWN
1876, August 25th: Thomas CROWE
1876, August 25th: Christos Emanuel BAUMBOS
1876, April 26th: John DALY
1877, January 2nd: Isaac MARKS
1877, March 12th: Francis TIDBURY & Henry TIDBURY
1877, March 26th: William CLARK
1877, March 27th: John McKENNA
1877, April 2nd: James BANNISTER
1877, April 17th: Frederick Edwin BAKER
1877, July 31st: John Henry STARKEY
1877, August 13th: Henry LEIGH
1877, August 14th: Caleb SMITH
1877, August 21st: John GOLDING
1877, August 21st: Patrick McGOVERN
1877, October 15th: John LYNCH
1877, November 12th: Thomas Benjamin PRATT
1877, November 19th: William HASSELL
1877, November 20th: Henry MARSH
1877, November 21st: Thomas GREY
1877, November 23rd: Cadwaller JONES
1877, November 27th: John SWIFT, John UPTON, James SATCHELL
1878, February 4th: George PIGGOTT
1878, February 11th: James CAFFYN
1878, February 12th: James TRICKETT
1878, February 13th: John BROOKS
1878, April 1st: Henry ROWLES
1878, April 15th: Vincent Knowles WALKER
1878, May 31st: Eugene Marie CHANTRELLE
1878, July 29th: Charles Joseph REVELL
1878, July 30th: Robert VEST
1878, August 12th: Thomas CHOLERTON
1878, August 15th: Selina WADGE
1878, October 3rd: William McDONALD
1878, October 8th: Thomas SMITHERS
1878, November 12th: Patrick John BYRNE
1878, November 18th: Joseph GARCIA
1878, November 19th: James McGOWAN
1878, November 25th: Henry GILBERT
1879, February 4th: Stephen GAMBRILL
1879, February 10th: Enoch WHISTON
1879, February 11th: William McGUINESS
1879, February 25th: Charles Frederick PEACE
1879, March 24th: James SIMMS
1879, May 12th: Edwin SMART
1879, May 20th: William COOPER
1879, May 26th: Catherine CHURCHILL
1879, May 27th: John D'ARCY
1879, May 28th: Thomas JOHNSON
1879, July 29th: Catherine WEBSTER
1879, August 11th: Annie TOOKE
1879, August 25th: James DILLEY
1879, August 26th: John RALPH
1879, December 3rd: Henry BEDINGFIELD
1879, January 10th: Thomas CUNCEEN
1880, January 5th: Charles SURETY
1880, February 17th: William CASSIDY
1880, March 2nd: Hugh BURNS & Patrick KEARNS
1880, March 22nd: John WINGFIELD
1880, May 10th: William DUMBLETON
1880, May 11th: John Henry WOOD
1880, August 16th: John WAKEFIELD
1880, November 16th: William BROWNLESS
1880, November 27th: William Joseph DISTON
1880, November 26th: Thomas WHEELER
1880, December 13th: William HERBERT
1880, December 13th: George PAVEY

1880, January 16th: Martin McHUGO
1880, April 14th: Peter CONWAY
1880, July 27th: Thomas BERRY
1881, February 21st: William STANWAY
1881, February 28th: Albert ROBINSON
1881, May 17th: Albert MOORE
1881, May 23rd: James HALL
1881, May 31st: Joseph Patrick McENTIRE
1881, August 15th: Thomas BROWN
1881, August 23rd: George DURLING
1881, November 24th: Alfred GOUGH
1881, November 28th: John Aspinall SIMPSON
1881, November 29th: Percy LEFROY
1882, January 31st: Charles GERRISH
1882, February 13th: Richard TEMPLETON
1882, April 28th: George Henry LAMSON
1882, May 16th: Thomas FURY
1882, May 22nd: William George ABIGAIL
1882, May 23rd: Osmond Otto BRAND
1882, August 21st: William TURNER
1882, November 13th: William Meager BARTLETT
1882, November 28th: Edward WHEATFALL
1882, December 4th: Bernard MULLARKEY
1882, December 12th: Charles TAYLOR
1882, September 11th: Francis HYNES
1882, September 22nd: Patrick WALSH
1882, December 15th: Pat CASEY, Miles JOYCE, Pat JOYCE
1883, January 2nd: Louisa Jane TAYLOR
1883, February 12th: Abraham THOMAS
1883, February 19th: James ANDERSON
1883, May 7th: Thomas GARRY
1883, May 8th: Patrick CAREY
1883, May 21st: Joseph WEDLAKE
1883, May 21st: George WHITE
1883, May 23rd: Henry MULLEN & Martin SCOTT
1883, August 6th: James BURTON
1883, January 15th: Patrick HIGGINS
1883, January 17th: Michael FLYNN & Thomas HIGGINS
1883, January 23rd: Sylvester POFF & James BARRETT
1883, April 30th: Timothy O'KEEFE
1883, May 14th: Joseph BRADY
1883, May 18th: Daniel CURLEY
1883, May 28th: Michael FAGAN
1883, June 2nd: Thomas CAFFREY
1883, June 9th: Timothy KELLY

Marwood, William (asst)
1873, August 26th: Thomas Hartley MONTGOMERY

Scott, Thomas
1892, January 12th: James HEANEY
1892, April 4th: James CAMPBELL
1892, April 19th: Daniel HANDLEY
1893, August 15th: John Thomas HEWITT
1893, January 6th: John BOYLE
1893, July 10th: Edward LEIGH
1893, September 2nd: James REILLY
1894, August 17th: John GILMOUR
1895, August 20th: Thomas BOND
1898, January 14th: Patrick HESTOR
1898, April 5th: Wilfrid F KENNY
1899, January 7th: Patrick HOLMES
1899, January 10th: Thomas KELLY
1899, January 13th: Philip KING

Scott, Thomas (asst)
1892, August 16th: James TAYLOR
1893, March 16th: Albert MANNING
1893, March 28th: William WILLIAMS
1893, December 21st: Frederick WYNDHAM
1895, June 18th: James CANNING
1895, July 2nd: Henry TICKNER
1895, December 17th: Elijah WINSTANLEY

Smith, George
1872, August 12th: Christopher EDWARDS
1873, January 7th: Edward HANCOCK
1873, August 4th: Henry EVANS
1873, August 20th: Laurence SMITH
1873, August 19th: Edward WALSH
1873, August 26th: Thomas Hartley MONTGOMERY

Smith, George (asst)
1868, September 8th: Alexander Arthur MACKAY
1872, August 13th: Thomas MOORE
1872, August 13th: James TOOTH
1872, August 13th: Francis BRADFORD

Speight, * (asst)
1884, December 8th: Arthur SHAW

Stanhouse, *
1879, August 25th: Joseph PRISTORIA

Thompson, * (asst)
1894, April 2nd: Margaret WALBER
1894, August 14th: Paul KOEZULA

Wade, Robert (asst)
1896, June 9th: Henry FOWLER & Albert MILSOM
1896, June 9th: William SEAMAN

Wade, Robert (asst)
1899, November 28th: Charles SCOTT

Warbrick, William (asst)
1893, August 16th: John DAVIS
1893, December 19th: Henry RUMBOLD
1895, June 4th: William MILLER
1895, December 24th: Henry WRIGHT
1896, February 4th: William James MORGAN
1896, February 25th: Alfred CHIPPERFIELD

Warbrick, William (asst)
1896, June 9th: Henry FOWLER & Albert MILSOM
1896, June 9th: William SEAMAN
1896, July 21st: Philip MATTHEWS
1896, July 21st: Frederick BURDEN
1896, July 21st: Samuel Edward SMITH
1896, August 5th: William PUGH
1896, August 11th: John ROSE
1896, August 11th: Samuel WILKINSON
1896, December 23rd: Joseph ALLCOCK
1899, December 6th: Michael DOWDLE

Hanged Index

Hanged Index

ABIGAIL, William George
1882, May 22nd

ADDINGTON, Richard
1871, July 31st

ALLCOCK, Joseph
1896, December 23rd

ALLEN, Thomas
1889, April 10th

ALT, Henry
1885, July 13th

ANDERSON, James
1883, February 19th

ANDERSON, John William
1875, December 22nd

ANDREWS, Frederick James
1899, May 3rd

ANSELL, Mary Ann
1899, July 19th

ARROWSMITH, William
1888, March 28th

BAILEY, Edwin
1874, January 12th

BAINS, John
1886, February 9th

BAKER, Frederick Edwin
1877, April 17th

BAKER, James
1886, February 8th

BAKER, William
1875, September 6th

BANBURY, John James
1892, October 11th

BANNISTER, James
1877, April 2nd

BARLOW, Silas
1876, December 19th

BARR, Thomas
1876, May 31st

BARRETT, James
1883, January 23rd

BARTLETT, Leir Richard
1888, November 13th

BARTLETT, William Meager
1882, November 13th

BARTON, James
1886, November 30th

BAUMBOS, Christos Emanuel
1876, August 25th

BEDINGFIELD, Henry
1879, December 3rd

BELL, Edward
1899, July 25th

BERRY, Ann
1874, January 12th

BERRY, Elizabeth
1887, March 14th

BERRY, Thomas
1880, July 27th

BETTS, William
1897, December 16th

BEVAN, Thomas Henry
1887, August 16th

BIGGADYKE, Priscilla
1868, December 28th

BLANCHARD, Peter
1875, August 9th

BLOXHAM, Thomas
1887, February 14th

BOND, Thomas
1895, August 20th

BOSWELL, Joseph
1890, March 11th

BOSWELL, Samuel
1890, March 11th

BOULTON, Thomas
1885, August 17th

BOWLING, George
1890, July 29th

BOWSER, Joseph
1897, July 27th

BOYLE, John
1893, January 6th

BRADFORD, Francis
1872, August 13th

BRADSHAW, Robert
1891, August 19th

BRADY, Joseph
1883, May 14th

BRAND, Osmond Otto
1882, May 23rd

BRAY, Peter
1883, November 19th

BRETT, Frederick
1889, December 31st

BRITLAND, Mary Ann
1886, August 9th

BROOKS, John
1878, February 13th

BROWN, Albert Edward
1886, May 31st

BROWN, Henry
1897, January 5th

BROWN, Thomas
1881, August 15th

BROWNING, Robert
1876, December 14th

BROWNLESS, William
1880, November 16th

BULL, William
1871, April 3rd

BULMER, Charles
1889, January 1st

BURDEN, Frederick
1896, July 21st

BURNS, Hugh
1880, March 2nd

BURTON, James
1883, August 6th

BURY, William Henry
1889, April 24th

BUTT, Charles Edward
1874, January 12th

BYRNE, Patrick John
1878, November 12th

CACCARIS, Giovanni
1876, May 23rd

CAFFREY, Thomas
1883, June 2nd

CAFFYN, James
1878, February 11th

CALADIS, Pascaler
1876, May 23rd

CAMPBELL, James
1892, April 4th

CAMPBELL, Michael
1871, April 24th

CANNING, James
1895, June 18th

CAREY, Patrick
1883, May 8th

CARLSEN, August
1896, December 22nd

CARR, Andrew
1870, July 28th

CARTER, John
1893, December 5th

CASEY, Patrick
1882, December 15th

CASSIDY, Peter
1884, August 19th

CASSIDY, William
1880, February 17th

CHADWICK, William Matthew
1890, April 15th

CHALMERS, George
1870, October 4th

CHANTRELLE, Eugene Marie
1878, May 31st

CHAMBERLAIN, Thomas
1874, March 31st

CHARLTON, Richard
1875, December 23rd

CHIPPERFIELD, Alfred
1896, February 25th

CHOLERTON, Thomas
1878, August 12th

CHURCHILL, Catherine
1879, May 26th

CLARK, William
1877, March 26th

CLARKE, George
1888, March 27th

CLEWES, Thomas
1889, January 1st

COATES, Richard
1875, March 29th

COLLINS, William
1871, August 17th

CONNOR, James
1873, September 8th

CONWAY, John
1891, August 20th

CONWAY, Peter
1880, April 14th

COOK, George Samuel
1893, July 25th

COOPER, Edward
1875, September 6th

COOPER, William
1879, May 20th

COPPEN, John Walter
1874, October 13th

CORGALIS, Matteo
1876, May 23rd

CORKERY, Jeremiah
1875, July 27th

CORRIGAN, Thomas
1874, January 5th

COTTON, John
1898, December 21st

COTTON, Mary Ann
1873, March 24th

COVINGTON, Arthur
1895, December 3rd

CRANWELL, James
1875, January 4th

CREAM, Thomas
1892, November 15th

CRONIN, John
1886, January 12th

CROSS, Phillip Henry Eustace
1888, January 10th

CROSSLEY, William
1894, July 31st

CROWE, Thomas
1876, August 25th

CROWTHER, Samuel
1888, December 11th

CROZIER, Samuel
1899, December 5th

CUDWORTH, Moses
1892, August 18th

CUNCEEN, Thomas
1879, January 10th

CURLEY, Daniel
1883, May 18th

CURRELL, Thomas William
1887, April 18th

D'ARCY, John
1879, May 27th

DAINTON, Henry
1891, December 15th

DALEY, Hugh
1874, December 28th

DALEY, Thomas
1898, December 14th

DALGLEISH, James
1876, December 19th

DALY, John
1876, April 26th

DANIELS, George Nathaniel
1888, August 28th

DAVIES, Frederick
1890, August 26th

DAVIES, Richard
1890, April 8th

DAVIS, John
1893, August 16th

DAWSON, Charles
1874, January 5th

DAY, Thomas Lyons
1883, November 13th

DEACON, Edward
1876, April 24th

DELANEY, Arthur Thomas
1888, August 10th

DELVIN, Henry
1890, September 23rd

DETHERIDGE, Jonah
1869, August 12th

DEWS, Alfred
1894, August 21st

DILLEY, James
1879, August 25th

DISTON, William Joseph
1880, November 27th

DOBELL, Charles
1889, January 2nd

DOCHERTY, Patrick
1875, October 5th

DOLAN, John
1869, March 23rd

DOWDLE, Michael
1899, December 6th

DOWNEY, Michael
1885, January 16th

DUCKWORTH, Cross
1893, January 3rd

DUKES, William
1889, December 24th

DUMBLETON, William 1880, May 10th

DURLING, George 1881, August 23rd

DUTTON, Henry 1883, December 3rd

DYER, Amelia Elizabeth 1896, June 10th

EBLETHRIFT, John 1876, August 29th

EDWARDS, Christopher 1872, August 12th

EDWARDS, Thomas 1892, December 22nd

EGGLESTON, Frederick 1892, March 17th

ELKINS, Samuel 1894, July 18th

ELLIOT, Augustus 1872, December 9th

ELLIS, Joseph Robert 1896, August 25th

EMERY, Samuel George 1894, December 11th

EVANS, Henry 1873, August 4th

EWERSTADT, Ernest 1884, December 8th

FAGAN, Michael 1883, May 28th

FAWCETT, Edward Henry 1891, August 25th

FENTON, Frederick William 1894, April 4th

FIDDLER, Mark 1875, August 16th

FISH, William 1876, August 14th

FLANAGAN, Catherine 1884, March 5th

FLANAGAN, Henry 1874, August 31st

FLANAGAN, William 1876, December 21st

FLYNN, Michael 1883, January 17th

FORDRED, Thomas 1876, April 4th

FOWLER, Henry 1896, June 9th

FURY, Thomas 1882, May 16th

GAMBRILL, Stephen 1879, February 4th

GARCIA, Joseph 1878, November 18th

GARNER, Philip 1894, April 3rd

GARRY, Thomas 1883, May 7th

GELL, John Alfred 1888, May 15th

GERRISH, Charles 1882, January 31st

GIBBONS, Patrick 1892, August 17th

GIBBS, James Henry 1874, August 24th

GILBERT, Henry 1878, November 25th

GILLINGHAM, Michael 1875, August 2nd

GILMOUR, John 1894, August 17th

GODWIN, John 1874, May 25th

GOLDING, John 1877, August 21st

GOODALE, Robert 1885, November 30th

GORRIE, Daniel Stewart 1890, June 10th

GOUGH, Alfred 1881, November 24th

GOUGH, Edward 1874, January 5th

GOWER, William 1889, January 2nd

GREEN, John 1876, December 20th

GREGSON, John 1870, January 10th

GREY, Thomas 1877, November 21st

GURD, John 1892, July 26th

HALE, William 1875, April 26th
HALL, James 1881, May 23rd
HAMER, Emanuel 1893, November 28th
HANCOCK, Edward 1873, January 7th
HANDLEY, Daniel 1892, April 19th
HARMER, George 1886, December 13th
HARRIS, Thomas 1884, October 6th
HARRIS, William 1894, January 2nd
HARRISON, James 1890, August 26th
HASSELL, William 1877, November 19th
HAYMAN, Robert 1897, February 9th
HAYES, Daniel 1888, April 29th
HAYES, John 1873, January 13th
HAYNES, Thomas 1882, August 22nd
HEANEY, James 1892, January 12th
HEAP, Alfred Thomas 1875, April 19th
HEMMINGS, Edward 1893, April 4th
HERBERT, William 1880, December 13th
HERDMAN, John 1898, March 12th
HESTOR, Patrick 1898, January 14th
HEWITT, Edward 1886, June 15th
HEWITT, John Thomas 1893, August 15th
HICKEY, Lawrence Maurice 1889, August 7th
HIGGENBOTHAM, Charles Lister 1890, January 7th

HIGGINS, Margaret 1884, March 5th
HIGGINS, Patrick 1883, January 15th
HIGGINS, Thomas 1883, January 17th
HILL, George 1876, April 10th
HILL, John 1885, November 23rd
HINSON, Frederick 1869, December 13th
HIRST, Joseph 1896, August 4th
HOBSON, Henry 1887, August 22nd
HOLMES, Charles 1872, August 12th
HOLMES, Patrick 1899, January 7th
HOOK, William Thomas 1889, December 31st
HORRY, William Frederick 1872, April 1st
HORSFORD, William 1898, June 28th
HORTON, George 1889, August 21st
HORTON, John 1886, February 1st
HOWARTH, Kay 1884, November 24th
HOWE, George William 1898, February 22nd
HUDSON, Benjamin 1873, August 4th
HUDSON, Robert Heseltine 1895, August 13th
HUNTER, George 1876, March 28th
HUNTER, William 1887, November 14th
HYNES, Francis 1882, September 11th
INNES, William 1884, March 31st
INSOLE, Richard 1887, February 21st

JACKSON, John
1888, August 7th

JACKSON, William
1874, August 18th

JAY, Horace Robert
1885, January 13th

JENKINS, Ebeneezer Samuel
1889, March 6th

JOHNSON, John Henry
1877, April 3rd

JOHNSON, John William
1891, December 22nd

JOHNSON, Michael James
1869, March 29th

JOHNSON, Thomas
1879, May 28th

JONES, Cadwaller
1877, November 23rd

JONES, Frederick
1872, January 8th

JONES, Harry Benjamin
1888, August 28th

JONES, James
1888, March 20th

JONES, James
1896, October 6th

JONES, Thomas
1898 August 3rd

JOYCE, Miles
1882, December 15th

JOYCE, Patrick
1882, December 15th

JUDGE, Patrick
1886, November 16th

KADI, George
1876, May 23rd

KEARNS, Patrick
1880, March 2nd

KELLY, Thomas
1899, January 10th

KELLY, Timothy
1883, June 9th

KENNEDY, Michael
1872, December 30th

KENNY, Wilfrid F
1898, April 5th

KESTEVEN, Edmund
1895, March 26th

KEWISH, John
1872, August 1st

KIMBERLEY, Henry
1885, March 17th

KING, Jessie
1889, March 11th

KING, Joseph
1887, March 21st

KING, Philip
1899, January 13th

KIRBY, James
1888, May 7th

KITCHING, Robert
1890, December 30th

KITE, Charles
1884, February 25th

KNIGHT, Cyrus
1894, December 12th

KOEZULA, Paul
1894, August 14th

LACE, William
1872, August 26th

LAMSON, George Henry
1882, April 28th

LANGFORD, John
1894, May 22nd

LAWSON, Joseph
1884, May 27th

LAYCOCK, Joseph
1884, August 26th

LE BRUN, Joseph Phillip
1875, August 11th

LEATHERBARROW, Thomas
1887, February 15th

LEE, James
1885, May 18th

LEFLEY, Mary
1884, May 26th

LEFROY, Percy
1881, November 29th

LEIGH, Edward
1893, July 10th

LEIGH, Henry
1877, August 13th

LEWIS, Joseph
1898, August 30th

LIPSKI, Israel
1877, August 22nd

LLOYD, Thomas   **Hanged Index**   **MULLARKY, Bernard**

LLOYD, Thomas
1897, August 18th

LYNCH, John
1877, October 15th

MacDONALD, John
1874, August 10th

MACKAY, Alexander Arthur
1868, September 8th

MAIDMENT, Charles
1899, July 18th

MANNING, Albert
1893, March 16th

MARKS, Isaac
1877, January 2nd

MARSH, Henry
1877, November 20th

MARTIN, James
1886, February 8th

MASON, George
1893, December 6th

MATTHEWS, Philip
1896, July 21st

McCONVILLE, John
1869, March 23rd

McDAID, John
1875, March 24th

McDONALD, Thomas
1890, December 30th

McDONALD, William
1878, October 3rd

McENTIRE, Joseph Patrick
1881, May 31st

McGILL, Owen
1886, February 22nd

McGOVERN, Patrick
1877, August 21st

McGOWAN, James
1878, November 19th

McGRAVE, John
1875, January 4th

McGUINESS, William
1879, February 11th

McHUGH, William
1875, August 2nd

McHUGO, Martin
1880, January 16th

McKENNA, John
1877, March 27th

McKEOWN, Arthur
1889, January 14th

McKEOWN, Steven
1876, August 21st

McKEOWN, William
1893, January 18th

McLEAN, Michael
1884, March 10th

McCRAE, Andrew George
1893, January 10th

McCULLOUGH, William
1875, August 16th

MELLOR, James
1892, December 20th

MEUNIER, Amie Holman
1893, July 19th

MILLAR, Walter
1870, August 1st

MILLER, William
1895, June 4th

MILSOM, Albert
1896, June 9th

MINAHAN, Daniel
1885, December 7th

MOBBS, William
1870, March 28th

MONTEAU, Francois
1890, August 27th

MONTGOMERY, Thomas Hartley
1873, August 26th

MOORE, Albert
1881, May 17th

MOORE, Thomas
1872, August 13th

MORGAN, John
1875, March 30th

MORGAN, William James
1896, February 4th

MORIARTY, Daniel
1888, April 29th

MORLEY, Joseph
1887, November 21st

MORLEY, Patrick
1895, December 31st

MUIR, James
1892, March 1st

MULLARKY, Bernard
1882, December 4th

MULLEN, Henry
1883, May 23rd

MULLEN, Michael
1875, January 4th

MUNCH, Franz Joseph
1891, July 21st

MURPHY, James
1886, November 29th

NASH, Thomas
1886, March 1st

NEAL, John
1890, March 26th

NEWELL, John William
1894, December 10th

NICHOLSON, George
1889, January 8th

NOBLE, John
1892, March 29th

NORMAN, Henry
1885, October 5th

NUNN, George
1899, November 21st

O'DONNELL, Charles
1876, December 11th

O'DONNELL, Patrick
1883, December 17th

O'KEEFE, Timothy
1883, April 30th

ORROCK, Thomas Henry
1884, October 6th

OWEN, John
1870, August 8th

PARKER, Joseph Cornelius
1899, July 11th

PARRIS, James
1876, August 1st

PARRY, Thomas
1885, January 20th

PATERSON, George
1897, June 7th

PAVEY, George
1880, December 13th

PAYNE, Thomas
1887, December 6th

PEACE, Charles Frederick
1879, February 25th

PEARSON, Elizabeth
1875, August 2nd

PICKERING, Henry
1892, June 14th

PIGGOTT, George
1878, February 4th

POFF, Sylvester
1883, January 23rd

POOLE, Joseph
1883, December 18th

POWELL, Henry
1883, November 6th

PRATT, Thomas Benjamin
1877, November 12th

PRESTON, Frederick
1899, October 3rd

PRISTORIA, Joseph
1879, August 25th

PRITCHARD, Edward
1887, February 17th

PUGH, William
1896, August 5th

PURCELL, Benjamin
1889, December 9th

PURCELL, John
1891, March 13th

RADCLIFFE, Thomas
1870, August 15th

RALPH, John
1879, August 26th

RAYNOR, Charles
1892, March 17th

READ, James Canham
1894, December 4th

REES, David
1888, March 13th

REILLY, James
1893, September 2nd

REVELL, Charles Joseph
1878, July 29th

RICHARDS, Thomas
1894, November 29th

RICHARDSON, James William
1888, May 22nd

RILEY, Thomas
1883, November 26th

ROBERTS, David
1886, March 2nd

ROBERTS, Edward
1872, March 18th

ROBERTSON, George 1899, March 28th	**SCOTT, Martin** 1883, May 23rd
ROBINSON, Albert 1881, February 28th	**SEAMAN, William** 1896, June 9th
ROBINSON, Joseph 1897, August 17th	**SHAW, Arthur** 1884, December 8th
ROBINSON, Walter 1897, August 17th	**SHEEHAN, William** 1886, January 20th
ROGERS, Henry 1877, July 31st	**SHEILD, Lawrence** 1870, May 27th
ROGERS, WIlliam 1894, December 12th	**SHEILD, Margaret** 1870, May 27th
ROSE, John 1896, August 11th	**SHEWARD, William** 1869, April 20th
ROW, William 1890, March 12th	**SHRIMPTON, Moses** 1885, May 25th
ROWLES, Henry 1878, April 1st	**SIMMS, James** 1879, March 24th
RUDGE, Anthony Ben 1886, February 8th	**SIMPSON, John Aspinall** 1881, November 28th
RUMBOLD, Henry 1893, December 19th	**SKEFFINGTON, Thomas** 1899, November 15th
RUSSELL, John 1875, April 9th	**SLANE, Hugh** 1873, January 13th
RYAN, John 1898, November 15th	**SMART, Edwin** 1879, May 12th
RYLANDS, Samuel 1889, March 13th	**SMEDLEY, William** 1875, December 21st
SABEY, Richard 1893, July 18th	**SMITH, Caleb** 1877, August 14th
SADLER, Thomas 1891, August 18th	**SMITH, Charles** 1887, May 9th
SAMUELS, William 1886, July 27th	**SMITH, Charles** 1898, March 22nd
SARGENT, George 1888, August 15th	**SMITH, Laurence** 1873, August 20th
SATCHELL, James 1877, November 27th	**SMITH, Samuel Edward** 1896, July 21st
SAUNDERS, Charles 1891, December 23rd	**SMITH, Thomas** 1874, November 16th
SAUNDERS, George 1886, February 16th	**SMITH, Walter** 1894, March 27th
SCANDRETT, Alfred 1888, March 20th	**SMITHERS, Thomas** 1878, October 8th
SCHNEIDER, John 1899, January 3rd	**SOWERY, Alfred** 1887, August 1st
SCOTT, Charles 1899, November 28th	**SPENCER, Arthur** 1891, July 28th

SPENCER, Richard
1873, January 8th

SPICER, Felix
1890, August 22nd

SQUIRES, Charles
1893, August 10th

STAFFORD, Peter
1889, April 8th

STANTON, John
1875, March 30th

STANWAY, William
1881, February 21st

STARKEY, John Henry
1877, July 31st

STEWART, Frances
1874, June 29th

STOCKWELL, James
1892, January 5th

STOREY, Frederick Thomas
1891, January 11th

SULLIVAN, Bartholomew
1891, February 2nd

SURETY, Charles
1880, January 5th

SWIFT, John
1877, November 27th

SWINDELLS, Harry Hammond
1884, November 24th

TAYLOR, Charles
1882, December 12th

TAYLOR, Frank
1896, August 18th

TAYLOR, James
1892, August 16th

TAYLOR, Louisa Jane
1883, January 2nd

TAYLOR, Robert
1874, December 29th

TAYLOR, William
1869, October 11th

TEMPLETON, Richard
1882, February 13th

TERRY, Benjamin
1887, February 22nd

THOMAS, Abraham
1883, February 12th

THOMAS, George
1885, December 9th

THOMAS, George
1894, February 13th

THOMPSON, Richard
1876, August 14th

THOMPSON, William
1874, January 5th

THURSTON, John
1886, February 10th

TICKNER, Henry
1895, July 2nd

TIDBURY, Francis
1877, March 12th

TIDBURY, Henry
1877, March 12th

TOBIN, James
1884, August 24th

TOBIN, William
1875, April 19th

TOOKE, Annie
1879, August 11th

TOOTH, James
1872, August 13th

TORR, Elias
1899, August 9th

TRICKETT, James
1878, February 12th

TUCKER, Joseph
1885, August 3rd

TURNER, Alfred William
1891, May 19th

TURNER, Walter Lewis
1891, August 18th

TURNER, William
1882, August 21st

TWISS, John
1895, February 9th

UPTON, John
1877, November 27th

UPTON, Robert
1888, July 17th

VEST, Robert
1878, July 30th

VICKERS, Robert Flockhart
1884, March 31st

VINALL, Martin Henry
1869, January 19th

WADDELL, William
1888, December 18th

WADE, Peter 1884, January 15th

WADELY, Enoch 1887, November 28th

WADGE, Selina 1878, August 15th

WAINWRIGHT, Henry 1875, December 21st

WAKEFIELD, John 1880, August 16th

WALBER, Margaret 1894, April 2nd

WALKER, Joseph 1887, November 15th

WALKER, Vincent Knowles 1877, April 15th

WALSH, Edward 1873, August 19th

WALSH, Patrick 1882, September 22nd

WARD, Robert 1899, October 4th

WARDLAW, David 1875, October 19th

WATERS, Margaret 1870, October 11th

WATT, James 1898, July 12th

WEBBER, Joseph 1876, April 25th

WEBSTER, Catherine 1879, July 29th

WEDLAKE, Joseph 1883, May 21st

WELLS, Thomas 1868, August 13th

WELSH, Joseph 1869, November 15th

WENZEL, John George 1892, August 16th

WEST, Robert 1889, December 31st

WHEATFALL, Edward 1882, November 28th

WHEELER, Mary Eleanor 1890, December 23rd

WHEELER, Thomas 1880, November 26th

WHELAN, James 1886, May 31st

WHISTON, Enoch 1879, February 10th

WHITE, George 1883, May 21st

WHITEHEAD, James Wilshaw 1894, November 27th

WILKES, William 1898, July 19th

WILKINSON, Samuel 1896, August 11th

WILLIAMS, James 1881, February 22nd

WILLIAMS, John 1876, July 26th

WILLIAMS, John 1885, November 23rd

WILLIAMS, Mary 1874, August 31st

WILLIAMS, William 1893, March 28th

WILSON, Joseph 1892, March 22nd

WILTON, William 1887, August 29th

WINGFIELD, John 1880, March 22nd

WINGROVE, Richard 1895, November 13th

WINSTANLEY, Elijah 1895, December 17th

WITHEY, John 1889, April 11th

WOOD, George Henry
1892, April 26th

WOOD, John Henry
1880, May 11th

WOOD, Walter
1887, May 30th

WOOLDRIDGE, Charles Thomas
1896, July 7th

WORTHINGTON, William
1875, January 4th

WRIGHT, Henry
1895, December 24th

WYNDHAM, Frederick
1893, December 21st

WYRE, Thomas
1888, July 18th

YOUNG, Henry William
1887, May 16th